SHIFTING STATES IN GLOBAL MARKETS

SHIFTING STATES
IN GLOBAL MARKETS

Subnational Industrial
Policy in Contemporary
Brazil and Spain

ALFRED P. MONTERO

The Pennsylvania State University Press
University Park, Pennsylvania

An earlier version of Chapter 3 appeared as "Making and Remaking 'Good Government' in Brazil: Subnational Industrial Policy in Minas Gerais," *Latin American Politics and Society* 43, no. 2 (Summer 2001): 49–80.
Reprinted by permission of the School of International Studies, University of Miami.
Copyright © 2001 School of International Studies, University of Miami.

Earlier versions of segments of Chapters 3–6 appeared in "Delegative Dilemmas and Horizontal Logics: Subnational Industrial Policy in Brazil and Spain," *Studies in Comparative International Development* 36, no. 3 (Fall 2001).
Reprinted by permission of Transaction Publishers.
Copyright © 2001 Transaction Publishers.

Library of Congress Cataloguing-in-Publication Data

Montero, Alfred P., 1969–
    Shifting states in global markets : subnational industrial policy in contemporary Brazil and Spain / Alfred P. Montero.
        p.   cm.
    Includes bibliographical references and index.
    ISBN 0-271-02189-6 (cloth : acid-free paper)
    1. Industrial policy—Spain—Case studies. 2. Industrial policy—Brazil—Case studies.
    3. Regional economics—Case studies. 4. Subnational governments—Spain—Case studies.
    5. Subnational governments—Brazil—Case studies. I. Title.

    HD3616.S483 M66 2002
    338.946—dc21   2001055950

To my parents, *con mucho amor y orgullo,*
Alfred and *Merysabel*

CONTENTS

FIGURES AND TABLES

ACKNOWLEDGMENTS

This book is the product of many conversations with myself. The ideas of others frequently intervened to sharpen my thinking or even to change its direction, however. Advisors, colleagues, interviewees, contacts, and students often turned a will-o'-the-wisp of an idea into a practicable argument or an important component of one. Although it is impossible to thank all those who affected my thinking process, if only because there are so many, I attempt here to name the most influential.

The financial support that helped sustain this project during the dissertation stage and beyond was considerable. I thank the Institute for the Study of World Politics, the Institute of Latin American and Iberian Studies at Columbia University, the Tinker Foundation, the Department of Political Science at Columbia, and Carleton College for supporting the Brazilian portion of the work. Carleton's Hildebrandt/Higinbotham Fund for Faculty Development in the Social Sciences proved particularly useful in updating my field work after the defense. The Spanish segment was supported by the Institute of Western Europe and the Department of Political Science at Columbia. The Fundación Juan March in Madrid granted me visiting scholar status on my frequent visits between 1994 and 1996, which significantly reduced the costs of my research in Spain. Finally, I am grateful for Carleton's support through the Keith Clark Memorial Fund for Faculty Development and the Hewlett Foundation during the time I transformed my manuscript into this book.

During my time at Columbia University, Douglas Chalmers, Robert Kaufman, Mark Kesselman, Arvid Lukauskas, and Patrick Heller all offered sage advice on the main argument and they provided careful and insightful reviews of my dissertation prior to defense. William C. Smith mentored me through the process of turning the dissertation into a book manuscript. Bill is a testament to the importance of having a patient teacher and advisor during the early years of an academic's career. Without him I would certainly have become a lawyer.

In Brazil, a number of friends, colleagues, and contacts provided assistance without which my fieldwork would surely have sputtered. In Rio de Janeiro, I enjoyed the considerable library resources of the Fundação Getúlio Vargas and the BNDES. At CODIN, Marco Antônio de Araujo Lima, Jorge de Paula Costa Avila, and Jorge Fernandes da Cunha Filho provided important documents and insights into Rio's industrial policy. At BNDES, Maria Christina Carneiro, Doris Lustman Meilman, Yolanda Maria Melo Ramalho, and Marcelo Nardim facilitated my access to internal documents and reports. Antônio Barros de Castro was an endless source of useful contacts in government and Brazilian academe. Eli Diniz at IUPERJ provided a useful introduction to *fluminense* politics. In São Paulo, Rui de Britto Alvares Affonso and Felipe de Holanda at FUNDAP-IESP were useful guides during my first forays into the study of Brazilian federalism. João Paulo Candia Veiga ("o Joca"), a great friend and colleague, made useful resources available at DESEP/CUT. Maria do Carmo Campello de Souza encouraged me to study the politics of regional disparities in Brazil, which directed me to the current project. She also facilitated my housing during my initial trips to São Paulo in 1993 and 1994. I also thank Pedro Jacobi, who offered access to CEDEC's library and other resources. In Minas Gerais, Clélio Campolina Diniz and Otávio Dulci provided invaluable advice and resources on the fascinating history of *mineiro* development and politics. Marilena Chaves at SEPLAN, Iran Almeida Pordeus at BDMG, Stefan Bogdan Salej at FIEMG, Carlos Alberto Teixeira, and Eduardo Mella da Costa and Kenneth Albernaz Barbosa at INDI provided many crucial documents and fantastic access to businesses and other institutions.

In Spain, special thanks goes to the directors, professors, staff, and students of the Fundación Juan March. José María Maravall and Leopoldo Calvo Sotelo graciously opened the doors of the institute and its splendid resources during my frequent trips to Madrid between 1994 and 1996. Both gave me useful contacts to initiate my research. Their generosity and the intellectual stimulation at the Fundación were of incalculable value. Martha Peach and her library staff were particularly generous with their time. José María provided the intellectual spark that stimulated my interest in Spain and he offered initial contacts to get my project off the ground. Fellow travelers in Madrid, Katrina Burgess and Rand Smith, provided feedback and additional contacts. Álvaro Espina Montero offered hours of insightful discussion on industrial restructuring and the Valencian experience. In Asturias, I wish to thank Rodolfo Gutiérrez Palacios who explained the labyrinthine politics of the region's industrial relations and provided generous access to the University of

Oviedo's library. María José Suárez Puente at IFR, Nieves Carasco at ITMA, Encarna Rodríguez Cañes at the Chancellery of Economy and Planning, Javier Fernández at CREP, and Rosa Corujedo made essential documents available. I gratefully thank Pedro de Silva Cienfuegos-Jovellanos, former president of Asturias, for his notable sacrifice of many hours on one afternoon in Gijón. In Seville, I thank the staff of the IFA who provided documents and insight on the workings of Andalusian industrial policy.

Many friends and colleagues commented on earlier drafts of the chapters or papers based on them. Although I retain full responsibility for any remaining errors of fact, omission, and interpretation, the project would not have cohered without their input. I thank in particular Renato Boschi, Douglas Chalmers, Bryan Daves, Eric Hershberg, Robert Kaufman, Richard Locke, Arvid Lukauskas, Scott Martin, Nicholas Onuf, Timothy Power, Hiram Ramírez, David Samuels, Rand Smith, William C. Smith, Richard Snyder, Judith Tendler, and Eliza Willis. Numerous conversations with others helped shape the project: Caren Addis, Gerard Alexander, Barry Ames, Antônio Barros de Castro, Katrina Burgess, Maria do Carmo Campello de Souza, Nadya Castro, Bruce Chadwick, Peter Kingstone, Scott Mainwaring, José María Maravall, Gabriel Saro, Steven Schier, Eduardo Silva, Steven Solnick, Pat Taylor, and participants in three meetings of the International Working Group on Subnational Economic Governance in Latin America in Comparative International Perspective (New York, 1997; São Paulo, 1999; and San Juan, Puerto Rico, 2000). Two anonymous peer reviewers for Penn State University Press provided very careful readings of the manuscript and made suggestions that greatly improved my working drafts. I thank Sandy Thatcher for seeing the project through to publication and Daniel Frank, Roy Grow, and Mar Valdecantos for help on some of the figures and the cover art.

My deepest debt of gratitude, of course, is reserved for my wife, María del Mar García-Valdecantos and our family. Mar accompanied me on numerous research trips and shared hundreds of little victories and setbacks. She also opened my eyes to a different way of life: one with plenty of *chorizo*, good wine, and enduring love. I am grateful to the loving support of her family in Madrid, especially her mother, Dolores (Lola) Navarro, and to my own family in Miami. I reserve my most profound gratitude for my parents, Alfred and Merysabel. They first introduced me to Brazil in 1986 and I was compelled to return many times thereafter. In the process, I became a student of Latin American politics. Without their love and devotion, I would never have developed as a scholar. For their support and unfailing inspiration, I dedicate this book to them.

ADL	Arthur D. Little Company
AD-RIO	Agência de Desenvolvimento do Rio
AP	Alianza Popular (Spain)
ARENA	Aliança Nacional Renovadora
BDMG	Banco de Desenvolvimento de Minas Gerais
BNDES	Banco Nacional de Desenvolvimento Econômico e Social
CCAA	Comunidades Autonomas
CCOO	Comisiones Obreras
CDI	Companhia de Distritos Industriais (Minas Gerais)
CEA	Confederación de Empresários de Andalucía
CEDEPLAR	Centro de Planejamento (Minas Gerais)
CEIM	Confederación Empresarial de Madrid
CEMIG	Centrais Elétricas de Minas Gerais
CIC	Centro Industrial Cearense
CIU	Convergència i Unió
CMN	Conselho Monetário Nacional
CODIN	Companhia de Desenvolvimento Industrial (Rio de Janeiro)
COIND	Conselho de Industrialização (Minas Gerais)
CPM	Companhia Paraibuna de Metais
CREP	Comisión de Representantes del Principado en la Empresa Pública
CSI	Corporación de la Siderurgia Integral
CSN	Companhia Siderúrgica Nacional
CVRD	Companhia Vale do Rio Doce
DEP	Departamento de Estudos e Planejamento (Minas Gerais)
EC	European Community
ECSC	European Coal and Steel Community

ENSIDESA	Empresa Nacional Siderúrgica
ERDF	European Regional Development Fund
ETA	Euskadi ta Askatasuna (Basque Homeland and Freedom)
EU	European Union
FADE	Federación Asturiana de Empresários
FIEMG	Federação das Indústrias do Estado de Minas Gerais
FIESP	Federação de Indústrias do Estado de São Paulo
FIND	Fundo de Industrialização (Minas Gerais)
FIRJAN	Federação das Indústrias do Estado do Rio de Janeiro
FJP	Fundação João Pinheiro (Minas Gerais)
FSE-PSOE	Federación Socialista Asturiana
FUNDES	Fundo de Desenvolvimento Econômico e Social (Rio de Janeiro)
HUNOSA	Hulleras del Norte
ICMS	Imposto sobre Circulação de Mercadorias e Serviços
IDB	Inter-American Development Bank
IFA	Instituto de Fomento de Andalucía
IFR	Instituto de Fomento Regional (Asturias)
IMADE	Instituto Madrileño de Desarrollo
IMPIVA	Instituto de la Mediana y Pequeña Industria Valenciana
INDI	Instituto de Desenvolvimento Industrial (Minas Gerais)
INI	Instituto Nacional de Industria
IPIA	Instituto de Promoción Industrial de Andalucía
ISI	Import-substitution Industrialization
IU	Izquierda Unida
JIT	Just-In-Time
LOFCA	Ley Orgánica de Financiación de las Comunidades Autónomas
MDB	Movimento Democrático Brasileiro
MERCOSUL	Mercado Comum do Sul
PAN	Partido Acción Nacional (Mexico)
PAUR	Programa de Actuaciones Urgentes de Reindustrialización (Asturias)
PDEA	Plan de Dinamización Económica de Asturias
PDS	Partido Democrático Social
PDT	Partido Democrático Trabalhista
PMDB	Partido do Movimento Democrático Brasileiro
PMDI	Plano Mineiro de Desenvolvimento Integrado
PNI	Plan Nacional de Industria (Spain)

PNIC	Programa Nacional de Interés Comunitario (Spain)
PP	Partido Popular (Spain)
PP	Partido Popular (Brazil)
PRD	Partido de la Revolución Democrática (Mexico)
PRI	Partido Revolucionário Institucional (Mexico)
PROIM	Programa de Indução e Modernização (Minas Gerais)
PROINDÚSTRIA	Programa de Integração e Diversificação Industrial (Minas Gerais)
PRONASOL	Programa Nacional de Solidaridad (Mexico)
PSA	Partido Socialista de Andalucía
PSD	Partido Social Democrático
PSDB	Partido da Social Democracia Brasileira
PSOE	Partido Socialista Obrero de España
PSP	Partido Social Progressista
PSPV-PSOE	Partido Socialista del País Valenciano
PT	Partido dos Trabalhadores
PTB	Partido Trabalhista Brasileiro
SADEI	Sociedad Asturiana de Estudios Económicos e Industriales
SAYPE	Servicio de Asesoramiento y Promoción Empresarial (Asturias)
SEDESOL	Secretaría de Desarrollo Social (Mexico)
SEPLAN	Secretaría de Planejamento (Minas Gerais)
SIC	Secretaría de Indústria e Comércio (Ceará)
SINDIPEÇAS	Sindicato Nacional da Indústria de Componentes para Veículos Automotores
SMJ	Siderúrgica Mendes Júnior
SODECO	Sociedad para el Desarrollo de las Comarcas Mineras (Asturias)
SOMA-UGT	Sindicato de Obreros Mineros de Asturias de la UGT
SOPREA	Sociedad para la Promoción y Reconversión Económica de Andalucía
SRP	Sociedad Regional de Promoción (Asturias)
SUIND	Superintendência de Industrialização (Minas Gerais)
UCD	Unión de Centro Democrático
UDN	União Democrática Nacional
UFMG	Universidade Federal de Minas Gerais
UGT	Unión General de Trabajadores
ZID	Zonas Industrializadas en Declive
ZPE	Zonas de Promoción Económica
ZUR	Zona de Urgente Reindustrialización

Introduction: The Political Origins of Synergy

One unexpected parallel to the widely held view that globalization has challenged the utility of national industrial policies is the finding that subnational governments have become more active in spurring industrial investment, higher productivity, and enhancing access to technological innovation. In the state of Minas Gerais in Brazil, an array of public agencies—utility companies, business information institutes, and industrial district companies—have facilitated the rapid expansion of auto-parts and assembly firms, chemical industries, and small and medium-sized enterprises in various sectors. In the Spanish region of Asturias, a similar set of public agencies with union and business association partners has promoted productivity-enhancing adjustments in small firms that were previously dependent on the now-eroding public steel and mining sectors. The experiences of Minas and Asturias dovetail a number of other cases around the world in different areas of economic policy (industrial, labor market, agriculture, and infrastructure) that have been reported by political economists.[1] Some scholars and policy

---

1. For example, in the Indian state of Kerala, Heller (1996) describes a regional government that has played a key role in facilitating the coordination of labor-management relations and providing welfare protection to unorganized workers. The result has been stable labor relations and an improved investment climate. In the poor northern state of Ceará in Brazil, Tendler (1997) chronicles the experiences of highly successful state and municipal programs in preventive health, public procurement, and agricultural productivity that were planned and executed in cooperation with citizen clients. In Taiwan, Lam (1996)

observers use these "success stories" to contest the popular notion that globalization of trade, production, and capital markets has reduced the importance of states and location of investment as factors in determining development patterns (e.g., Evans 1996, 1997b; Swyngedouw 1992). Moreover, these case studies correct the analytical bias in favor of national institutions and policy-making apparent in much political economic scholarship (Snyder 2001).[2] These experiences suggest that subnational comparisons can reveal important *heterogeneous* characteristics in countries many have previously regarded as having certain strictly homogenous, national-level qualities.

When these cases are compared to other subnational regions in Brazil and Spain, however, or when they are compared to each other, the successes of industrial policy in Minas and Asturias require additional explanation. For example, the experience of Minas Gerais stands out in a country that has a long history of political clientelism associated with the mismanagement of development policy resources. Brazil's governors are particularly liable for administering what many scholars of the country see as the most powerful clientelistic networks in Brazil (Abrúcio 1998; Samuels 1998, 2000; Schwartzman 1973). Due to the weakness of national party labels, political institutions are chronically unable to limit the governors' influence on federal legislators and public firms (Mainwaring 1997, 1999; Ames 1995, 2001; Garman, Haggard, and Willis 2001). In states such as Rio de Janeiro, populist governors have historically developed political dynasties that invoke comparisons to the *caciques* of Mexican politics or the notorious local party bosses of Tammany Hall and Chicago. If political clientelism is as common as studies of policy-making in Brazil commonly attest (e.g., Weyland 1996; Hagopian 1996), then subnational industrial policy remains vulnerable to these short-term political interests. Subnational party bosses have strong incentives to manipulate industrial reform to enhance their own short-term interests at the cost of the long-term *economic* performance such policy seeks to enhance. In other words,

---

describes subnational government agencies that have improved the administration of irrigation systems by coordinating farmers in a sector that is notorious for its inefficiency in most of the developing world.

2. Studies of "adjustment" to global constraints have tended to assume that national governments are the only relevant stewards of policy change. The major studies of economic adjustment in advanced capitalist and developing economies invariably focus on the reform strategies pursued by *national* governments. See Katzenstein (1978, 1985), Gourevitch (1986), Stallings and Kaufman (1989), Nelson (1990), Haggard and Kaufman (1992, 1995), Bates and Krueger (1993), Haggard and Webb (1994), Garrett (1995, 1998), and Kitschelt, Lange, Marks, and Stephens (1999). Notable exceptions include Willis (1996), Snyder (1999a), and Locke (1995).

the management of subnational industrial policy in Brazil suffers from a kind of delegative dilemma. Self-serving populist governors would be reluctant to waste politically valuable economic policy resources by devolving control over industrial policy to public development agencies. Populists could more easily manipulate economic policy resources by continuing to *centralize* control over the policy-making apparatus. Without delegation, public agencies and private firms could not coordinate resources in ways that would enhance long-term economic performance.

Where Rio de Janeiro reflects these seemingly endemic qualities in Brazilian politics, Minas Gerais does not. In Minas, the governors created a decentralized network of technocratic industrial policy agencies and they delegated politically useful authorities and resources to them from the 1960s through the 1990s. The *mineiro* agencies proved successful in promoting industrial investment and in enhancing productivity under both a state-led, developmentalist framework from the 1960s to the mid-1980s and a market-oriented model during the late 1980s and throughout the 1990s. The case of Minas suggests that the experience of subnational economic policy-making in Brazil does not follow a uniform pattern. It takes more of a patchwork, composite shape (Montero 2000, 2001a).

We might expect a more uniform pattern in Spain. In contrast to Brazil's fragmented political party and federal system, Spain's new democracy during the 1980s and 1990s developed highly disciplined national parties and a well-organized federal state structure (Bermeo 1994; Agranoff 1996). Yet, like Brazil, the pattern of subnational industrial policy-making in Spain is also composite. Different regional experiences with industrial policy are the rule. For example, while Asturias's regional development agencies avoided the contentious politics of labor union mobilization against national downsizing in the public mining and steel sectors, Andalusia's regional agencies became devices for collecting labor support for the governing Socialist Party. Although both regions were governed during most of the 1980s and 1990s by the same national party, Andalusia's industrial policy was plagued by populist intervention and clientelistic exchange; Asturias's industrial policy was not. Disciplined national parties and a highly organized federal structure in Spain led to the same patchwork distribution of effective and politicized subnational economic programs evident in Brazil.

The composite pattern of subnational industrial policy-making in these two very different countries highlights the need for scholars to peer below national-level data and the national unit of analysis to explain within-country variation. This mandate is particularly challenging to the dominant analytical tendencies in the study of economic policy in federal or decentralized states. Scholars in this research program have divided into two competing camps: those who argue that decentralization enhances economic policy (the optimists) and those who posit that it endangers it (the pessimists). The optimistic view typically sees decentralization as a means for improving the economic performance of markets by limiting central intervention, encouraging policy innovation among competing subnational units, and enhancing allocative efficiency through the local provision of goods.[3] The pessimists argue that political factors impede the realization of these benefits. Pervasive subnational clientelism, especially in developing countries, leads to the misappropriation of resources.[4] The benefits of decentralization cannot be realized at the subnational level if patronage-maximizing local incumbents centralize control over policy resources and fail to delegate authority to technocratic agencies.

Both competing views suffer from the tendency to treat subnational governments and the process of decentralization as systems with *endemic* positive or negative attributes. However, these explanations are challenged by the existence of highly *composite* configurations of subnational policy performance within countries. This finding highlights the role of variables endogenous to subnational politics, including the interests of politicians and the structure of bureaucracies. Rio's experience with industrial policy differs from Minas's because of its particular legacy of populist government, conflict over patrimonial politics, and highly centralized economic bureaucracy. Similarly, Andalusia's industrial policy has from its initiation been governed by populist ideology, labor union politics, and bureaucratic centralization.

These comparative experiences challenge both the optimistic and pessimistic views of economic policy in decentralized states. The cases

---

3. Many of these arguments are based on the notion that local governments have better information than national governments about local tastes and preferences. Although this idea was discussed by Jean-Jacques Rousseau in his *Government of Poland*, contemporary scholars of federalism have done much more with this core principle. Two major theoretical insights have emerged in the more recent literature. The first emphasizes the "allocative efficiency" of decentralizing policy decisions to "better informed" local governments. See Oates (1973) and IDB (1994: 178; 1997: 153). The second argues that competition among subnational units enhances distributional efficiency by parceling out goods and services according to interregional preferences. This approach is most associated with the work of Charles Tiebout (1956), but it is also a core principle of contemporary work on fiscal federalism. See Brennan and Buchanan (1980); Musgrave and Musgrave (1989); López Murphy (1995).

4. This view is supported through case studies of subnational populism (e.g., Conniff 1981), subnational clientelism and policy performance (e.g., Prud'homme 1995; Hagopian 1996), and intergovernmental conflicts and their effects on economic adjustment (e.g., Treisman 1999; Remmer and Wibbels 2000).

of Rio and Andalusia confound optimistic expectations that decentralization will produce subnational innovation and allocative efficiency. These goals are laudable, but they are, as the pessimists argue, politically vulnerable to clientelistic manipulation. Meanwhile, the pessimistic view of decentralization cannot explain the political sources of subnational policy innovation and allocative efficiency in Minas Gerais and Asturias. These experiences suggest something other than the presence of endemically clientelistic subnational politicians and dysfunctional bureaucracies.

Systemic/endemic approaches must be replaced by comparative cross-national and cross-subnational studies of decentralized public sectors to reveal the politically contingent conditions affecting policy performance. This is the main enterprise of this book. The remainder of this chapter outlines the main argument, the theoretical framework, and the format of the empirical study.

THE ARGUMENT
The Dependent Variable

The empirical finding of composite patterns of subnational industrial policy-making in Brazil and Spain begs a broader question that is central to the focus of this book: *Why do some subnational governments produce productivity-enhancing cooperation between public agencies and firms while others do not?* This dependent variable is captured by the term "synergy." As Peter Evans (1997b: 3) explains, "the idea of `synergy' implies [that] . . . the actions of public agencies facilitate [the] forging of norms of trust and networks of civic engagement among ordinary citizens and [the use of] these norms and networks for developmental ends." The presence of synergy reduces the costs of transacting business by facilitating cooperation between state agencies and capitalists. Synergy minimizes the costs of bargaining to smooth out disagreements since all parties can rely on a reservoir of social trust. These conditions limit the opportunity costs of bargainers' time, the price of surveillance, and the cost of arbitration when cooperation threatens to collapse. Trust will also reduce future costs by lessening uncertainty. Consequently, in the presence of high levels of synergy, firms deem government officials more credible and they demonstrate more confidence in public sector decision-making.

Another way to think about synergy is to regard it as highly reciprocal transfers of information between agencies and firms; close collaboration on the setting of goals and the implementation of policy. Elinor

Ostrom (1997) illustrates this relationship by first making a distinction between a "regular producer" and a "client" of a public good such as education. Typically, she argues, government agencies are the "regular producers" of education while ordinary citizens are the "clients." This relationship describes an active provider and a passive user. Synergy exists where these distinctions are blurred; where citizens participate actively in the conception and provision of the public good and government agencies are not simply producers but clients of "citizen-produced" information and other resources.[5]

In this study the public good in question is industrial policy, namely, public policies designed to enhance the productivity and growth of firms in the industrial sector. In typical studies of industrial policy, the firm or the industrial sector is conceived of as the "client" of the financing, import protection, research and development programs, and any of the other common instruments of industrial policy that the state provides. Industrial policy, however, that is conceived and implemented through synergistic relations between public agencies and firms is the product of *reciprocal* exchange of information and resources and close collaboration. Agencies and firms coordinate common resources (e.g., information, financing, etc.) to produce a desired economic outcome (e.g., productivity improvements, positive externalities, growth, etc.).

The main purpose of this study is not to explain the causes of positive economic outcomes, but to examine the political causes of the cost-effective forms of public-private cooperation described by Ostrom and Evans as "synergy." My concern is specifically with two questions: (a) Under what political conditions will such associations *emerge?*; and (b) Under what conditions will these relations be *maintained?* The study treats synergy as both a dichotomous variable (it exists or does not) and as a variable with more continuous qualities. For example, synergy can be said to be high in cases in which public agencies and firms continually cooperate in the setting of common goals for policy; share information and resources such as finance, technology, and personnel; and work in tandem to produce positive externalities. In these cases, the distinction between the roles of producer of industrial policy and client is blurred. Conversely, sporadic or absent forms of cooperation in which public agencies have few or no contacts with firms and impose policy goals unilaterally are cases of low synergy. These are the experiences that will generate more costly forms of policy implementation.

---

5. Ostrom calls this relationship "coproduction." See Ostrom (1997: 100–102).

Coping with the Delegative Dilemma:
The Political Determinants of Synergy

Producing synergy is complicated by a public-goods logic that is magnified in the area of industrial policy. The actors and policies that are responsible for generating synergy operate within a political context. In that context they are subject to the classic problems of public-private interactions. Each intervention by the public sector in private markets creates incentives for business to influence economic policy and therefore to transform the state into an arena of distributive conflict (Rueschemeyer and Evans 1985: 69; Knight 1992). Diverse interests vie for the retention of protection, subsidies, or some other mechanism that defends an allocative outcome favorable to them (Krueger 1974; Buchanan, Tollison, and Tullock 1980; Olson 1982).[6] This extends most notably to the politician herself/himself. In the short term, a politically optimal strategy (that is, one that assures the political survival of incumbents) may require politicians to manipulate state resources and make patronage appointments to the bureaucracy in return for support. This calculation creates a tradeoff between employing economic policy resources for political purposes in the short term versus risking political survival in the hope of promoting collective economic efficiencies over the long term. Garrett and Lange (1996: 50) describe this tradeoff simply: "Politicians cannot afford to ask what is good for society as a whole in the long run, lest they lose power in the interim."

Following Barbara Geddes's (1994) game-theoretic work on political interests and economic reform, I argue that the conflict between short-run and long-term political interests constitutes a "delegative dilemma." Incumbents will maximize their chances of political survival in the short term by centralizing their control over policy resources and distributing these goods to cultivate clientelistic support (Bates and Krueger 1993). Delegation of authority over economic policy and resources to agencies would increase the political opportunity costs to incumbents of manipulating these resources. Yet as Geddes and other scholars in the "political survival" literature attest (see Ames 1987; Bates 1989), the incentive structure of short-term versus long-term tradeoffs is not constant. Changing socioeconomic constraints and institutions mediate "between [these] raw preferences and government behavior" (Garrett and Lange

---

6. This point does not assume that it is either possible or desirable to search for a policy or a set of property rights that can eliminate "wasteful rents." Nor does it assume that economically efficient policy outcomes are impossible in the absence of such structures. Rather, this argument only concludes that allocative rights and distributional outcomes are politically contested. See Samuels and Mercuro (1984: 59–60) and Bates (1989).

1996: 51). These factors may take many forms. They may include formal institutions such as electoral rules that favor the emergence of large programmatic parties and strategic situations in which all potential political rivals are weak.[7] These contextual factors alter politicians' expectations of the costs and benefits accrued from delegation. The chief analytical advantage of highlighting under what conditions political expectations take the shape they do is that this approach links in a *generalizable manner* the interests of political leaders, the institutions and socioeconomic factors that affect the content of their interests, and policy outcomes (Geddes 1994: 8).[8]

A more specific and universally applicable formulation of this logic focuses on political security. Under conditions in which the tenure of governing elites is not in jeopardy and time horizons can be extended, political leaders are more likely to delegate politically useful resources to technocratic agencies. Where levels of polarization among elite groups are high, incumbents feel vulnerable and are likely to discount future gains from economic policy success.[9] Elite conflict occurs both in terms of partisan competition over votes and social conflicts involving labor and business. These two dimensions of elite competition can intersect, generating cases in which majority parties/coalitions that might otherwise make incumbents more risk-accepting eschew delegation when faced with significant union and business opposition. Where both partisan and

---

7. This argument is based on the existence of incentives causing politicians to abandon or at least minimize *particular* interests for the sake of pursuing more *universal* goals. For empirical operationalizations of this argument in Brazil and Spain, see Weyland (1996) and Lukauskas (1998), respectively.

8. Analysis of actor expectations and the strategic environment have become particularly crucial in the study of institutional change. For example, scholars of electoral systems explain how partisan expectations following periods of electoral instability affect reform choices among electoral rules. See Boix (1999). Like the argument proposed here, these works rely on microfoundational assumptions about politicians' behavior that incumbents are reluctant to waste resources, *ceteris paribus* (e.g., Cox 1997). By specifying the contextual factors that explain how distinct patterns of strategic coordination generate diverse approaches to policy-making, this research can produce more nuanced observations. For an extended defense of this approach, see Carey (2000).

9. Alternatively, politicians in positions of dominance may seek to further their security by *not* delegating. This is a core principle of liberal thought that is aptly reflected in the case for the "separation of powers" and federalism in *The Federalist Papers*. Applied more broadly, however, this idea is problematic as it makes no distinction for changes in political context or the connections politicians readily make between long-term political interests and economic growth. A context-sensitive "political survival" argument presents a more nuanced and, as the empirical comparisons will attest, a more accurate depiction of political behavior across countries. Evidence of delegation by politically dominant incumbents in Minas Gerais and Asturias contradicts the counter-assumption, as does the overall composite pattern of political interests and policy outcomes *within* Brazil and Spain.

social polarization are muted, incumbents lead what I call *delegative governments*. Where partisan or social polarization are high or increasing, incumbents face incentives to cultivate personal support in the short term by rewarding their backers through clientelism. Incumbents in this case will not forego potential sources of patronage by delegating control over economic policy to technocrats. They will reduce their political opportunity costs by centralizing their authority over these politically useful resources. These conditions are typical of *populist governments*.

The delegative dilemma is similar to one Barbara Geddes terms the "politician's dilemma." While industrial policy does not ask politicians to forsake patronage altogether, the kind of industrial policy that generates positive externalities in the market requires that clientelistic exchange be minimized. Geddes argues that this is more likely to occur under conditions in which contending political parties are roughly equal in power. Parity reduces the relative political costs of delegation by requiring all political rivals to pay these costs equally. However, the argument I posit here suggests that parity may not be necessary and that politicians in a more secure position will have incentives to delegate.[10] Political security adjusts incumbents' perceptions of the costs of delegation in the short term. Delegative governments, as the empirical cases in this book demonstrate, do not discount the future as heavily as populist governments do. On the contrary, they estimate that the opportunity costs of delegation are low. Therefore, while delegation increases the opportunity costs of using politically useful resources later, incumbents in delegative governments believe that they have made investments and that they will be able to claim credit for improved economic performance over the long haul.[11]

The primary utility of both the partisan parity argument and that of political dominance is that they highlight the importance of low elite polarization. Highly competitive or conflictual political games are more likely to be associated with incentives to pursue clientelistic support than those in which the political opportunity costs of delegation are low. Politically vulnerable subnational incumbents will minimize the opportunity

10. This position is highly plausible. For example, scholars of the political economy of authoritarianism and democratic transitions have noted that authoritarian parties/elite groups in politically dominant positions will delegate authority to technocrats (e.g., Haggard and Kaufman 1995; Boylan 1998).

11. Geddes's argument implies that politicians "give up" these resources when they delegate, hence they would generally avoid doing so. Delegation in industrial policy might also be considered a political investment, however, in that a secure incumbent would survive to take credit for the greater productivity and growth emerging from synergistic industrial reform. Delegation, therefore, does not *necessarily* imply that incumbents discount future political gains produced by the initial act of delegating resources.

costs of mustering personal support by centralizing control over clientelistic resources, while less vulnerable subnational elites will entertain secondary incentives to decentralize. The primary incentives to delegate, therefore, are determined by the relative level of *intraregional conflict.*

Secondary incentives to delegate operate in the absence of high levels of intraregional political conflict and they are based on the nontrivial benefits of delegation. The act of delegation provides its own political returns, as regional leaders can tell their constituents that they are "doing something" about persisting economic problems and can thus justify the need for additional resources and authority from central government managers. Alternatively, if things go wrong, incumbents can blame the agencies to which they delegated their authority, covering their own responsibility for policy failure under a cloak of ambiguity (Alesina and Cukierman 1990: 846). Doing nothing may become politically costly in the face of eroding economic performance and competition with rival subnational governments over the same pool of fiscal resources. These executives will be motivated to delegate by growing concern for the larger economic welfare of their region, in addition to the expected political benefits accrued from ostensibly addressing these problems.

The Intervening Variable: Horizontal Embeddedness

Delegation empowers "political technocrats" who have broader reservoirs of technical experience than politicians. These actors are also more politically savvy than careerist technocrats.[12] Political technocrats are "swing agents" in the bureaucracy. They sit atop key bureaucratic agencies as figures pivotal to the delegation of political authority and the coordination of technical resources (Schneider 1991). As in all principal-agent models of this type, the agent (political technocrat) recommends a strategy that he or she views as the best response to economic problems. Governing politicians (the principals) that are not vulnerable to their political opponents but are less informed about technical responses will support their subordinates' proposals to avoid the risks of worsening the economic situation through their own inaction or through poorly planned action (Aghion and Tirole 1997). By doing so, in-

12. The emerging literature on political technocrats, or "technopols," has gone farthest in connecting ideas to political agents. See Dominguez (1997) and Schneider (1991 and 1993). In this book, I refer to political technocrats as appointed or selected members of the economic bureaucracy. While I agree with Domínguez (1997: 6) that technopols may also be elected and hold executive office, such elites face tradeoffs very different from those political technocrats confront in the policy-making bureaucracy.

cumbents will see the delegation of authority and resources to political technocrats as being in their best political interests.

Nevertheless, delegation is a necessary but insufficient condition for producing synergy. Two dangers may continue to threaten the emergence of cooperative agency-firm relations over time. First, incumbents may overcome the "delegative dilemma" at one point in time (t0) but face a new set of political opportunities later. Incumbents may become vulnerable to rivals at t1, compelling them to recentralize resources and authorities in ways that weaken the institutions producing synergy. That makes the maintenance of delegation contingent upon the politician's ex post evaluation at t1 of political costs and benefits. Previous commitments and institutional constraints will certainly reduce the ability of incumbents to renege, but these are not infallible (Samuels and Mercuro 1984). In short, the existence of contingent delegation keeps bureaucracies under the threat of pervasive rent-seeking.

Second, delegation gives political technocrats opportunities to advance their own interests. Since these "technopols" "are not marionettes of other politicians" (Domínguez 1997: 5), they may develop an interest in hiding information about their effort levels and performance from supervisors, politicians, and their constituents, thus contributing to "bureaucratic dysfunction."[13] As in all principal-agent relations, every incentive system allows individuals to pursue their own narrow interests or "shirk." Information asymmetries produce higher "costs of hidden action and hidden information" that facilitate shirking (Miller 1992; Solnick 1996).[14] Moreover, even when politicians favor delegation, private interests will continue to prod for special protection and subsidies ("rents"), producing incentives for bureaucrats to act in their own self-interest (Schneider 1993; Bates and Krueger 1993: 464).

I argue that the *form* interagency relations take is a crucial intervening variable in linking political interests with the creation of productive patterns of cooperation between public agencies and firms. The literature on agency-firm cooperation suggests that these relations develop from the creation of strong "vertical ties": associations that produce reciprocity,

13. This is the subject of a vast literature on bureaucracies. Its key premise is that, in the absence of oversight or some other type of constraint, bureaucrats will pursue their own career or political agendas instead of directives from their political leadership. See McCubbins, Noll, and Weingast (1987) and Niskanen (1971).

14. This is also known as the "Sen Paradox," which argues that all devolved systems of decision-making with multiple subunits produce the possibility for inefficiencies in the principal's assessment of loyal action by the agents. Due to information asymmetries within the organization, subunits will pursue their own interests at the expense of the larger organization's efficiency. See Miller (1992: 86–91) and Moe (1984).

mutual understanding, and goal-setting. I argue, however, that this is only half the story. A more important dimension lies above the domain of these vertical associations, at the level of public agencies themselves and, in some cases, decision-making partners such as unions and business associations. The most important aspects of this dimension are the patterns of contacts among these actors and the operation of these ties in conceiving and implementing economic policy.[15] I call these contacts among policy-making agencies *horizontal embeddedness*.[16]

Horizontal embeddedness minimizes the costs of political intervention and bureaucratic dysfunction by enfranchising a cross-cutting policy constituency broader than is normally the case in strictly vertical forms of cooperation between bureaucratic agencies and firms. Clientelism can develop more easily within vertical networks, while horizontal embeddedness produces the cross-agency monitoring that raises the costs of bureaucratic shirking. Horizontal embeddedness also raises the costs of intervention by politicians by creating alternative sources of political support through the expansion of the constituency of public agents and private clients involved in industrial policy-making. For example, horizontal ties increase the number of alarm bells that may sound if policy goals are not being met, preventing incumbents from hiding evidence of patrimonial exchange (McCubbins and Schwartz 1984). In sum, subnational governments will implement and maintain industrial policy, generating allocative efficiencies and minimizing clientelism, only when delegative government and horizontal embeddedness are present. *Both are necessary and cumulatively sufficient.*

The Incidence of Delegative Government with Horizontal Embeddedness: The Interregional Determinant

The combination of delegative government and horizontal embeddedness emerges in cases where incumbents delegate authority and re-

---

15. The "horizontal" dimension among policy-making agents that I describe here is similar to Hilderbrand and Grindle's (1997: 37) "task networks." These networks include both public and nonpublic sector agents whose capacity to communicate and coordinate their efforts are the *sine qua non* of their performance.

16. In the exposition of the argument I use the term "agencies" to describe mostly decision-making units of the public economic bureaucracy. But as the empirical cases in Spain will demonstrate, unions and business organizations can also play a policy-making role in partnership with public agencies. Since the argument emphasizes the interrelations among these actors and not their organizational attributes, I subsume the roles of unions and business associations in policy decision-making under the rubric of "agencies." Of course, these actors also play a role in mediating social conflict.

sources to political technocrats but are themselves exposed to incentives to divide the governance of economic policy among an array of different agencies rather than to invest control in just one. Following the work on competitive federalism in American politics, scholars attribute the shape and content of subnational policy to competition among subnational governments for investment. They argue that competition provides incentives for innovation in public policy to attract consumer-voters and businesses (Fosler 1988; Dye 1990).[17] These conflicts also create political inducements to attract federal funding lest other states acquire relatively larger shares. By creating an array of public agencies to design and implement industrial policy, incumbents can bolster their arguments for more resources from the central government with references to the immensity of the economic crisis and the related need to fund an expansive industrial policy structure. Given that industrial policy includes multiple tasks and policy skills, from utility management to labor retraining, logistical exigencies produce additional incentives for subnational governments to create numerous and connected public agencies to satisfy firm-clients and consumer-voters. Where political incentives to delegate are present, such horizontally embedded structures will be more common than in cases in which populist elites are in command of subnational government. Under populist management, the incentives to centralize control over policy resources will override the inducements created by competitive federalism to decentralize. Elite polarization will continue to tip political institutions in directions that favor clientelistic exchange. Hence, horizontal embeddedness is more likely to emerge where intraregional elite competition is low but interregional elite competition is high.

Figure 1.1 illustrates the interplay of these two independent variables and the occurrence of the intervening variable, horizontal embeddedness. Spain and Brazil are decentralized states with relatively high interregional competition. These conditions generate incentives for the development of horizontal embeddedness. In these cases, intraregional competition determines which subnational cases develop *both* delegative government and horizontal embeddedness. In Chapter 6 I explore change in the same decentralized state over time to illustrate the two

---

17. While I find this observation useful, this study challenges the general conclusion of the competitive federalist work: that intergovernmental competition produces better subnational developmental policies. This, I argue, is contingent upon subnational politics (e.g., elite and alliance interests, partisan competition, social polarization, etc.). A competitive federalist model is insufficient for analyzing these factors as these arguments tend to see subnational governments as unitary actors or "black boxes" (Chubb 1991).

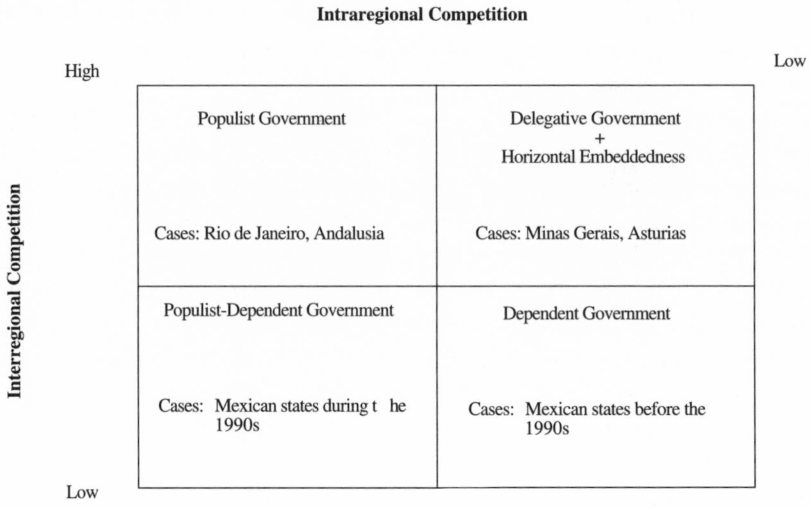

Intraregional Competition

	High	Low
Interregional Competition High	Populist Government Cases: Rio de Janeiro, Andalusia	Delegative Government + Horizontal Embeddedness Cases: Minas Gerais, Asturias
Low	Populist-Dependent Government Cases: Mexican states during t he 1990s	Dependent Government Cases: Mexican states before the 1990s

FIG 1.1　The independent variables

other possible combinations. The Mexican states prior to the 1990s faced little interregional competition but also little intraregional elite conflict. Most states were governed by the Institutional Revolutionary Party (PRI). While the opportunity to delegate existed, low levels of inter-regional competition due to tight federal controls over economic policy-making and spending by the states produced few incentives or resources for the creation of subnational, horizontally embedded economic agencies.[18] Where delegation did occur, subnational bureaucracies were un-derdeveloped and tended to follow or be governed by national government mandates. They were, as the figure indicates, "dependent governments." During the 1990s, a more competitive political party system and decentralization reforms created incentives for the governors to use slowly expanding economic policy resources to cultivate their subnational constituencies. Most fiscal and economic policy authorities, however, remained centralized; governed by federal mandates that weakened incentives for subnational executives to create extensive subnational development bureaucracies. Continued control over inter-regional competition in a polity experiencing greater intraregional elite conflict produced "populist-dependent governments," which, like the

18. Comparative studies have recently shown that the preferences of subnational elites in the pursuit of economic policies are strongly determined by the decentralization of re-sources and opportunities to pursue political and economic self-interest. For example, see Chhibber and Eldersveld (2000: 361).

"populist" and "dependent" types, developed neither delegative government nor horizontal embeddedness.

Unpacking Horizontal Embeddedness

Once created, horizontal embeddedness protects the decentralized connections between public agencies and private firms that are necessary for producing developmentally successful forms of cooperation. Even if intraregional elite polarization becomes more intense over time, making political leaders more vulnerable, their ability to intervene in these encompassing networks will be diminished. Horizontally embedded bureaucracies are more difficult to disassemble since they can move their resources around with relative flexibility. Public agencies in these networks can also cultivate broader constituencies for industrial policy, creating countervailing political support that raises the costs of intervention for political executives. Horizontal embeddedness also creates cross-cutting networks of surveillance *within* the bureaucracy that reduce the risk that political technocrats will abuse their authority. Therefore, horizontal embeddedness allows public-private cooperation to persist even after the end of the mandates of the politicians who first made these productive associations possible.

Horizontally embedded policy networks are also flexibly reactive. Since information flows are symmetric and frequent, policy-making agencies can solve problems collectively in the most efficient manner possible. Continuous monitoring facilitates continuous experimentation and learning in a manner akin to that identified by scholars of flexible production systems (e.g., Sabel 1995). Consequently, horizontally embedded networks are less likely to become ossified. They are prone to develop responses to economic and political change as these transformations occur.

As the cases will demonstrate, delegative governments may produce horizontal embeddedness that varies according to the structure of interagency relations, based upon (a) the frequency of interagency contact and (b) the degree of centralization of the interagency network. The most developed form of horizontal embeddedness is characterized by continuous contacts across agencies that are decentralized but coordinated under a common development plan that specifies targeted sectors or regions and agency responsibilities. The plan establishes a framework for setting goals and timetables for joint action (for high-level functions) and, in practice, requires the sharing of personnel and information as a routine matter. No single agency maintains supremacy over the others, although an interagency council on which all are represented might have priority-setting powers. I label this ideal type "plan-oriented" horizontal embeddedness.

The second form of horizontal embeddedness created by delegative government is the "project-oriented" type. The agencies still coordinate high-level functions and oversee each other's operations, but contact is less frequent than in the plan-oriented system. Strategic planning is co-ordinated among the agencies, but usually without an interagency council or a development plan supported by a ministry. Planning is done as project opportunities emerge. As in the plan-oriented variety, no agency is supreme or able to see a firm project through to completion without the involvement of the others. As the cases will demonstrate, project-oriented forms of horizontal embeddedness are more likely to exist when politicians have de-emphasized the creation of industrial development plans and have left these functions to the agencies under an extant set of priorities.

Populist and populist-dependent governments do not produce horizontal embeddedness, but they do foster the development of two types of interagency relations that are evident in the cases. These are summarized in Figure 1.2 and compared with the types described above. The first is a "hierarchical-functional" type in which interagency relations are highly centralized. A dominant planning agency will devolve operations to more specialized units, but each of these subagencies will have only low-level functional duties (e.g., distributing finance, building infrastructure, etc.) without the authority to participate in strategic planning. Strategic planning will most likely be defined by politicians with command over the dominant agency. Contacts are "continuous" but asymmetrical between the dominant agency and the subagencies. Hence few opportunities exist to generate feedback or produce checks on potential abuses of power at the top.

The second type of interagency network evident in populist or populist-dependent cases is the "nonfunctional" type. Like the hierarchical-functional system, this type has the concentrated interagency structure favored by populist governments. But in addition to the problems of reduced checks on executive decisions, low levels of interagency contact generate high costs of hidden information. This type maximizes bureaucratic dysfunction and clientelistic misappropriation of resources.[19]

19. One other possibility not depicted here involves "dependent governments." Interagency networks in these cases are not likely to be developed on either of the dimensions of horizontal embeddedness. Most important, there are no opportunities for *inter*agency contact since dependent governments are less likely to create multiple agencies and will have few resources to delegate. These might also be considered "nonfunctional" cases.

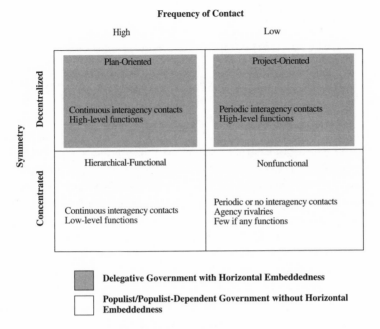

Frequency of Contact

FIG 1.2   Ideal types of interagency networks

Both the plan-oriented and the project-oriented types of horizontal embeddedness produce coordinated and accountable relations among the agencies, reducing the possibilities for politicization and abuse of resources. These systems are most likely to maintain themselves in the face of subsequent elite polarization and therefore are more likely to sustain cooperative, efficiency-enhancing relations with firms. Contacts in both of these systems will be maintained and they will generate common goals between agencies and firms and collaborative use of resources. The hierarchical-functional and nonfunctional systems, however, are more open to being politicized by incumbents. These are the interagency relations most likely to be favored by populists who seek to minimize the costs of mustering clientelistic resources in the face of threats to their political survival. For populists, the concentration of control over development agencies is the most convenient way of maximizing their control over patronage.

ALTERNATIVE APPROACHES TO EXPLAINING THE CAUSES OF SYNERGY

The problem of how to create and sustain cooperation between public agencies and firms has been the focus of a great deal of scholarship in the social sciences. In recent years, much of this work has highlighted patterns of cooperation based on mutual understanding and trust, rather than on market-based efficiency. Whether they use evocative terms such as Mark Granovetter's (1985) "embeddedness" or Robert Putnam's (1993) "civic-ness" and "social capital," these scholars see close trust-based associations between states and firms as developmentally effective. Judith Tendler (1997) illustrates the importance of these close ties in her study of state and municipal programs in preventive health, public procurement, and agricultural productivity in Ceará, Brazil. In addition to the role of favorable publicity and the meritocractic distribution of rewards within the state bureaucracy, Tendler emphasizes the way in which public sector officers and private clients maintained a capacity to listen to each other and adjust goals through the exchange of information. Such demonstrated reciprocity, Tendler claims, explained the effectiveness of Ceará's innovative economic and social policies. In a similar way, Elinor Ostrom has highlighted the role of close ties between public servants and clients in the creation of systems of "coproduction." In these cases, clients hammer out the details of projects in close consultation with officials, thereby reducing the costs of arbitrating prices and citizens' complaints after public monies have been committed.[20] The success of consultation emerges from the proximity of the actors and the frequency of their meetings, conditions that "deepen" their mutual understanding. The emphasis in these cases is on making the representatives of public agencies part of the community in which they work. Close ties are strong ties, and strong ties create confidence.

These approaches, however, overplay the importance of "close ties" while underplaying the role of bureaucratic structure. Some do specify the relevant organizational attributes of the public sector, but these tend to highlight factors that deal inadequately with the delegative dilemma and bureaucratic dysfunction.

Close vertical ties may enhance economic policy performance, but may also reinforce rent-seeking by recreating dozens of concentrated systems of discretionary power.[21] Dense associative ties, like those advo-

20. Ostrom (1997) identifies cases in the planning of condominial sanitation systems in which citizens became involved in making decisions. Lam (1996) reports similar levels of close public agency-client ties in the management of irrigation systems in Taiwan.

21. By placing causal emphasis on the motivations of public agents, Tendler's (1997) nuanced approach to synergy seeks to explain how normative structures can block rent-seeking. Yet by ignoring how politicians may gain control over these vertical networks in the future, she begs the question of how synergy can be *politically* sustained once it is created. Normative ties may explain the proper functioning of vertically and even horizontally elaborate networks, but Tendler does not explain how they may defend against the incursions of political agents who are not included in these normative networks.

cated by Putnam and Richard Locke (1995), produce their own dangers. In their multicountry test of Putnam's thesis, Knack and Keefer (1997) found that associational activity built reservoirs of trust, but also facilitated rent-seeking by expanding the organizational base of societal interests. Of course, associations that are broad-based and encompassing may produce cross-cutting cleavages that prevent "Olsonite distributional coalitions" (Schneider 1998: 111; Garrett 1998), but these multisectoral organizations, which are best known in the "democratic corporatist" cases of Western Europe, are either absent or barely coherent in most developing countries. In the context of developing economies with "porous" state structures, encompassing associations are more likely to abuse their market power and exert pressure for rents on the economic bureaucracy.[22]

Associational approaches also suffer from the tendency to sublimate the role of the state (both central and subnational) to one of many relevant sociopolitical actors, or to ignore it altogether by focusing analysis on relations among firms.[23] Yet in poor regions in developing countries where labor and business groups are often weak, the state is invariably the key actor in providing crucial resources for economic adjustment. The sociopolitical associations that do emerge are likely to be initially created by public officials and political leaders rather than by a preexisting coherent network of well-organized political, economic, and societal actors (Schmitter 1997: 248–49; Fox 1996).[24] Moreover, how these public agencies organize is an important determinant of agency-firm cooperation. Studies that conflate these variables gloss over this causal

---

22. See Hagopian (1996), Bates (1989), Callaghy (1988), and Migdal (1988).

23. One major example is the literature on "industrial districts," which focuses on the emergence of networks of innovative small- and medium-sized firms, some with familial associations, that became more productive and internationally competitive during the 1970s and 1980s. The preeminent cases in this literature include the developed regions of northeastern and central Italy (the so-called "Third Italy"), most notably Emilia-Romagna; the cases of Silicon Valley and Route 128 in the U. S.; and that of Baden-Württemberg in Germany. See Piore and Sabel (1984), Sabel (1989), Brusco (1982), Pyke, Becattini, and Sengenberger (1990), Castells (1989), Saxenian (1994), and Herrigel (1995). These regions are among the most developed in these countries, making them poor models for lesser developed regions in Third World countries. Analysts looking for the same dynamic small firm associations in the developing world have encountered few cases and formidable political and economic obstacles to the broad application of the Third Italy model. See Fuhr (1993). Fiscal crises in developing countries also make problematic the U.S. model of pumping large outlays into university systems to create a milieu of ideas and skilled personnel.

24. By contrast, much of the literature on industrial districts reverses the causal chain by highlighting the preexistence of "a climate of social consensus and strong credibility" as a means of facilitating subnational industrial policy. See Brusco and Righi (1989).

relationship. For example, Evans's (1995) use of the term "embedded-ness" includes the linkages between agencies and firms but it fails to disaggregate the interagency dimension.

Other works place emphasis on the professional and organizational attributes of the public sector. According to these arguments, professionally staffed, corporately coherent, and "autonomous" bureaucratic agencies guarantee that economic policy will be designed and implemented in an economically rational manner.[25] Autonomy alone, however, is insufficient for providing state agencies with the information and political resources needed to create synergy. Moreover, bureaucrats may sacrifice economic efficiency in defense of their career interests, particularly when they are induced by politicians and societal actors who have been known to breach the wall of bureaucratic autonomy. Evans (1992, 1995) argues that a mixture of autonomy and embeddedness can produce synergy, but he is unclear about how the proper balance of the two emerges in distinct political settings. The creation of one can sap the other, especially when self-interested actors are involved in the game of institution-building.

Available analytical approaches to synergy either "oversocialize" by discounting the role of state interests (politicians and bureaucrats) or they "undersocialize" by ignoring the dangers and insufficiencies of autonomous state intervention.[26] The prescriptions of associational, social capital, and autonomy arguments remain vulnerable to the problems of the "delegative dilemma" that can cause synergy to fail or not develop in the first place. Even if synergy emerges, these continued problems will threaten its maintenance. How then can the political interests of politicians and bureaucrats be reconciled with the collective action required by synergy? The answer lies in putting off the chimerical search for pre-existing networks of civic engagement and taking the political interests and strategies of state managers seriously.

---

25. Patterns of recruitment from elite university systems, the existence of meritocractic advancement, long terms of service, the circulation of bureaucrats among different policy agencies, and the development of an effective esprit de corps are all factors that increase the autonomy of the professional economic bureaucracy. See Schneider (1993). Some approaches to embeddedness, such as Evans's (1995), impute such importance to Weberian bureaucracies that these factors tend to overshadow the role of embedded ties between state and society. The political economic literature on the sources of East Asian development is most explicit about linking the corporate organization of the state to the success of the growth model. See Johnson (1982), Amsden (1989), Deyo (1987), and Wade (1990).

26. The distinction between approaches that "oversocialize" and "undersocialize" can be found in Granovetter (1985). I will expand on this critique in my final chapter.

THE STUDY

Explaining the political causes of synergy has led me to compare subnational regions in Brazil and Spain, two countries literally an ocean apart. My initial expectations for the availability of synergy in either country could not have been more different. In terms of its level of national development, Spain is now, without a doubt, a member of the advanced capitalist world. Although Spanish industrialization followed a state-led path similar to that of Brazil during the postwar period, Spain's leaders were able to reorient the country's development model along more market-oriented lines earlier than in Brazil, and with more success. Spain's fiscal crisis during the 1980s was severe, but not at all on a par with the external debt crisis that decimated Brazil's fiscal accounts and ended the country's experiments with "deepening" import-substitution industrialization. By 1986, Spain, along with Portugal, became a member of the European Community (EC) (now, the European Union or EU). EC structural funding and a recovering fiscal capacity allowed the Socialist government to launch a costly and politically risky restructuring of the country's major industrial sectors. By contrast, Brazil's industrial adjustment was ad hoc, orchestrated by a gradual opening of the domestic market to foreign competition and complicated by repeated bouts with mega-inflation. Given these differences, it would be no mystery why Spain by the end of the 1990s was able to consolidate its position in global markets as a developed market economy while Brazil continued to struggle with the exigencies of economic adjustment at great cost to domestic industry.

Several political factors favored Spain's ability to adjust. Following the death of longtime dictator Francisco Franco in November 1975 the transition to democracy produced a stable parliamentary system with coherent parties. The Socialist Party (Partido Socialista Obrero Español, PSOE), led by Felipe González, was the most organizationally disciplined and successful. Under González, the PSOE won an absolute majority in the Spanish Cortes (parliament) and held it for two terms (1982–89). Although in 1993 the PSOE would be forced to forge a parliamentary alliance with the Catalonian nationalist party, Convergència i Unió (CiU), to retain a governing majority, the Socialists would remain in power until 1996. Under these conditions, the PSOE government was effective in mediating the numerous economic and political conflicts in the Spanish regions that might threaten the stability of democracy.[27]

---

27. The PSOE's powerful position in Spanish politics was, in part, due to the sequencing of the democratic transition. Bermeo (1994) argues that the centrist Union of the Demo-

Such coherent and stable party rule was completely missing in Brazil, where electoral laws and clientelism continued to erode party identity.[28] Ad hoc alliances for reform routinely fell apart as parties were unable to maintain a loyal following either among the voters or the "political class" (*clase política*).[29] Once again, decentralization played a destabilizing role as personalist party leadership tied to subnational political machines further fragmented parties in the national legislature (Mainwaring 1997: 83–84), compelling Brazilian presidents to exert their considerable authority through decree powers (Power 1991, 1998; Figueiredo and Limongi 1997). Yet even here, policy resulting from these "hyperpresidentialist" efforts was often diluted by the need to distribute patronage to subnational elites in order to consolidate legislative support at the federal level (Smith and Messari 1998).

Spain and Brazil could not be more different in their reservoirs of social capital. In their study of social capital in twenty-nine market economies, Knack and Keefer (1997) found that Spain was only slightly below the average score for the level of trust (34.5; the mean was 35.8) and ranked among the advanced industrial countries in levels of civic engagement and associational density. Brazil, by contrast, was ranked dead last on these indicators. Given the tendency for social capital to concentrate in countries with greater and more equal distribution of income, the fact that Brazil remained one of the world's most unequal countries helps to explain these results.

Despite such national differences between Spain and Brazil, both countries maintained a composite subnational pattern of synergy. Synergistic ties emerged in some regions and not in others *within* both countries. Associative networks became the basis for innovative industrial policy-making in certain regions; these had incumbents interested in delegating authority to subnational political technocracies with developing

---

cratic Center (UCD) that preceded the PSOE in power paid the primary political costs of initiating the democratic transition, thereby providing the Socialists with a stable democratic order in which the PSOE could implement costly economic adjustment policies. Many of the costs of these reforms fell upon regional economies, making the PSOE's "autonomous position within the various institutions of the Spanish [central] state" crucial to implementing the national reform agenda. See Bermeo and García-Durán (1994).

28. The literature on how Brazilian electoral laws weaken party labels by creating incentives for "candidate-centric" voting and organization is extensive. See Mainwaring (1992–93: 682–83, 700–701), Ames (2001), Samuels (1998), and Mainwaring (1999).

29. In the Brazilian cases I use the term "political class" to refer to the narrow clientelistic networks that dominate the arena of political competition. See Schneider (1999: 289–91). For an examination of the Brazilian political class and regional inequalities in the Brazilian federation, see Schwartzman (1973, 1975).

levels of horizontal embeddedness. Other regions without these factors failed to develop synergy. The presence of more favorable economic conditions, greater fiscal resources, the existence of stronger and more coherent parties, EU membership, and more voluminous reservoirs of social capital in Spain cannot explain the failures. Likewise, the absence of these factors in Brazil cannot account for the emergence of synergy in certain cases.

Such composite patterns of subnational adjustment require that scholars put aside analyses of national policy-making and utilize a more precise subnational comparative method (Snyder 2001).[30] Given the complexity of "composite economies" and the importance of the qualitative features of variables such as horizontal embeddedness and synergy, my chosen method of study utilizes qualitative subnational case study comparisons. While some of the aspects of synergy and horizontal embeddedness are quantifiable (for instance, heightened productivity and frequency of contacts), I agree with Locke and others in maintaining that these quantitative aspects are less important than their qualitative attributes. The emergence of mutual understanding and cooperation among agencies, and between agencies and firms, depends upon human perceptions of complex interactions over time, which are only poorly quantifiable. This does not mean that such objects of study cannot be assessed using a rigorous comparative method and utilizing concrete indicators of the variables.[31] Having fleshed out my main variables and their indicators in this chapter, I will use the case studies to demonstrate how these variables operate in comparative perspective. I substantiate these variables in the empirical cases through careful use of interviews of politicians, agency directors, middle-level policy-makers, firm managers, labor union organizers, and other actors. The analysis is also based on government documents, internal memos, secondary sources, and periodicals.

In this study, I focus on two subnational cases in each country: in Brazil, the states of Minas Gerais and Rio de Janeiro; in Spain, the regions of the Principado de Asturias and Andalusia. Minas Gerais and Asturias

---

30. This argument is also central to Locke's (1995) approach to studying the political economy of Italy. For a discussion of the "micropolitical" approach, see his Chapter 6. Additional support for this approach can be found in Krugman (1991: 99), who writes that "regional comparisons offer a huge, almost untapped source of evidence about how our economy really works."

31. Of course, countless studies in comparative politics have done just that. One of the leading works in the subfield of methodology has provided the strongest case to date that the rules of scientific inference and rigor are the same for qualitative and quantitative studies. See King, Keohane, and Verba (1994).

FIG 1.3 States of Brazil

developed significant levels of synergy during the 1980s and 1990s while Rio de Janeiro and Andalusia failed to create viable systems of public-private cooperation. Although attempts were made in all four cases, the political interests and level of horizontal embeddedness governing sub-national industrial policies favored the emergence of synergy in Minas and Asturias. Histories of pervasive clientelism and political polarization in state politics hindered the creation and maintenance of industrial policies in Rio and Andalusia.

Selection of these subnational cases was influenced by the complexity of the economic problems they faced. I chose subnational cases that could be considered "hard cases"—secondary industrial regions facing sweeping political and economic change that would present challenges to subnational industrial policy-making. Asturias and Minas Gerais were unlikely places for synergy. Each was a secondary location of industrial investment, unlike the core economies of Madrid/Catalonia and São Paulo. Severe economic crises in both regions challenged the efficacy

FIG 1.4   Regions of Spain

of subnational policy responses. Moreover, these regions were either ordinary or impoverished in their supply of the ideal-typical cooperative
norms of Putnam's theory. Asturias remained a hotbed of labor conflict
throughout the period under study. Minas Gerais's development continued to be based on a combination of socially undifferentiated and isolated industrial towns and significant levels of labor repression.

   I subject the role of elite polarization and horizontal embeddedness in
explaining the unlikely emergence of synergy in Asturias and Minas
Gerais to a more rigorous test by comparing these experiences across
both countries. Despite the economic and political characteristics re-
viewed above that should place Spanish regions in a position superior to
that of Brazilian states, the comparison of Asturias and Minas demonstrates that levels of elite polarization and horizontal embeddedness explain the advent of synergy in these two cases. Figure 1.5 illustrates the
distribution of the cases, which I preview briefly below.

   In Chapter 2, I compare the political and economic histories of Brazil

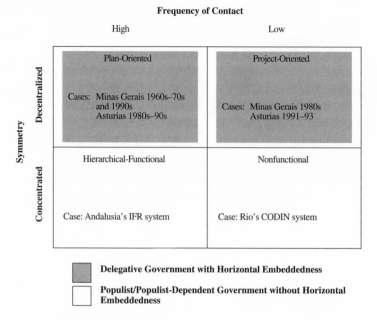

FIG 1.5   Distribution of Cases

and Spain. The analysis focuses on transformations in both countries dating from the 1970s through the mid-1990s. I outline the substantial differences between the two countries in the development and reform of industrial markets, the evolution of economic crises, the management of institutional reforms (particularly democratization and decentralization), and relations with supranational entities. Despite these differences in national institutions, both countries experienced growing inter-regional competition and composite subnational patterns of synergy.

Chapter 3 examines economic policy-making in the Brazilian state of Minas Gerais. In Minas, industrial policy emerged as a focus of the state's cohesive political class of traditional elites during the 1960s. At that time, the state government developed strong political interests in breaking the economy's dependency on São Paulo's larger and more dynamic industrial markets bordering Minas's south. Amid a fiscal reform initiated by the military, Minas Gerais's political leadership positioned itself to claim new resources and authorities for the state's development policy. Intergovernmental conflicts with other states and the federal government encouraged Minas's leaders to construct an elaborate economic technocracy designed to attract new investment to the state. These public agencies established close relations with numerous large investors, including the Italian multinational Fiat, which formed the core of the state's most important industrial sector. Horizontal embeddedness in this period was plan-oriented.

Minas's economic bureaucracy expanded, but the fiscal crisis of the 1980s decimated Brazil's state-led developmentalist model, threatening Minas's industrial policy and calling for a revision to the state's development mission. As these conditions changed, political technocrats seized the opportunity to reorient the state's industrial policy to support productive changes in the region's automotive industry. Horizontal ties across the state's development agencies produced the interdisciplinary knowledge required by automotive projects, but they also established lasting political ties. During the mid-1980s, a populist governor attempted to scavenge fiscal resources from the Minas Gerais agencies. Without the support of a delegative government, Minas's plan-based horizontal embeddedness became more project-focused. Persisting horizontal ties linking the state development bank, the entrepreneurial information agencies, and the state's utility companies created a tight-knit constituency within the bureaucracy that helped preserve the industrial policy system. Later, these horizontal ties provided communicative links among agency elites that made possible a dramatic reform in Minas Gerais's economic bureaucracy and development policy, returning it to a plan-based form of horizontal embeddedness. The state's industrial policy was reoriented, directed away from developmentalism and toward a market-oriented approach. As market criteria became more important in economic policy-making, horizontal ties proved more valuable in limiting clientelistic exchange.

The nature of horizontal ties was both formal and informal. Legislation provided Minas Gerais's industrial policy agencies with different authorities and resources that called for coordination among them on complex projects. Relations across the state secretariats of planning and the economy created regular executive-level communication among agency administrators. These contacts also operated at an informal level as technocrats communicated routinely and across agency hierarchies at the executive and middle management levels. Given such close and constant ties across agencies, the costs of cross-agency monitoring were low, limiting the opportunities for politicians and bureaucrats to pursue their parochial interests. Moreover, these ties created a lasting level of confidence among firms and agencies that, despite changes in the economic model and the threat of political intervention, cooperation would persist. These conditions produced industrial policies that greatly enhanced the productivity of Fiat and its suppliers during the 1990s.

Chapter 4 analyzes the industrial policy network in the Principado de Asturias in Spain. The Asturian economy depended upon two declining publicly owned industries: mining and steel. Due to the problems of these sectors, labor unions with strong ties to the Socialists remained the most powerful voices in regional politics. This gave the PSOE a solid base of organized support, allowing one Socialist regional president, Pedro de Silva, to govern Asturias for most of the 1980s.

In Asturias, the development mission formed around a set of assumptions emerging from decades of public intervention in mining and steel. For much of the 1960s and 1970s, Asturian politicians and the economic bureaucracy accepted the fact that the inefficient mining and steel sectors could not be weaned off national subsidies. Periodic fiscal problems in Spain, and the long, slow decline of public mining and steel in neighboring European countries, convinced the Asturian leadership that this was an unsustainable situation. The government also assumed that the region's powerful labor unions would not change their preferences in the future; they would attempt to keep public mining alive in Asturias by defending its subsidies and their jobs. Once Spain became mired in a "stagflationary" crisis after 1973 and the pace of political change accelerated with the death of Francisco Franco and the transition to democracy, the Asturian government believed that the time had come to change the direction of the region's economy.

By delegating economic authority and fiscal resources to a handful of bureaucratic agencies, the Asturian leadership believed that it could develop alternative industries in the mining and steel districts. At the same time, building a complex industrial policy and delegating authority to its technocratic management satisfied several political interests of the Asturian leadership. Like their nationalist counterparts in Catalonia and the Basque Country, Asturias's governing politicians wanted greater political autonomy for the regional government during the transition to democracy. While the Asturian leadership could not credibly use nationalist arguments as the Catalonians and the Basque did in their campaign for regional autonomy, and thus could not access the fiscal authority that would go along with it, the Asturians could compete against other regions for national resources by referring to Asturias's severe economic crisis. Promoting a regional industrial policy would justify the constitutional devolution of authority and resources to the Asturians, a position that both the Socialists and their political opponents favored. In order to place additional pressure on Madrid, the regional government framed the new Asturian industrial policy as a "compensatory" program for jobs soon to be lost in public mining.

Knowing that the labor unions would resist national restructuring of the public mining firms and that their claims would have to be addressed by national politicians in the new democracy, Asturias's industrial policy-makers deftly used references to "social compensation" to piggyback their interests on those of the region's unions and position themselves for garnering additional authorities and fiscal resources from the central government.

Empowered with substantial resources and political support, the technocrats at the helm of the Asturian development agencies created an array of new programs designed to improve the productivity of small- and medium-sized firms, the region's chief source of employment. The plan-based network matured, producing heightened confidence among the region's firms in the role of the regional public sector; this was an unlikely outcome in a Spanish region haunted by the destructive role of the national public sector in mining and steel. Even when the Socialists lost control of the regional government in the mid-1990s, ties among the industrial policy agencies, firms, and labor unions preserved these confidence-building effects, although the system became more project-based.

Chapter 5 outlines two cases that form a sharp contrast to the experiences of Minas Gerais and Asturias: Rio de Janeiro (Brazil) and Andalusia (Spain). In these two cases, chronic and polarizing political conflicts among elites created strong incentives for governing politicians to centralize their control over economic policy-making. The logic of populist politics led these politicians to manipulate industrial policy to satisfy their constituencies and isolate their rivals. The results for the economy were the generation of severe inefficiencies in the management of fiscal resources and inaction on the needs of firms.

In comparison to Minas's political leadership, Rio de Janeiro's political class was highly conflictual. It depended upon the rise and fall of numerous populist governors such as Antônio de Pádua Chagas Freitas and Leonel Brizola. These politicians centralized their control over industrial policy agencies and used them to cultivate clientelistic networks of support. As a result, the development mission in Rio was weak and interagency ties were nonfunctional.

Vertical ties emerged in some sectors, but these became mechanisms for building a clientelistic constituency. A prominent example were the "industrial districts" managed by the state's Company of Industrial Development (CODIN). Brizola, and his successor between 1986–90, Wellington Moreira Franco, centralized control over the districts and used them to subsidize land speculation. CODIN also became a clientelistic resource as a center of political appointments in state government. As a result, the CODIN could develop few workable linkages with national or state-level agencies, business, or labor groups. Firms continued to distrust the agency, even as a new governorship during the mid-1990s attempted to salvage the state's industrial policy system.

Andalusia's governing Socialists were a powerful presence in the region, but early nationalist opposition and periodic confrontations with the region's chief business association threatened to erode the PSOE's constituency soon after the region gained statutory autonomy during the Spanish transition to democracy. Socialist leaders were forced to buttress their support base with populist-style distribution. They manipulated industrial policy to build their constituency among the working class during a time of great economic uncertainty in Andalusia. This practice created incentives for regional elites to centralize administration, facilitating the control incumbents could exert over the region's industrial reforms.

The resulting hierarchical-functional form of interagency ties that developed in Andalusia generated high costs in the implementation of industrial policy. Andalusia's politicians embraced unsustainable big-ticket industrial policies that were fiscally and economically costly. As the Socialists moved to consolidate their electoral constituency through the use of industrial policy, loyalists manipulated the resources of the region's chief development agency, the Andalusian Institute of Promotion (IFA). Social pressure from the region's labor unions and chief business association generated incentives for politicians to embrace wasteful distribution of subsidies and public buy-outs. While these actions accrued political benefits to the governing Socialists, they produced few lasting examples of cooperation between regional agencies and private firms.

In Chapter 6, I reconsider the causes and incidence of synergy by comparing the data cross-regionally and cross-subnationally and with reference to other subnational cases in Spain, Brazil, and other countries. I then examine the populist-dependent and dependent types with a longitudinal comparison of the Mexican states. Finally, I assess the theoretical significance of these findings for emerging research on the political economy of decentralization.

Dual Transitions in Spain and Brazil

Spain and Brazil each maintained models of growth in which public sector investments shaped development patterns. During the 1980s and 1990s, these state-led models declined and required extensive economic reform. Both countries also engaged in transitions from long periods of authoritarian rule to democracy. These "dual transitions" produced new pressures and opportunities for subnational governments to become more active in economic policy.[1] First, the erosion of the state-led growth model and liberal structural reform produced a series of hardships in subnational economies. Such hardships created demand among local governments for the authorities and resources needed to address them. Second, democratic transitions in Brazil and Spain facilitated political and fiscal decentralization of central government functions. This process empowered subnational government with new economic policy-making authorities and resources. Finally, this process fomented greater levels of interregional competition. These tensions created strong incentives for subnational governments to demand more resources and to develop their own differentiated economic bureaucracies.

These general similarities aside, dual transitions in both countries progressed in very different ways. The Spanish state and economy were successfully reformed during the 1980s and 1990s in ways that dramati-

---

1. "Dual transitions" are cases of democratic transition that coincide with liberal structural reforms. See Bermeo (1994), Bermeo and García-Durán (1994), and Encarnación (1997).

cally improved Spain's level of development and reinforced democratization. The reform experience in Brazil was decidedly different. Economic crises remained a part of the political landscape well through the 1990s while anemic political parties and endemic clientelism threatened nascent democratic institutions. Associational life in Spain, despite its problems, continued to evolve in ways that favored programmatic reform. Coherent and disciplined national parties reinforced these trends. In Brazil, associations and politicians continued to defend their own particular interests, hindering reform efforts by some national parties such as the leftist Workers' Party. Other national parties and legislatures were unable to discipline these constituencies to support a national reform agenda. Finally, Spain's membership in the European Union greatly expanded the resources national governing parties had to consolidate economic and political reforms. Brazil could count on no such entity to help it through its dual transition.

This chapter argues that, despite these differences between Spain and Brazil, dual transitions created a range of opportunities *in both countries* for the development of synergy. Democratization, economic crises, and decentralizing state reforms opened the way for numerous subnational experiments with industrial policy during the 1980s and 1990s. Nevertheless, no national models of synergy materialized in either case. The rest of this book demonstrates that composite patterns emerged within and between both countries, suggesting that factors endogenous to subnational politics are the key explanatory variables.

The next section of this chapter contrasts the distinct experiences of Spain and Brazil with the reform of state-led development models. The comparison highlights the apparent advantages of Spain over Brazil. The section that follows argues that, despite these differences, subnational government in both countries developed opportunities for implementing industrial reforms of their own.

THE DECLINE OF INDUSTRIAL COORDINATION FROM ABOVE: SPAIN AND BRAZIL COMPARED

If the state plays a key role in the development of late-industrializers (Gershenkron 1963), then Brazil and Spain are archetypal cases of the famous argument. Import-substitution and public sector investments in steel, mining, and petroleum, guided by nationalism and reasons of military defense, dominated the early phases of heavy industrialization in the 1930s and 1940s in Spain and Brazil. In Brazil, statism found ideological support in Getúlio Vargas' *Estado Nôvo* (1937–45) and its doctrine of using the state to exploit the wealth of the country.[2] Similarly, the military regime that ruled Brazil between 1964 and 1985 justified state intervention in sectors such as oil and steel as an effort in breaking the country's dependency on foreign sources and preserving the national security interests of the state and the nation (Evans 1979).

In Spain, General Francisco Franco's dictatorship (1938–75) created the Instituto Nacional de Industria (National Institute of Industry, INI) in 1941 as a holding company of state firms largely concentrated in petroleum, steel, mining, and transportation.[3] Inspired by the fascist Istituto per la Recostruzione Industriale (IRI) in Italy, the main goals of INI industrial policy were industrial autarky and national defense. Juan Antonio Suanzes, the influential first president of the INI, argued that Spain's dependency on foreigners for basic industrial commodities such as steel and its industrial "backwardness" required that the state become the steward of the country's industrialization (Aceña and Comín 1991: 78–84).

The expansion of the public sector was a key tool for building a domestic industrial class in both countries. For example, the state made possible an important role for Brazilian private capital in the creation of the Companhia Siderúrgica Nacional (National Steel Company, CSN) in 1941 (Baer 1969: 103). The creation of the Banco Nacional de Desenvolvimento Econômico e Social (National Development Bank—BNDES) during the early 1950s established a powerful financial partner for private entrepreneurs willing to invest in the new "mixed-enterprise" steel companies, Usiminas and Cosipa (Evans 1979: 92; Martins 1985). In a similar way, the INI followed a "Prussian" style of economic development that married the interests of large private banks (the "financial aristocracy") with INI firms and "mixed companies" (Aceña and Comín 1991: 136–40; Pérez 1997: 169–71). During the 1950s, the Spanish state created a national ruling class from the government banking and industrial sectors (Maravall and Santamaría 1986: 75–76). After a landmark liberalization of the economy by Franco in 1959, the INI abandoned autarkic, public

2. The literature on this period in Brazilian economic history is voluminous. For a good review, see Skidmore (1967).

3. Not all Spanish public firms were governed by INI. After 1970 the Franquist state created two more holdings—the Dirección General del Patrimonio del Estado (the General Direction of the Patrimony of the State, DGPE), a collection of film, communications, food, and tobacco companies—and the Instituto Nacional de Hidrocarburos (National Institute of Hydrocarbons, INH), a collection of energy firms. INI, however, remained the most important public sector holding company. The current study focuses mainly on INI firms since they are representative of the crisis of the Spanish public sector as a whole.

production and adopted policies that favored the involvement of private initiative. Mixed firms became a more common form of INI intervention in the market. A new industrial law in 1963 opened the door to economic planning designed to aid private enterprises in sectors where private capital was weak. Inspired by the ideas of the French Massé Plan, the 1963 Plan de Desarrollo 1964–1967 (Development Plan I) argued that the private sector was the main engine of economic development and that the state should play a tutelary but auxiliary role. Cooperative arrangements soon emerged between private and public capital in previously autarkic sectors such as steel, ship construction, and mining. Overall, however, the INI firms continued to dominate Spain's industrial economy well into the 1970s (Boyer 1975: 95–96).

The combination of import-substitution and industrial promotion of domestic and foreign investment through state-led initiatives in both countries led to a period of intensive industrialization and rapid growth during the 1950s, 1960s, and early 1970s. The Spanish industrial economy grew 7.2 percent between 1960 and 1973, reaching a peak of 8 percent between 1971 and 1973, while its European neighbors grew 4.7 percent during these years (Angel Rojo 1987: 193). The Brazilian real industrial product increased 262 percent between 1947 and 1961 (Baer 1965: 69–71). During the early 1970s, Brazilian growth rates, fueled by industrial expansion, produced a period known as the "Brazilian miracle" in which growth rates reached 13 percent and industrial output rose 109 percent (Frieden 1991: 115–18).

Economic slowdowns during the 1970s threatened national state-led growth models in both countries. The primary causes of these crises were international in both cases. In Brazil escalating external debt and the end of the "miracle" led to a fiscal crisis of the state during the 1980s (Bresser Pereira 1993). Public-sector–led growth policies under the military's Second Development Plan generated the largest external debt in Latin America, averaging 35.5 percent of GDP between 1980 and 1992.[4] Growing deficits and financial speculation led to mega-inflation during the 1980s. In the case of Spain the cause of economic crisis was stagflation in Western Europe resulting from the first oil price shocks of 1973. Although the Spanish economy began its liberalization in 1959 when Franco invoked a shift in macroeconomic policy, Spain's public sector still represented a growing burden on official accounts that would need to be reduced to avoid soaring deficits and promote the country's entry into the European Community (EC) in 1986. In both countries, growth

4. Figure prepared from data in *Indicadores DESEP* (1994: 46, 56–57).

rates plummeted. Spanish growth rates fell from 7.2 to 1.6 percent during 1975–83. Brazilian growth rates collapsed from the high of the "Brazilian miracle" to 1.3 percent in 1980 and negative 4 percent in 1990.[5]

The fiscal crisis of the state in Brazil forced policy-makers to reduce the autonomy and entrepreneurial role of public firms (Castro 1994: 201–4; Werneck 1991). Public production as a percentage of gross investment fell from 21 percent in 1982 to 6 percent in 1990. The sharp reduction in the entrepreneurial capacity of the Brazilian public sector, however, did not produce a more stable economy in the medium term. The continued postponement of extensive fiscal and administrative reform during the first civilian governments of the transition to democracy (José Sarney 1985–90; Fernando Collor 1990–92; and Itamar Franco 1992–94) led from one failed stabilization plan to another. Monthly mega-inflationary rates exceeding 60 percent were not uncommon for much of the late 1980s and early 1990s. As a result, industrial policy became a secondary consideration. Between 1985 and 1991, no fewer than 10 different proposals for an "industrial policy" were circulated by Brazilian ministries and hyped by the presidents and cabinet officers they served. Each of these proposals, however, did not get past the position paper stage (Suzigan 1992). Inflation control remained the political priority of national politicians through the election of Fernando Henrique Cardoso in 1994 and his reelection in 1998. Even when the inflationary spiral was halted in mid-1994 by Cardoso's Real Plan, the stabilization program required attacking Brazil's burgeoning fiscal deficits (Castro 1999). Persistent capital flight during 1998–99 forced a maxi-devaluation of the real in January 1999.

Spain's monetary and fiscal problems were not as severe as Brazil's. The management of Spanish industrial policy was more sensitive to the inflationary symptoms of rapid growth than was Brazilian industrial policy.[6] Spanish industrial promotion swung between restrictive phases when inflation was reheated and accelerated phases when stagnation loomed (Tamames 1986: 215).[7] Despite a more careful macroeconomic

---

5. For a more thorough treatment of the crisis periods in both countries, see Fuentes Quintana and Requeijo (1984) for Spain and Baer (1995) for Brazil.

6. Brazilian industrial policy, by contrast, did not prioritize macroeconomic stabilization over growth. The reverse was true. The demand for growth was greater than the perceived need to curb inflation. For more on this point, see Baer (1965: 79–81 and 1989: 92–93), and Castro (1994: 192).

7. This point does not mean that relatively high annual rates of inflation did not accompany the growth evidenced in the 1960s, since they certainly did. It only suggests that there was more concern in Spanish planning with macroeconomic instability. The 1959 stabilization policy epitomized this concern by instituting a series of fiscal, monetary, and commer-

policy, the Spanish economy could not avoid a severe industrial crisis in 1973 when the first oil price shocks threatened stagflation in Western Europe. The INI industries stagnated as foreign and domestic demand declined during the decade, generating inflation, large trade deficits, and high levels of unemployment. Continued INI losses and chronic trade deficits created the conditions for a fiscal crisis in Spain in the early 1980s. The budget deficit grew from 1.7 percent to 5.5 percent of GDP in the short period from 1979 to 1982 (Angel Rojo 1987: 196; Segura 1989).

The fiscal and macroeconomic exigencies of reducing inflation and the public budget deficit soon outweighed the priorities of planning. Following policies first established under Franco, the first civilian government of Adolfo Suárez and his centrist Unión de Centro Democrático (UCD) reaffirmed the commitment to control inflation with a monetarist devaluation of the peseta and a fiscal reform. These goals were institutionalized in 1977 in the Pacts of Moncloa, which provided for crucial economic reforms just before the acceleration of the transition to democracy.[8] Despite the election in October 1982 of the Socialists (PSOE) led by Felipe González, whose party once entertained the idea of launching an expansionary policy designed to create 800,000 new jobs, tight monetary and incomes policies were continued over from the previous UCD government. Like the Socialists in France, PSOE would go much further than their center-right predecessors in implementing fiscal reform and restructuring public firms.

Several factors explain the superior ability of the Socialists to implement economic reform. First, in contrast to the UCD's minority government, the PSOE was able to maintain an absolute majority in the Cortes. Second, the PSOE enjoyed a democratic system that had been relatively mature and stable for several years before the Socialists came to power in 1982. UCD, by contrast, was forced to balance the need for economic reforms with the need to build and consolidate democratic institutions. This careful juggling act sapped the alliance's political capital and contributed to its stunning electoral defeat at the hands of the Socialists

---

cial controls. Maintaining positive export balances and low domestic inflation became priorities governing industrial policy during the last decade and a half of Franco's rule (1960–75). See Aríztegui (1988).

8. Among some of the anti-inflationary policies contained in the Moncloa Pacts were a tight monetary policy and reductions in public expenditures on pensions, social security, and the civil service. See Fuentes Quintana (1990) and Trullén i Thomàs (1994). Most important, the Moncloa agreements institutionalized a market economy in Spain—a process that was considerably furthered the following year, in 1978, with the promulgation of the Constitution (Maravall 1993: 100).

(Bermeo and García-Durán 1994). Finally, the PSOE engaged in the restructuring of the public sector under more favorable economic conditions (EC accession in 1986, recovering growth rates, and increased foreign investment during the late 1980s) while the UCD policies were thwarted by the second energy crisis in 1979 (Bermeo and García-Durán 1994; Fuentes Quintana and Requeijo 1984: 28).

UCD and PSOE policy-makers alike were convinced that they had to prepare domestic industry for competition from more advanced European economies while they redressed the fiscal imbalances and monetary instability that could prohibit accession to the EC.[9] They also viewed accession to the EC as crucial to consolidating Spanish democracy and improving the competitiveness of Spanish industry (Maravall 1993: 93; Lukauskas 1997). Although the dominance of EC policy priorities, which followed a generally neoliberal line, limited the scope of industrial policy by disassembling the entrepreneurial projects of the INI, EC fiscal transfers also made a more extensive restructuring of the public sector possible, and this expectation emboldened Socialist reformers.[10]

The Socialists pursued a wide-ranging industrial "reconversion" (restructuring) policy that premiered in a White Book report (Libro Blanco) in July 1983, delivered by the minister of industry, Carlos Solchaga. Both the White Book and its legislative successor, the Law of Reconversion and Reindustrialization (1984), targeted certain sectors in industrial decline for subsidized credit and structural aid.[11] The key sectors of the reconversion—steel, metallurgy, appliances, and textiles—all received large amounts of state aid. Zones of Urgent Reindustrialization (ZURs) surrounding the most hard-pressed sectors were provided with preferential credit and subsidies and were the beneficiaries of funds for labor

9. Author interview with Ignácio Bayón, UCD minister of industry (1980–82), July 7, 1994, Madrid; Holman (1989: 95).

10. Author interview with Álvaro Espina, former secretary of state for industry, Ministry of Industry, June 29, 1994, Madrid; and author interview with Fernando Maravall, former general technical secretary, Ministry of Industry, and adviser to the Socialist minister of industry, Carlos Solchaga (1983–86), June 27, 1994, Madrid.

11. Key aspects of the PSOE's approach to industrial reconversion simply extended ideas into practice that had circulated within the UCD government, particularly during the period that Ignácio Bayón was minister of industry for the Calvo-Sotelo government (1980–82). Under Bayón's leadership, the government focused on a sectoral reconversion policy for steel, textiles, ship-building and other sectors that were "in crisis" (Subirats Humet 1992: 102; Segura 1989: 411–12; author interview with Bayón, July 7, 1994, Madrid). Like the UCD, the PSOE concentrated its attention and its spending on key sectors—steel, metallurgy, ship-building and appliances—the so-called *núcleo duro* (hard core) of Spanish industry (Navarro Arancegui 1990: 118).

relocation, retraining, and unemployment support (Navarro Arancegui 1990).[12]

Led by Solchaga and Miguel Boyer, the minister of the economy, the industrial reconversion became an extension of a larger neoliberal policy designed to consolidate the stabilization of the economy by reducing inflation and containing public sector losses. The INI spent large amounts of public money to remodel and eliminate entire lines of production, which had the effect of reducing jobs and salaries. Total employment in the INI fell from 216,700 workers in 1983 to 154,500 in 1989, almost a 30 percent reduction (Smith 1998: 118; Aceña and Comín 1991: 542). Spain's public firms were downsized in the 1980s, subdivided in 1992 into "profitable" and "nonprofitable" firms, private buyers were found for the few that could be sold, and the INI was dissolved in July 1995. The ZURs were a particularly important component of the total financing and administration of Spanish industrial policy between 1984 and 1988, although the zones had their most transformative effects early. By the end of 1984, the ZURs had successfully implemented 76 percent of the workforce reductions foreseen in the reconversion law (Smith 1998).

The social effects of industrial restructuring were only partially and temporarily ameliorated by compensatory policies. The ZURs, for example, which provided funds for labor relocation, succeeded in "pre-retiring" workers over 55 years of age. Yet the ZURs could only create jobs for one-fourth of all laid-off workers under 55 (Navarro Arancegui 1990: 181). The ZURs in Madrid and Barcelona enjoyed the most positive results in relocating workers due to already diversified local economies, while zones in other regions more dependent upon declining public

12. The Socialists, led by Solchaga, supported the ZURs and wrote them into the 1984 reconversion law due to the earlier experience of reconverting the steel works, Altos Hornos Valenciana (AHV), in Sagunto, Valencia. PSOE reformers established a "Zone of Preferential Location" in Sagunto in 1983. The policy was effective in reducing the production capacity of Altos Hornos, relocating laid-off workers, and attracting foreign investors to Sagunto. Based on this experience, Solchaga became convinced that a "zonal" element of this type had to be added to the 1984 law. This point was made by Fernando Maravall, one of Solchaga's advisors and the idea founder of the ZURs, in an interview, June 27, 1994, Madrid. Seven ZURs were established in 1985, each with a projected life of three years: Asturias, Barcelona (Catalonia), Cádiz (Andalusia), Ferrol (Galicia), Vigo (Galicia), Madrid and Nervión (Basque Country). Each was designed to establish a pool of risk capital and subsidized financing to promote reduction of workforces, projects to increase productivity and attract new investment. For a thorough overview of the economics of the ZURs, see Mata Galán (1988) and Lafuente Félez and Pérez Simarro (1988). Although Spanish accession to the EC occurred in January 1986, Madrid asked Brussels for monies from the European Regional Development Fund (ERDF) to cofinance the ZURs before final membership. For more on EC structural funds and how they were used, see Tsoukalis (1993: 238–48) and Allen (2000).

firms, particularly those in the industrial north of Spain (Asturias, Galicia, and the Basque Country), registered disappointing results (Navarro Arancegui 1990: 168–70, 185–86). The modest effects of the ZURs were a function of their limited character; particularly the fact that they were not designed to last more than three years nor become the basis for a more comprehensive and long-lasting national industrial policy. As Fernando Maravall, former general technical secretary of the Ministry of Industry, adviser to Solchaga (1983–86), and former president of several ZURs, noted:

> The ZURs were designed to attract firms in these zones, where laid-off workers were located. Subsidies and other fiscal mechanisms were used to attract firms to the ZURs. But, as was realized later, these measures were not very effective. Due to the fiscal limits on the national state, these measures had nominal effects. . . . Not enough workers were let go. Many of the workers that were let go, could not be relocated. Lack of infrastructure was another problem. The key problem was that the ZURs needed to have more of a coordinated direction. . . . There should have been more public works, more infrastructure, and more subsidies to construction on infrastructure, railroads and highways. . . . It was not a global, coordinated policy of the government, you see, it was a series of policies that came out of the Ministry of Industry, and that did not allow for a comprehensive approach. (Author interview, June 27, 1994, Madrid)

After 1986, both sectoral and ZUR reconversion were phased out when the EC compelled the Ministry of Industry to comply with the Community's prohibitions on "excessive" state aid to industry under the Treaty of Rome's competition articles.[13]

The Spanish Socialists employed an industrial policy that sought to ease the social and political contradictions of a social democratic yet neoliberal project. At first this meant garnering the support of the PSOE's chief ally among Spain's labor confederations, the Socialist Unión General de Trabajadores (General Union of Workers, UGT). UGT, however, moved away from the national party's reconversion strategy after initially signing a series of national pacts before 1985. As a result of PSOE's

---

13. Author interview with Álvaro Espina Montero, former secretary of state for industry, Ministry of Industry, June 29, 1994, Madrid; and author interview with Fernando Maravall, former general technical secretary, Ministry of Industry, and adviser to Solchaga (1983–86), June 27, 1994.

embrace of membership in NATO, the downsizing of social security allotments, and the reluctance of national party leaders to negotiate a "second reconversion" after 1986, UGT increasingly embraced the dissent stance (clearly the "exit option" in the politics of party-union ties) of the Communist unions, Comisiones Obreras (Worker Commissions, CCOO) (Burgess 1999). Likewise, shop floor leaders who controlled the third major union force, the factory councils, gained control of CCOO. The influence of the more concessionary factory councils oriented CCOO after 1987 to a more moderate position in keeping with UGT (Wozniak 1993: 84). In 1988, UGT and CCOO saw the need for common action. Both unions organized a general strike that momentarily brought the Spanish economy to a halt.

Yet even the party-union split did not threaten the Socialists' industrial reconversion program or lead to a sustained national opposition to restructuring. By 1990, the government had achieved more than 90 percent of all anticipated job cuts. The Socialists had also reduced severance payments but expanded spending on retraining and "reindustrialization" expenditures—subsidies to regional governments to find alternative employment for the jobless. Smith (1998: 128–29) suggests that these policies were designed primarily to mollify Spanish labor and that they proved successful since the government was able to complete the industrial reconversion without serious disruptions. As a result, for the unions, both the strategy of negotiation and outright opposition failed. The PSOE appeared firmly in control of industrial reform.

By contrast, the Brazilian state was in no position to grant generous payouts to laid-off or retired workers of public firms. The exhaustion of ISI, so evident in the fiscal crisis of the public sector and the decline of the internal market in the 1980s, motivated policy-makers to promote exports.[14] The partial recovery of Brazilian industry, the positive performance of commodity exporters during the late 1980s and early 1990s, and the scarcity of external financing help to explain why the Brazilian debt as a percentage of GDP did not increase to the extent it did in Spain. Con-

---

14. Returning the Brazilian state to creditworthiness became the principal aim of policy-makers in the BNDES and the *Conselho de Desenvolvimento Industrial* (CDI), the latter being the chief implementor of Brazilian industrial policy under the military's Second National Development Plan (author interview with José Afonso Castanheira, former executive of the BNDES and former director of the CDI, March 6, 1995, São Paulo). Later, during the Fernando Collor and Itamar Franco governments, liberalization of imports became a more important mechanism for governing trade as it was seen by government leaders as a means of reducing inflation (Author interview with Gesner Oliveira, former adjunct secretary of political economy for the Itamar Administration, Ministry of the Economy, December 7, 1994, Brasília, Distrito Federal).

versely, the availability of European credit markets and structural funding from the EC after 1986 helped the Spanish government finance INI losses and downsize public sector producers.

Industrial reconversion in Brazil was limited to public firms engaged in key commodity exports. Mining, steel, aluminum, petroleum, petrochemicals, autoparts, machine tools, and pulp and paper—sectors with a history of state ownership or intervention—showed positive export competitiveness throughout the 1990s as a result of public restructuring prior to privatization or private adjustment shaped by government policy (Kingstone 1999; Coutinho and Ferraz 1994: 261–81). Consequently the most productive public firms in these sectors (e.g., Usiminas (steel); Acesita (special metals); and CVRD (mining)) were the initial targets of Fernando Collor's and Fernando Henrique Cardoso's privatization policies. Privatization was designed to restructure these firms through infusions of public and private investment (Montero 1998). These conditions were absent in Spain, where privatization was relatively limited under Socialist management, mature sectors such as steel and mining were uncompetitive by European standards, and where annual trade deficits were the rule rather than the exception.

These few cases of restructuring aside, more elaborate economic reforms in Brazil were hamstrung by the weakness of reform efforts in Congress, the anemia of political parties, and the widespread particularism of business, labor, and other political interests. Organizational fragmentation in all of these arenas of collective action favored the persistence of personalism and conflicts over access to patronage (Weyland 1996; Hagopian 1996; Mainwaring 1997, 1999; Ames 2001). These tendencies continued to impede central control and coordination, weakening the Brazilian state's ability to respond to widening economic problems. As a result, these problems overshadowed all attempts to define a new industrial trajectory for the country. As former BNDES executive, José Afonso Castanheira remembered:

In the BNDES we focused on this question of constructing a means for negotiating with capitalist actors. We wanted to construct an "active policy" which included fiscal incentives, tax breaks, wage policy, and liberal market opening. So within a year, the commercial deficit became a commercial surplus. The idea was to return Brazil to creditworthiness. Active policies were "in the air" but Tancredo [Neves, the first civilian president,] did not have designs on changing [the military's] policies. His focus was on political reform—the transition and the new constitution. [José] Sarney, his successor, was very weak. Like [the military], he had little popular support. So the result was an erratic policy. There was no clear objective except for stabilization at all costs. . . . When Cruzado failed in 1987, the government had no direction. When Collor took over in 1990, the new economic model was very concentrated and closed. There was absolutely no decision-making in favor of articulating an industrial policy. The president had political interests in attacking industrialists. There was no chance given to a coordinated policy. What was eventually done was disastrous. What little was done was concentrated in the area of monetary policy and privatization. (Author interview, March 6, 1995, São Paulo)

If at one time both Spain and Brazil embraced state-led growth, the crisis and reform of these development models would later cause both countries to take different trajectories. Spain's initial fiscal crisis was overcome through a concerted and largely successful downsizing of the public sector. The PSOE's internal coherence and parliamentary majority helped ease reforms from formulation through implementation despite significant labor opposition. Brazil's debt crisis, by contrast, was much more severe than anything the Spanish reformers faced, but unlike the Spanish reformers, Brazil's politicians proved less capable of launching a response. The fragmentation of Congress and the weakness of Brazil's political parties limited reform efforts. Despite these differences, however, subnational governments in both countries took advantage of opportunities granted them to create their own responses. These experiences were possible given the context of democratization with decentralization of the state in both countries.

SHIFTING THE STATE: THE POLITICS OF DECENTRALIZATION

During the late 1970s and 1980s in Spain and the 1980s in Brazil, transitions to democratic rule generated unintended consequences for the structure of the state. Regime liberalization and democratization in both cases encouraged decentralization of authorities and resources once controlled by the central government. Subnational governments could claim new abilities to implement economic reforms of their own in response to the economic crises central governments seemed incapable of redressing completely. Greater levels of interregional competition created additional incentives for subnational governments to act. In neither country, however, did the pattern of decentralization and democratization dictate strictly the kinds of policies subnational governments would pursue or how effective these policies would be in creating synergy. Moreover, the differences between Spain and Brazil that were highlighted above were not borne out in Spanish regions having an advantage initiating subnational industrial policies. Opportunities and incentives for implementing these policies and creating a subnational economic bureaucracy to govern these programs became widespread in both countries.

Brazil

The Brazilian military, which had originally embraced a politically centralized formula of authoritarianism after the coup of 1964, decentralized taxes and intergovernmental transfers through the 1966–67 tax reform. The act was an attempt to counterbalance the power of the southern and southeastern states where much of the opposition to authoritarianism first emerged (Selcher 1990).[15] Yet it also set a precedent for expanding subnational autonomy in perverse ways. The reform allowed the state governments control over the new Imposto sobre Circulação de Mercadorias (Tax on the Circulation of Goods—ICM) and the Tax on the Exchange of Real Estate.[16] Since ICM was a value-added tax on goods (and eventually, services, thus ICMS), differences in ICMS rates across states created administrative confusion that aided tax evaders and allowed states to grant tax concessions in competition with each other.[17] The latter tendency was partially controlled by the military government, which

15. Fiscal transfers were particularly important in this respect since the north and northeast were more dependent upon these transfers than revenues from taxation. Unlike the states of the industrialized southeast and south which could generate vast quantities of revenue from taxes on a diversified local economy, the poor states in the north and northeast relied more heavily upon federal transfers to finance expenditures. In this way, centralized disbursal of federal transfers gave the military a powerful tool for assuring the political support of patrimonial elites in these states.

16. The ICMS improved on the state sales taxes it replaced by charging only on the added value in each stage of production. The reforms also allowed the cities to manage their own taxes, primarily the *Imposto sobre Serviços de Qualquer Natureza* (Tax on Services—ISS), which did not apply to the services already taxed by the ICMS. The federal government retained the other major tax on business, the *Imposto sobre Produtos Industrializados* (Tax on Industrial Products—IPI), also a value-added tax. The major differences between the IPI and the ICMS are that ICMS taxes interstate and intermunicipal transport services, communication, minerals, electrical energy, petroleum, and capital goods in addition to goods and services. IPI is a tax on value added to the production and distribution of goods and services.

17. This does not apply to ICMS rates on interstate trade, transport, and communication, which are established by the federal Senate and changed by unanimous agreement of all the state governments. Yet, as we shall see, these safeguards tended to break down during the 1980s.

managed how the states and cities spent transferred resources, linking transfers to specific budget items (Arretche 1996: 52; Medeiros 1983). States seeking to increase expenditures were forced to depend upon the accumulation of debt to finance local development. By one estimate, in 1981 over one-third of Brazil's total external indebtedness was held by the state governments (Graham 1990: 87). As the military's constraints on state fiscal financing were loosened during the transition to democratic rule, additional distortions in Brazil's fiscal structure would emerge.

The combination of the fiscal crisis of the state and the growing inability of authoritarian institutions to deal with these problems opened the door to a gradual transition to democracy. But this process proved to be a conflictual one. No national program of decentralization with demarcated rules and timetables developed. The result was a distribution of authorities and resources based on the circumstances of political conflict and not on a national (or even rational) process of negotiation (Afonso 1995: 321).

Although the liberalization of the authoritarian regime was initiated by "lights" within the Brazilian military (officers who envisioned and planned a return to civilian rule), the process increasingly became driven by the emergence of civilian leadership in the state and municipal governments. The first critical juncture of the liberalization process occurred during the 1982 governors' election, which saw the stunning defeat of the pro-military party (Partido Democrático Social/Democratic Social Party—PDS)[18] and the resounding victory of opposition parties in nine states, including the key economically developed states of São Paulo, Rio de Janeiro, Minas Gerais, Espirito Santo, and Paraná. Several of these governors had been nationally prominent during the liberalization of the regime in the post-1974 period and were often mentioned as potential presidential candidates. Tancredo Neves in Minas Gerais and Leonel Brizola in Rio de Janeiro headed the list. The rise of these well-known opposition governors during the early part of the transition to democracy contrasted with the absence of a *democratically elected* executive with which the terms of political decentralization could be negotiated. Military leaders avoided the subject of decentralization as it played directly into the hands of the political opposition, which by 1984 was demanding

18. This party was formally known as the Aliança Nacional Renovadora (National Renovation Alliance, ARENA). The military changed the name of ARENA to the PDS in order to alter the popular perception of Brazilians that the ARENA was associated with the most repressive of the post-1964 military governments. PDS was created, along with multiple opposition parties that were previously organized collectively as the Movimento Democrático Brasileiro (Brazilian Democratic Movement, MDB), in 1979 as part of a party reform act designed by General Golbery do Couto e Silva to fragment the opposition. See Skidmore (1988: 219–20) and von Mettenheim (1995: 106–7).

direct elections for the presidency as part of the Diretas Já! (Direct Elections Now!) campaign.

Interested in exploiting the contradictions of a liberalizing military regime that maintained authoritarian control over the central government, the governors and the opposition municipal and federal representatives (also elected in 1982) moved to expand their local bases of support. These politicians mobilized partisans through broad distributional and patrimonial networks at the subnational level and controlled the career trajectories of federal legislators (Abrúcio 1998; Hagopian 1996; Samuels 1998b). The rise of the "politics of the governors" *before* citizens had the right to vote for a democratic executive became one of the essential, early foundations of the Brazilian transition to democracy.

The persistence of centralized authoritarian control over the process of democratization *from above* and the surprising acceleration of civilian, non-PDS, penetration of the process *from below* created a host of contradictions. One of the most prominent of these contradictions was the continued control that the central government had over taxation and expenditures. Democratic leaders in the state governments could not, on the one hand, claim to be independent of the military government and, on the other hand, continue to depend on the same government for fiscal resources. This obvious paradox catalyzed a movement at the municipal and state levels in 1983 and 1984 to expand the size of the ICMS and the states' control over it. Multiparty congressional alliances at the national level carried the fight by supporting a series of constitutional amendments dictating changes in the laws governing taxes and transfers to the states and municipalities (Affonso 1988; Souza 1997). These attempts to engineer change from below in the distribution of fiscal authorities would evolve as a highly influential political force in the years to come.

Indicative of the emerging strength of regional interests was the fact that these groups became more influential once executive authority finally shifted to the first civilian (although indirectly elected) president, Tancredo Neves, in 1985. Neves's death on the eve of his inauguration brought his vice-president, José Sarney, to power. Sarney, who had been linked with the previous military government, commanded little respect among Brazil's nascent and fragmented political society. The new democracy's party system tended to break down into groups organized around individuals and patrimonial alliances.[19] These institutional weaknesses further empowered local networks of influence as alternative

---

19. For a useful review of the literature on the weakness of the Brazilian political party system, see Mainwaring (1999).

bases of political power (Mainwaring 1997). Sarney attempted to woo these networks by increasing nontax federal transfers to the states and municipalities 23 percent from their 1980 level. In this way, the weak president cultivated support among Brazil's governors and their local patronage machines in his campaign for a five-year term and the preservation of presidential rule on the eve of the drafting of the 1988 Constitution (Serra and Afonso 1991: 49).

By the time the Constituent Assembly, the elected body charged with the responsibility of drafting the new Constitution, first convened in 1987, regional interests were all but dominant in Brazilian political society. As a result, the Assembly became a forum for regional and local interests, particularly on the subcommittees reviewing taxation and revenue sharing arrangements (Souza 1997: chaps. 3, 4). The support of the governors whose power continued to grow with the democratic transition strengthened the regional blocks (*bancadas regionais*). These political forces were all buoyed by their new-found political access: to achieve the decentralization of fiscal resources they could not extract from the military. The states of the northeast and north formed alliances in favor of redistributive tax rules aimed at addressing the problems of regional disparities in wealth. Explicit in this debate was the condemnation of central government policy on taxation and spending which was seen as favoring the continued concentration of industry in São Paulo (Rodriguez 1994: 437). In response, politicians from the southeastern and southern states moved to block these efforts and solidify their own command over fiscal resources. As a result of these distributive conflicts in the Constituent Assembly, the Constitution of 1988 would make Brazil one of the most fiscally decentralized federalisms in the world, but one comparable to Spain, the U. S., and Germany in this respect (Rodden 2000).[20]

Most remarkable in the Brazilian case was the shifting of significant taxation authorities to subnational government. The states gained more control over the ICMS and both states and municipalities increased their

20. The structure of public sector spending in Brazil is typical of fiscal federalisms in the most advanced countries. For example, the states and municipal governments in Brazil accounted for 49 percent of public sector expenditures in 1992, a figure comparable to the United States (50.5 percent) and Germany (45.7 percent). It might also be noted that the *type* of taxes reserved to the Brazilian states, indeed the overall distribution of tax functions in Brazil, is not unique. In fact, Lagemann (1995: 330–31) points out that it is internationally common for national states to administer progressive taxes on income while subnational governments administer taxes on property, both traits common to the Brazilian case. The aforementioned distortion of having two value-added taxes administered by two different levels of government continues to be a particularity of the Brazilian case, but in terms of tax and spending functions, Brazil is generally within the bounds of the traditional cases of fiscal federalism.

share of federal transfers from national tax collection.[21] After figuring for revenue sharing and transfers, in 1974 the national state disposed of 50.2 percent of all revenue, the states 36.2 percent, and the municipalities 13.6 percent. By 1988, the national state disposed of 33.4 percent of revenue while the states boosted their share to 50.7 percent and the municipalities to 15.9 percent (Shah 1991: 17).

The 1988 Constitution served to lock in these fiscal commitments to the states and municipalities by endowing them with a "democratic legitimacy." It could be (and was) said, that the Constituent Assembly, "the representatives of the people," had bestowed upon the states and municipalities greater financial autonomy. The greater authority of the states and municipalities to tax and spend was thus consecrated as a democratic "entitlement." In this way the political expectations of the governors and the mayors became intertwined with national fiscal reform and the consolidation of Brazilian democracy (Sola 1995: 40). Based on arguments such as these, efforts to reform the Constitution during the mid-1990s would encounter significant political obstacles.

Most important, the 1988 reform gave the states reserved authorities to engage in economic policies not within the jurisdiction of the national state. The open-endedness of this provision granted the states almost carte blanche to direct spending at an array of development needs. As federal responsibilities in health, education, and industrial policy declined during the 1980s and 1990s, subnational commitments in these areas expanded (Affonso 1995). By the end of the 1990s, subnational governments in Brazil accounted for 44 percent of all spending on health, 69 percent of all spending on education, and provided public investments two times the size of those of the federal authority (Afonso, Ramundo, and Araujo 1998). Over 90 percent of intergovernmental fiscal transfers were not earmarked for particular purposes by Brasília and were free to be spent at the discretion of state and municipal governments (Afonso 1994: 356; Affonso 1995: 66). Over 30 percent of these transfers were

21. The 1988 Constitution eliminated federal taxes on transportation, electricity, fuel, and mining and combined these into the ICMS. Although the state governments could set ICMS rates, these powers were governed by certain federal laws. Ceiling rates were placed on lists of products specified by federal legislation. In this way, the average ICMS rate on consumer goods fluctuated around 17 percent. States could set rates slightly above or below the average depending on how federal law governed the taxed transaction. For more on ICMS rates in Brazil, see Longo (1994). The Constitution also expanded a previous piece of legislation from 1983, the Passos Porto Amendment, which increased intergovernmental revenue sharing. State and municipal transfers were augmented and reorganized into the Fundo de Participação dos Estados (FPE) and the Fundo de Participação dos Municípios (FPM), respectively.

considered "free" since they could be applied generically to elementary education and health, areas that could be more specifically defined by state and municipal governments (Afonso 1995: 318).[22] This liberalization of spending authority was the essential difference between fiscal decentralization during the democratic period and the preceding authoritarian regime.

The result of the decentralization of development policy resources and authorities was the proliferation of a wide array of new subnational economic institutions and policy mechanisms designed to promote industrial investment, employment, and innovation among the Brazilian states. Most Brazilian states created new or adapted old development agencies and banks in order to implement industrial policy. Fiscal, financial, infrastructural, and technical mechanisms composed the repertoire of the emerging subnational system of industrial promotion. Table 2.1 illustrates this institutional and policy diversity by state.

The emergence of new economic ideas also facilitated the transfer of fiscal authority and resources to the Brazilian states. The growing popularity of federal policy prescriptions favoring "decentralization, privatization, deregulation, and liberalization" strengthened the view among governors and mayors that the central government was retreating from its traditional development responsibilities, compelling subnational governments to take a more aggressive role (Affonso 1995: 59).

Perhaps the most telling evidence for an expansion in the responsibilities *and* resources of the state and municipal governments is the array of policies they designed to address social, educational, and economic issues in the years following the transition to democracy. The expanding command of the governors, mayors, and city councils was in part a product of their capacity for producing innovative responses to persisting problems when the federal government seemed stymied and ineffective. Many of these so-called "innovations from below" (*novidades vindas de baixo*) appeared in the areas of health, education, housing, and public procurements (Arretche 1996: 55; Tendler 1997).

Although policy innovations at the subnational level became more

22. Some Brazilian specialists have argued that the Constitution of 1988 provided the states and municipalities with more fiscal resources but it failed to *delegate* official duties to these levels of government. However, data presented by Affonso (1995: 65) demonstrates that the state and municipal governments presently account for close to 80 percent of all public investment and 67 percent of current public consumption, excluding expenditures on national public firms. In the category of fixed capital formation, the states made tremendous headway in assuming more responsibility over public investment during the 1980s.

Table 2.1 Subnational development agencies and policy mechanisms,
Brazil 1998

State	Development Agency(ies)	Fiscal Incentives	Financial Programs	Infra-structure	Technical Support
Acre	Codisacre	Yes	Yes	Yes	Yes
Alagoas	Codesen, Codeal	Yes	Yes	Yes	Yes
Amapá	Adap	Yes	Yes	No	Yes
Amazonas	BEA[1], Government[2]	Yes	Yes	No	No
Bahia	Desenbanco[1]	Yes	Yes	No	Yes
Ceará	CDI	Yes	Yes	Yes	No
Distrito Federal	Codeplan, Terracad	Yes	Yes	Yes	No
Espírito Santo	Bandes[1]	Yes	Yes	Yes	No
Goiás	Government	Yes	Yes	Yes	Yes
Maranhão	CDI, BEM[1]	No	Yes	No	Yes
Mato Grosso	Government	Yes	Yes	Yes	Yes
Mato Grosso do Sul	Codems	Yes	Yes	Yes	Yes
Minas Gerais	BDMG[1], CDI, INDI	Yes	Yes	Yes	Yes
Pará	CDI	Yes	Yes	Yes	Yes
Paraíba	CINEP	Yes	Yes	Yes	Yes
Paraná	Government	Yes	Yes	No	No
Pernambuco	Government	Yes	Yes	No	No
Piauí	Comdepi	Yes	No	Yes	Yes
Rio de Janeiro	Codin, AD-Rio	Yes	Yes	Yes	Yes
Rio Grande do Norte	Government	Yes	Yes	Yes	No
Rio Grande do Sul	Cedic, Pólo	Yes	Yes	Yes	Yes
Rondônia	Prodic	Yes	Yes	Yes	Yes
Roraima	Codesaima	Yes	Yes	Yes	Yes
Santa Catarina	Codesc, Badesc[1]	Yes	Yes	No	No
São Paulo	Government	Yes	Yes	Yes	Yes
Sergipe	Codise	Yes	Yes	Yes	No
Tocantins	ADT	Yes	Yes	Yes	No

SOURCE: Based on information contained in CNI (1995, 1998) and author's field research.
All programs are state-level, but in most cases municipalities offer additional support.

[1] State development bank.
[2] Indicates that subnational secretariats (usually Secretariat of Industry and/or of Economy) administered policy directly.

possible, the potential for squandering newfound resources was also great, as many governors and mayors had already proven adept at maneuvering fiscal resources to their clientelistic bases during the transition (Hagopian 1996; Samuels and Abrúcio, 2001). Some of the governors' authorities were also contested by central government agencies. Control over state banks, including some development banks, would pit the governors against the national monetary authorities—the Central Bank and the Conselho Monetário Nacional (CMN).[23] During the 1980s, the governors used the state banks to finance their growing subnational deficits. Such practices threatened the liquidity of the banks and challenged the ability of the Central Bank and the CMN to regulate the financial system (Sola 1995). As the fiscal conditions of the state governments worsened, the Central Bank was forced to bail out the states annually in response to political pressures placed on national politicians by the governors and their Secretaries of Economy (Silva and Costa 1995: 270–72; Werlang and Neto 1995). Along with seigniorage—the inflationary practice of printing money to finance public expenditures—the states' use of the subnational banking system generated massive amounts of debt. By 1998 total state bank debt exceeded $96 billion while total state debt "accounted for 8 of the 10 percentage point increase in domestic public debt from 1994 to 1997" (Dillinger and Webb 1998: 3).

More important, state elites faced perverse incentives during the post-Constitutional period to use their newly acquired resources to compete with each other in the attraction of multinational investment. The 1988 Constitution granted the states the authority to grant tax incentives on ICMS and many states did so in an attempt to attract automotive firms during the 1990s. This process was accelerated by a new automotive tax incentive regime launched by the Cardoso government in 1995. Tax abatement added to the fiscal pressures created by accelerated spending on health care, education, and the civil service. Between 1986 and 1995, state level expenditures increased 33 percent in real terms but subnational GDP grew only 14 percent (Dillinger and Webb 1998: 26). While the worst of these fiscal problems have been slowed or reversed by stopgap and ad hoc efforts by the Fernando Henrique Cardoso government (Montero 2001b), the states in Brazil still reflect both innovative and perverse sides to the decentralization of economic policy-making.[24]

23. Twenty-four of the twenty-seven states own commercial and/or development banks.

24. The effects of decentralization in Brazil cannot be fully assessed here, nor need they be. For our purposes it is only important to point out how decentralization, democratization, and the erosion of the state-led model made greater devolution of economic policy-making authorities and resources possible.

Spain

From the beginning of the regime transition, the question of regional autonomy dominated the emergence of Spanish democracy. This was a product of historical memory. The regional question overshadowed most of the major transitions in Spanish politics for over 150 years. Three civil wars in the nineteenth century, the contested liberal Restoration (1875–1923), and the Second Republic (1931–36) had all been irrevocably influenced by the political assertion of the Spanish regions. These sentiments continued to simmer just under the surface of Francoism's embrace of Catholic unity and authoritarian centralism. Thus it was not surprising that the two most developed historical nationalities among the regions—the Basque Country and Catalonia—would once again force Spaniards to revisit this historical bugbear during the Spanish transition to democracy.

The Basque and Catalonians mobilized soon after Francisco Franco's death in 1975 for a reinstatement of their statutes of political autonomy, institutions originally abrogated by *el Caudillo* during the 1930s. Lingering nationalist resentments in the Basque Country and Catalonia, and separatist violence in the former led by ETA (Basque Homeland and Freedom) threatened to derail Spain's delicate transition to democracy. At the same time, other regions began to assert their claims to autonomy, regardless of whether these claims had historical correlates. The fear shared by the regions was that special concessions would be granted to the Basque Country and Catalonia, leaving the rest of the regions more dependent upon the central government (Maravall and Santamaría 1986). The timing of these claims was essential since the transition to democracy provided the regions an opportunity to assert their claims precisely when the institutions of Spanish democracy were not yet established (Agranoff 1996; Diaz-López 1981). As a result of these conflicts, the political assertion of nationalist sentiments in two key regions broached a wider debate concerning the structure of the state (Pérez Díaz 1984: 49).

The official response to these historical and political pressures was the creation of a system of autonomy for all of the Spanish regions. The parties of the emerging Spanish democracy, particularly UCD and PSOE, sought an institutional solution. The 1978 Constitution guaranteed the regions "autonomy for the administration of their respective interests" (Article 137) and the controversial Title VIII authorized a negotiated route to autonomy based upon the development of statutes of autonomy for each region which would divide up responsibilities for taxation, shares of intergovernmental transfers, and corresponding spending duties. The result was the emergence of a new state structure known as the "state of the autonomies."

The system conceived by the 1978 Constitution was meant to be flexible, to build the "state of the autonomies" gradually, over time and through a process of negotiation between the central government and the regions (Subirats Humet 1991: 107; Serrano Sanz 1988: 503).[25] Nevertheless, different needs and political interests among the regions thwarted central government ambitions to generalize a model of autonomy to be applied to all cases (Ballesteros 1989: 176). The negotiation of statutes of autonomy with each region further compartmentalized the autonomy process. Different regions obtained distinct and sometimes "exclusive" rights. The governments of the Basque Country and Navarra, for example, asserted their historic "special regime" (*régimen foral*) in taxing and financing themselves. Catalonia, Valencia, Andalusia and Galicia gained additional control over education and other social expenditures under the "fast track" (*vía rápida*) to autonomy. The other Spanish regions were placed on the "slow track" (*vía lenta*) which provided a less extensive array of capacities, yet still a significant number. The evolving composite system of fiscal rules would be institutionalized in the *Ley Orgánica de Financiación de las Comunidades Autónomas* (Organic Law of Financing for the Autonomous Communities—LOFCA).

Although there were differences in degree, all the regional governments successfully gained increases in fiscal resources during the long evolution of the statutes of autonomy and LOFCA.[26] Although taxation functions were not as decentralized in Spain as they became in Brazil and despite the regions' greater dependence on fiscal transfers than on their

25. The period of negotiation was known as "preautonomy." During this period, the administrative apparatus of each region was built in accordance with the responsibilities and resources mandated in the statute of autonomy. The preautonomy process began with the inauguration of statutes of autonomy in Catalonia and the Basque Country in December 1979 (Organic Law 4 and 3, respectively). These were followed by the promulgation of statutes of autonomy in the other regions between 1981 and 1983: Galicia (1981), Andalusia (1981), Asturias (1981), Cantabria (1981), La Rioja (1982), Murcia (1982), Valencia (1982), Aragón (1982), Castilla-La Mancha (1982), Canary Islands (1982), Navarra (1982), Extremadura (1983), Balearic Islands (1983), Madrid (1983) and Castilla y León (1983). See Ballesteros (1989) for a more complete description of the process.

26. The "autonomous communities" received their financing from five sources stipulated by the Constitution and then later elaborated upon by LOFCA: 1) taxes ceded by the central government in part or completely; 2) autonomously administered regional taxes; 3) fiscal transfers from the central government that are specified in the annual budget of Spain; 4) all profits and capital produced by firms and agencies owned by the regional governments; and 5) all financial operations administered by the regional governments. It is not possible here to specify the evolution and workings of the LOFCA system. For a more complete analysis, see CEOE (1992).

own tax revenues, the "autonomies" accounted for an expanding share of total public expenditures (Castells 1990: 450–67). Between 1984 and 1994, the Spanish regions increased their spending as a percentage of GDP from 4.8 percent to 10.9 percent. As a percentage of total public expenditures during the first twelve years of the Estado de las Autonomías the central government went from administering 90 percent of public spending to 65 percent, while the regions increased their share to 25 percent (Curbelo 1994: 7).[27] As we will see, these aggregate numbers are deceptive since many national and EU programs in infrastructure and industrial promotion would come to be administered almost completely by the regions. In practice, therefore, the regions commanded a broader range of resources than simply those delegated to them by the Spanish Constitution.

Another indicator of the expanding role of the regional autonomies became the sheer number of laws and decrees the regions issued vis-à-vis the central government. Between 1981 and 1990, the regions went from administering 30 percent of all laws and 15 percent of all decrees to promulgating 85 percent of all laws and over two-thirds of all decrees (Agranoff 1996: 388–89).

The sustainability of the decentralization of Spanish fiscal resources also differed from the Brazilian case. Whereas in Brazil national restrictions on subnational fiscal policy were routinely flouted and only rarely reinforced by extraordinary federal intervention in state banks during the 1990s, in Spain, LOFCA standards were continually enforced. Periodic reforms to LOFCA were necessary during the 1980s and early 1990s in order to limit regional debt and to bring tax collection activities in line with spending responsibilities (Corona, Alonso, and Puy 1998). Yet the Spanish system evolved without the institutional disruptions seen in Brazil.

More than simply shifting greater resources to the Spanish regions, the "state of the autonomies" depended upon the shifting of greater authorities over policy-making to subnational government. The Constitution of 1978 and the statutes of autonomy recognized that the regional governments should have the capacity to promote technological development, address the financial needs of industries located in their territories, and engage in logistical support of local firms (Rosell and Viladomiu 1991: 286–87). The Constitution gave the regions authority

27. For more on these changes, see Ministerio de Economía y Hacienda (1995). These percentages are roughly equivalent to the other three-tiered decentralized government in the EU, Germany. See Castells and Bel (1991: 222).

Table 2.2 Subnational development agencies and policy mechanisms, Spain 1995

Region	Development Agency(ies)	Subsidy and Financial Programs	Infra-structure	Technical Support
Andalucía	IFA	Yes	Yes	Yes
Aragón	IAF	Yes	Yes	Yes
Asturias	IFR, SODECO, SRP, SAYPE	Yes	Yes	Yes
Basque Country	SPRI and Public Firms	Yes	Yes	Yes
Catalonia	Cidem	Yes	No	Yes
Extremadura	SOFIDE	Yes	No	No
Galicia	IGAPE	Yes	No	Yes
Madrid	IMADE, Arpegio/Irmasa	Yes	Yes	Yes
Murcia	IFRM	Yes	Yes	Yes
Valencia	IMPIVA and Technology Institutes	Yes	No	Yes

SOURCE: IFA (1993) and author's research.

over the "fomenting" of industrial growth. Certain statutes of autonomy elaborated on "foment," specifying "planning" and "promotion." In all cases, the statutes of autonomy granted regional governments the authority to maintain their own public sectors. Accordingly, many regions launched an array of agencies and economic policies designed to promote industrial investment during the 1980s (Table 2.2). Although the juridical parameters within which these subnational apparatuses operated were governed by the qualification that all policy must be "in accordance with the general economic objectives of the central government," these terms retained a certain open-endedness that allowed regional governments and their agencies to set their own priorities (Jimenez Blanco 1989: 399–410).

The open-endedness of the stipulated political economic rights of the regions allowed for a great deal of leeway in the interpretation of the capacity of the regions to promote industry. The negotiated process allowed the regions to claim authority through their statutes of autonomy that were not specifically contained in the 1978 Constitution (Serrano Sanz 1988: 511–12; Pérez Díaz 1984: 54–55; Subirats Humet 1991: 112). The regional governments effectively had the authority to develop their competencies in the area of industrial promotion and reconversion and even to expand them beyond the range the central government reserved for itself. Moreover, the central government was able to transfer competencies to the regions that, in theory, were not specifically contained within their statutes of autonomy (Serrano Sanz 1988: 519).

The evolution of the economic policy-making capacity of subnational government in Spain was also propelled by nonjuridical factors. Although the regional governments did not maintain a key financial role in the ZURs, the experience was important for developing the administrative side of industrial policy-making in the regional governments. Central government authorities from the Ministry of Industry managed the Executive Office, which was charged with the responsibility of establishing initial contacts with entrepreneurs, both foreign and domestic. The regional governments had representatives who sat on Administrative Commissions along with central government representatives. These Administrative Commissions decided on the size of the subsidies and the criteria for their disbursement (Lafuente Félez and Pérez Simarro 1988: 220). The commissions handled all the follow-through on initial contacts with investors. In this way, Spanish industrial policy in the ZURs was decentralized into a two-tiered administrative structure with multiple centers of decision-making among the regions (Brú Parra 1988: 42).

Other aspects of the ZUR experience, however, validated the notion that regional governments would eventually need to go it alone with their own policies. As noted above, the scope of ZUR activities was too sectorally concentrated and temporally limited to provide a basis for long-term institution-building. The ZURs' questionable performance raised doubts as well. Firms located in the ZURs often complained of the prolonged administrative and technical procedures that were required in order to receive official support.[28] Regional governments complained of their inability to represent their interests in ZUR administration. These deficiencies in the ZURs would be used by regional leaders to justify the development of their own industrial policies in subsequent years.

Perhaps the most damning aspect of the ZURs was their transitory nature. By law, the ZURs were not designed to last beyond 1986.[29] Yet the phasing-out of the ZURs also marked a more general decline in other national industrial promotion policies. The total of funds for industrial policy directly administered by the central government (mostly the Ministry of Industry), declined over time and increasingly concentrated not in

---

28. Central government ZUR officials even admitted these shortcomings publicly. See the interview with José Sánchez Junco, general director of industry, MINER, *El País*, January 14, 1990.

29. Despite the law and the intentions of key central government leaders such as Carlos Solchaga to limit the ZURs, some ZUR activities continued until 1990.

secondary regions in economic decline or crisis, but in the core economies of Madrid and Catalonia. Table 2.3 shows these trends. Faced with a declining pool of national resources for industrial promotion, many regional governments, particularly those in Spain's secondary regions, would find an additional justification for pursuing their own industrial policies.

Another noninstitutional factor that propelled the expansion of subnational industrial policy was the evolution of union and business support for alternatives to national reconversion policy. By the end of the official period of reconversion in 1986, unions and business organizations had increasingly allied themselves with regional governments to demand changes in national policy.[30] Often this meant calls to slow down plans to complete sectoral downsizing and increase compensatory benefits. Faced with local economic crises, regional leaders often took up the demands of business and labor groups. These relations had the effect of creating regional lobbies (Subirats Humet 1992: 109; Brú Parra 1988: 42). By shaping industrial reconversion policy to serve regional political interests, local governments were able to construct continuing alliances with economic actors.

Splits between the Socialist party and the UGT at the national level reinforced the closeness of the UGT with PSOE leaders at the regional level. Regional Socialist leaders who sought a more prominent role for themselves in the PSOE found ready allies within the UGT. Nicolás Redondo, the national leader of the UGT, publicly declared that he felt closer to Joaquín Leguina (Madrid) and Joan Lerma (Valencia) than to Felipe González.[31] The relationship served Redondo, who could now gain influence within the PSOE in sensitive regions with strong Socialist support. Regional leaders such as Leguina and Lerma gained a natural ally in their campaign to combat the "political centralism" they perceived within the party and to gain access to national policy-making.

A final factor promoting the economic policy-making capacities of the Spanish regions was Spain's accession to the EC in 1986. Despite EC constraints on member states to work within neoliberal parameters, the Commission mandated in 1985 that regional governments could invoke

30. The argument of many of the regional governments was that subnational government had to promote industry since the central government had effectively abandoned industrial policy after 1986. This argument was repeated continually by regional leaders. See *El País*, August 8, 1988. Business leaders joined the regional governments in criticizing Madrid for lacking an industrial policy after the end of the "official reconversion." See *El País*, January 24–25, 1990. Union leaders in both UGT and CCOO echoed the charge. See *El País*, February 8, 1991.

31. See Redondo's comments in *El País*, May 30, 1987.

Table 2.3 Distribution of national spending on industrial promotion/"reconversion" programs, 1991–1995 (regional figures in percentages; total figures reported in millions of dollars)

Region	1991	1992	1993	1994	1995
Andalucía	8.48	4.40	5.72	3.57	3.66
Aragón	2.35	1.07	.63	3.34	.86
Asturias	2.36	5.45	2.52	.27	.44
Baleares	1.05	.35	.29	.29	.66
Canary Islands	8.24	5.42	7.29	.08	.34
Cantabria	.97	.35	.68	.28	.47
Castilla–La Mancha	2.00	1.03	1.89	1.35	1.10
Castilla y León	4.96	1.72	1.85	2.04	.71
Catalonia	14.66	10.54	12.12	12.67	47.55
Extremadura	2.60	.83	.27	.26	.18
Galicia	4.36	6.24	2.70	1.89	2.33
La Rioja	.42	.11	.15	.18	.11
Madrid	31.87	47.81	51.86	61.62	34.01
Murcia	1.23	.31	.41	.53	.29
Navarra	1.66	.98	.99	1.64	.30
Basque Country	8.19	8.23	3.92	4.12	4.73
Valencia	4.61	5.16	6.70	5.87	2.27
TOTAL	$236	$270	$218	$154	$228

SOURCE: Esteban and Velasco (1996: 291).

more active industrial policies than their national governments. Socialist leaders saw this as a strong incentive to devolve additional policy responsibilities to the regions.[32]

The end result was a two-tiered strategy of industrial adjustment—a national policy of reconversion following broad neoliberal principles and a subnational strategy of selective intervention based on local politics and the overarching process of decentralizing policy responsibilities and fiscal resources to the regions. And both strategies carried the EC's stamp of approval. As Óscar Fanjul, a former advisor to Minister of Industry Carlos Solchaga, recalls:

When the rights of the Comunidades Autonomas (CCAA) began to increase, the regional governments became a counterweight to

32. Author interview with Fernando Maravall, Spanish economist, June 27, 1994, Madrid; author interview with Gervásio Cordero Mestanza, subdirector general of regional planning, Ministry of Economy, July 11, 1994, Madrid; and author interview with César Molinas Sans, director general of planning, Ministry of Economy, July 11, 1994, Madrid.

the central government. They could lobby the government to acquire funds. . . . When the CCAA increasingly acquired economic competencies, they began to copy some of the actions of the central government. They created their own public sectors, their own INIs, if you will. . . . The regions did all of this because they had to justify their own existence. They departed from neoliberal principles and engaged in more direct management of industry. The central government certainly couldn't stop it since the autonomy process had gone too far to go back. (Author interview, July 18, 1994, Madrid)

In 1988 the EC initiated a regional development program that qualified certain European regions in industrial decline for structural funding. Spain soon implanted its own regional promotion plans under EC guidelines, forming Zones of Economic Promotion (ZPEs) and Zones in Industrial Decline (ZIDs). Spanish regions approved by the EC were instantly declared ZIDs.[33] The ZIDs financed technological promotion programs in declining sectors such as steel. The ZPEs and ZIDs also financed programs targeted toward the promotion of small- and medium-sized firms, programs designed to improve professional and vocational skills, and projects to protect the environment and provide infrastructural investments.

Unlike the ZURs, the ZPEs and ZIDs gave the Spanish regional governments greater administrative control over the disbursement and management of program funding. On one level, the influx of EC structural funding concentrated authority over the disbursement of funds in the Spanish central government (Navarro Arancegui 1990: 213). Madrid tended to fund projects that were already underway as central government projects in the regions. Most of these projects were dedicated to infrastructure and education. In this way, EC structural funding became a means of cofinancing national public sector spending. The autonomous communities administered approximately one third of these EC structural funds (Rosell and Viladomiu 1991: 294–95). Yet in other areas such as the promotion of small- and medium-sized firms and industrial employment, where central government resources declined, regional government became more active (Lerena 1988). The sheer number and diversity of industrial projects at the regional level testifies to

---

33. These initially included the Basque Country, Catalonia, Cantabria, La Rioja, Aragón, Navarra, and Madrid. After prolonged lobbying by the regional government of the Principado of Asturias and the Spanish central government, that region was granted EC approval as a ZID.

this trend. New technology parks were established in the Basque Country, Valencia, Andalusia, Asturias, and Catalonia.[34] Regional governments, newly empowered by Madrid's decision to devolve to them the administrative responsibilities of the ZPEs and the ZIDs, enjoyed an influx of financing for new projects. Although the regions were spending a total of 35 perent of the national budget, they accounted for 75 percent of the expenditures allocated to promoting industrial investment by late 1988 (Rosell and Viladomiu 1991: 290).[35] Even EC officials traveling through the Spanish regions would claim that the capacity of the EC to promote industrial development in Spain depended almost entirely on the capabilities of the regional governments.[36]

COMPARATIVE PERSPECTIVES ON DUAL TRANSITIONS IN BRAZIL AND SPAIN

The crisis of state-led growth and the evolution of political decentralization in Spain and Brazil suggest that the former was a stronger candidate for successful adjustment. The Spanish state's fiscal crisis, the coherence of the PSOE and its capacity to govern the industrial reconversion, the carefully negotiated decentralization of the state, and the country's inclusion in the EC/EU provide a sharp contrast to the Brazilian experience. Brazil's debt crisis presented a more severe predicament, economic adjustment and political decentralization were governed by ad hoc agreements and intergovernmental conflicts that threatened to spiral out of control, and Brazil's political leaders and parties remained mired in the pursuit of clientelistic advantages.

Despite these differences, subnational governments in both countries developed new opportunities for producing their own strategies of industrial reform. The dialectical links between democratization and political decentralization in Brazil and Spain created open-ended institutions and a level of conflict in intergovernmental and interregional relations

34. The parks were the Technology Park of Andalusia in Málaga, the Technology Park of Asturias in Llanera, the Technology Park of Vallés (Catalonia), the Technology Park of Madrid at Tres Cantos and the Science and Technology Park at Alcalá de Henares, the Technology Park of Zamudio and the Technology Park of Alava (the Basque Country), and the Technology Park of Valencia. For more on these cases, see *El País*, February 26, 1989, and IFA (1993).

35. The figure is an estimate, but one that became widely accepted. See *El País*, August 8, 1988.

36. Author interview with Ronald Moys, Directorate General 16, Regional Policy, European Commission, June 23, 1995, Oviedo, Asturias.

that both empowered subnational governments and induced them to pursue industrial policy.

To be sure, the evolution of decentralized economic policy-making in Spain and Brazil generated both challenges and opportunities for subnational government. While on the one hand subnational governments could now direct significant resources and policy attention to their own economic problems, not all subnational governments were able to mount a consistent and effective set of policies. The result was a composite structure of capable and inept subnational policy systems. A closer look at subnational cases in Spain and Brazil reveals that synergy emerged from a particular configuration of political interests and institutional constraints.

Remaking Industrial Policy in Minas Gerais

Minas Gerais is an unlikely state to initiate an industrial policy. Unlike São Paulo, the state that borders it to the south, Minas is not Brazil's most industrialized state. Historically it has been linked to São Paulo's industrialization, but always as a secondary location for new investment. During the 1980s, Minas Gerais faced severe economic problems: lagging growth, a state government in fiscal crisis, and the emergence of a populist governor who was more interested in accumulating and distributing patronage than in improving Minas's economy. Even so, by this time, Minas's state government could boast an array of public agencies with a solid record of industrial policy. Despite uneven political support during the 1980s, the *mineiro* agencies survived to put scarce resources into innovative industrial policies during the early to mid-1990s.

Mineiro political leadership is divided into a traditional elite descended from the oligarchical period and a political technocratic segment with ties to national public firms and the state's industrial policy agencies. Significant conflicts within the political class of traditional elites was infrequent in Minas's politics. The political oligarchy ruled the state government with few challenges from subaltern or rival classes such as labor or business. While these traditional elites ruled Minas, economic policy remained in the hands of the political technocracy. Yet Minas was challenged externally by competition for federal resources from neighboring states, and particularly São Paulo. These pressures compelled both politicians and political technocrats to develop an array of connected industrial policy agencies. During the developmentalist period of the 1960s and 1970s, this emerging economic bureaucracy became highly coordinated through state-wide industrial plans, common goal-setting, and routine collaboration among specialized agencies. Plan-oriented horizontal embeddedness produced significant achievements in attracting new investors and producing externalities in the *mineiro* economy that buttressed the most impressive industrial growth rates in Brazil during the 1970s.

The crisis of developmentalism and the transition to democracy, however, did not disable these agencies. Even as intraregional elite conflict became more intense during the first years of democratization, horizontal embeddedness preserved the technocracy from becoming fragmented by the clientelism of a populist governor. Nevertheless, the end of delegative government at that time reduced the agencies to a project-oriented form of horizontal embeddedness that produced modest results compared to the state's developmentalist past. When delegative government returned in 1991, the agencies were able to utilize their unbroken associations to restructure *mineiro* industrial policy along more market-oriented lines. A new plan-oriented horizontal embeddedness made possible externalities in sectors such as auto manufacturing that were first established in the state during the developmentalist period.

This chapter explores this evolution of industrial policy in Minas Gerais. The first section examines the origins of the *mineiro* industrial policy agencies and the political factors that led traditional elites to delegate authority to these organizations. The second section analyzes how horizontal ties among the agencies protected them from the clientelism of a populist government and created possibilities for policy innovation during the 1980s and 1990s. The final section highlights how cooperative exchanges of information between the *mineiro* agencies and the multinational automaker, Fiat, and its auto parts suppliers enhanced productivity and transformed the industrial structure of key economic areas of Minas Gerais during the latest phase of plan-oriented horizontal embeddedness.

REVERSING EXPECTATIONS: THE POLITICS OF CREATING DEVELOPMENTAL AGENCIES IN MINAS GERAIS

Minas Gerais had a direct role in Brazilian national politics since the beginning of the twentieth century. In the highly decentralized "politics of the governors" that dominated the Old Republic (1889–1930), the coffee and ranch barons at the head of Minas's political machine became prominent members of the *café com leite* power-sharing arrangement with São Paulo between 1894 and 1930. After 1930, *mineiro* support for Getúlio Vargas's *Estado Nôvo* preserved Minas's access to national policy-making.[1] In the subsequent struggle between Vargas and the governors, the dictator replaced all the governors with appointed "interventors" but rewarded Minas's loyalty by allowing it to retain its governor, the only state to be so privileged.

In return for access to the policy-making process and a share of national resources, Minas's political oligarchy backed Vargas.[2] This patrimonial relation would soon produce results for Minas Gerais's economy. In 1944, Vargas negotiated an agreement with British and American mining interests that allowed the Brazilians to nationalize the mining industry, mostly located in east-central Minas Gerais, in return for guarantees of iron ore supplies for the Allied war machine. With this deal the Companhia Vale do Rio Doce (Company of the Valley of Rio Doce, CVRD) was born as a public conglomerate with rights to Minas's mineral riches. Public investments in heavy industry and the country's rapid postwar industrialization accentuated the importance of CVRD's iron ore, and by corollary, Minas Gerais's role in the Brazilian economy.

Other factors such as the decline of the coffee and agricultural economy of the southeast during the Great Depression made the diversification and industrialization of the *mineiro* economy a more salient ambition of the state government. Following the model of CVRD's creation, the preferred tool of the *mineiro* elite became official planning. The creation of the planned "industrial city" of Contagem close to Belo Horizonte, the capital of Minas Gerais, epitomized the *mineiro* elite's interest in applying official planning to their goal of diversifying the state's economy. Consequently, the end of the Estado Nôvo and the beginning of a period of redemocratization in 1945 did not see a return to the liberal economic policy of the pre-Depression era, but to new models of state management of industrial development.

Minas's governor during the late 1940s, Juscelino Kubitschek, who would in 1955 become president of the republic, launched a Recuperation

---

1. Minas's political backing and commitment of its state militia gave Vargas the necessary resources to overcome an attempted revolution by São Paulo in 1932. Minas's support also allowed Vargas to counterbalance other autonomous movements in Rio Grande do Sul. See Hagopian (1996: 54) and Dulci (1988: 26).

2. The relationship between *mineiros* and their federal contacts was based on systemic patronage. See John D. Wirth's (1977: 178–84) description of the early development of patronage networks between Minas's elite and the federal government. Also see Hagopian (1996: chap. 2).

Plan in 1947 that defined areas of Minas's economy to be targeted with public programs for industrial development. Kubitschek created a technocracy modeled after professional state agencies at the national level. His 1947 plan included massive public investments in electrification that paved the way for the creation of Centrais Elétricas de Minas Gerais (Electrical Centers of Minas Gerais, CEMIG), the state electric company in 1952. CEMIG acted as a development agency for the state government, providing electricity to new industrial investments and promoting Minas Gerais's private sector. The agency was conceived and controlled by a score of professional engineers and administrators who had extensive experience in managing international corporations. Many of these elites, among them Mário Bhering, John Reginald Cotrim, and Mauro Thibau, had served with CEMIG's first president, Lucas Lopes, on the Mixed Brazil-U.S. Energy Commission, which employed planning techniques to address development issues in the utility sector. These elites employed similar ideas to structure CEMIG as a public firm autonomous from the recruitment and budgeting functions of the rest of the *mineiro* state apparatus (Brito 1984: 242).[3] Despite the dominance of the political oligarchy in Minas, CEMIG's administration remained one of several *bolsões de eficiência* (pockets of efficiency) within state government.

These initial attempts to industrialize Minas Gerais did not succeed in addressing the state's development problems. Despite all the hopes stemming from CVRD's importance in Brazil's industrialization model, the mining company's extractive and transportation operations in Minas Gerais were concentrated in the "Valley of Steel" area located in the east-central region of the state. Beyond reviving Minas's mining industry, CVRD did little to foster the development of new industries. Minas's agricultural economy remained highly dependent upon consumers in more industrialized neighboring states. The ranching economy was helping to feed the emerging working class and the growing urban population of São Paulo during the 1940s and 1950s, but these activities did not diversify the *mineiro* economy as quickly as state leaders hoped. The *mineiro* business class remained a small, marginal group as producers in traditional sectors such as textiles and agriculture. State elites became convinced that they needed to concentrate their efforts on attracting additional investment by the central government to produce a big push for Minas's industrialization. The *mineiro* political oligarchy once again turned to their associations with national elites, and mounted a cam-

3. For a more complete description of CEMIG's genesis and its subsequent evolution, see Tendler (1968: 36–37, and chap. 6).

paign to place major public firms in Minas Gerais. Under direct pressure from state government elites, Kubitschek's national government placed a large public steel producer, Usiminas, in Minas Gerais in 1957 (Schneider 1991: chap. 6).[4]

This dependence on public investments by the central government continued to be the basic model of *mineiro* economic policy. When the military came to power in 1964 *mineiro* political leaders supported them as the price for the placement of other public firms in the state. Minas Gerais became a key part of the developmentalist industrial policy of the military during the 1970s as the home of other large public steel firms (Açominas and Acesita) (Schneider 1991). As a result of *mineiro* bargaining the public sector remained a dominant fixture in Minas's early industrial development. By 1976, 57 percent of the largest 185 companies operating in Minas Gerais were public; 23 percent of the remaining companies represented private national investment; and 20 percent were foreign direct investors (C. Diniz 1981: 202; C. Diniz 1986: 337). As a result, much of the stunning growth of state-led industrialization during the "Brazilian miracle" could be observed within the political boundaries of Minas Gerais (Hagopian 1996: 74).

Mineiro politicians up through this period had developed into two separate but complementary political classes due to the logic of intergovernmental cooperation with national dictators and democratic leaders. First, a patrimonial, "traditional" class of politicians emerged from landed families who continued to play key roles in electing governors and running political machines in local politics (Horta 1986). The second class of *mineiro* politician developed within or linked to the national public sector and the technocratic development agencies of the state, CEMIG in particular. During Brazil's developmentalist period, the second group of elites began to dominate the thinking governing Minas's economic policies (Starling 1986; C. Diniz 1986: 335–36; C. Diniz 1981; Gama de Andrade 1980). The circulation of these elites between the state government's planning apparatus and that of the national state provided an additional link between the interests of *mineiro* economic policy and national developmentalist programs.[5]

4. *Mineiro* interests had mobilized much earlier for the placement of the National Steel Company (CSN) in Minas Gerais. They lost CSN when Vargas decided to place the new steel mill in Volta Redonda, Rio de Janeiro. Usiminas and Mannesmann, a second steel project, were supported by federal authorities in the 1950s as compensation for Minas's earlier loss of CSN (see Dulci 1992: 149).

5. This was particularly true of CEMIG's political technocracy. Lucas Lopes, the first president of CEMIG, eventually served as Kubitschek's minister of finance. John Cotrim

These professional administrators were not an apolitical group. Observers of Minas's technocracy such as Gama de Andrade (1980), Tendler (1968), C. Diniz (1981), and Hagopian (1996) argue that key segments of the *mineiro* political-technocracy had technical as well as political proficiency and that some of the most technically adept had considerable control over economic policy. Schneider (1991) argues that these technocrats were `hybrids'—political technocrats who were capable of forming valuable political connections to support technically competent development policies.[6] Their hybrid quality made these elites more effective implementors of industrial policy since they could coordinate both political and technical arguments for the allocation of resources. Prime examples included the CEMIG administrators and *mineiro* executives of the national public firms who remained just as concerned with maintaining themselves politically well-connected as technically proficient (Tendler 1968: 179–80).

To be sure, "traditional" elements of the older political class remained in key political positions within state government, particularly those that controlled political patronage (Hagopian 1996: 105).[7] Yet in areas of economic policy, these elites did not develop a similar level of influence. The military governments helped to displace many from state government in Minas with the expressed goal of empowering "technocrats." Nevertheless, political technocrats in the *mineiro* economic bureaucracy were already in positions of great influence well before the military came to power in 1964. In the pre-1964 period, traditional elites had little reason to intervene in economic governance since technocratic maintenance of developmentalism in Minas guaranteed them political influence in national and regional politics, placing them in strategic positions to defend oligarchical privileges.

Elite conflict within the oligarchy in the pre-1964 period was limited to minor partisan contests that in no way threatened the rule of the oligarchy as a political class. Indeed, this level of elite accommodation within the oligarchy was essential to forging the high levels of internal

---

was CEMIG's technical director until 1956 when he became president of the national Furnas electrical project. Benedicto Dutra, CEMIG's commercial director, became a chief deputy in the Ministry of Mines and Energy in 1964. Mário Bhering, vice president of CEMIG, was appointed by the military to head up Eletrobrás in 1967. See Tendler (1968: 175).

6. Hagopian (1996: 126–28) agrees, arguing that these were not "technocrats" in the sense that they devalued the interests of political elites in favor of a monolithic, "technical" agenda.

7. Although Hagopian (1996: chap. 3) is clear about the dominance of "traditional elites" in Minas, she fails to explain the maintenance of a professional and technopolitical class in agencies such as CEMIG and others developed during the 1960s and 1970s.

unity the *mineiro* elite required to minimize ideological or issue-oriented conflicts among the members of its crucial *bancada mineira* (Minas's delegation of national representatives) (Wirth 1977). Despite the persistence of a multiparty system during the 1945–64 period, the use of populism and clientelism preserved a coherent set of dominant, oligarchical interests in Minas's state government. Solid evidence of this group's consolidated grip on power was the fact that these interests easily closed ranks in support of the military coup of 1964 (Hagopian 1996: 61–70).

The military government accentuated the role of political technocrats within the economic bureaucracy but at no time did this threaten the hold of traditional elites over other segments of the state government. As a consequence, there was little conflict between the oligarchy and the political technocracy during the bureaucratic-authoritarian period. Hagopian (1996) offers an important corrective to the notion that the military period produced "technocratic governments" in Minas. She demonstrates, instead, that the top political leadership of Minas Gerais remained firmly in the hands of traditional politicians, although many had technical as well as political backgrounds. Each administration included a substantial technocratic component. The technocratic composition of cabinet positions increased during the first half of military rule (29 percent and 55 percent during the governorships of Israel Pinheiro (1966–71) and Rondon Pacheco (1971–75), respectively) and decreased during the second half of the dictatorship (30 percent and 15 percent during the governorships of Aureliano Chaves (1975–79) and Francelino Pereira (1979–82), respectively).[8] During the transition to democracy, the composition of traditional politicians in Minas Gerais's government rose precipitously (Hagopian 1992).

Hagopian's findings are important for the current study since they highlight the period of early military rule during which the state government created an array of development agencies that were controlled by the state's political technocratic economic bureaucracy. Nevertheless, it should be pointed out that political technocrats had voiced plans for an expanded industrial policy before this time. And despite a decline in the technocratic composition of the cabinet in subsequent years, the development agencies continued to function without serious conflicts between the oligarchy and political technocrats in the economic bureaucracy. Hagopian (1996: 137, n. 21) confirms the low level of conflict between traditional elites and political technocrats when she notes that "no politician that I interviewed in 1981 or 1982 complained of an inability to

8. See Table 4.2 in Hagopian (1996: 119).

work with technocrats." Consistent with the argument in this chapter, these trends reflect not so much a change during the period of military rule but a *continuation* of larger patterns of elite accommodation around common interests from the pre-1964 period.

The role of the political technocrats in Minas's economic policy became more prominent as traditional leaders remained sensitive to the state's dependency on the more advanced industrialized states of the South and Southeast (C. Diniz 1986: 336; C. Diniz 1981: 185–86). In their eyes, these linkages continued to depreciate Minas's role in the larger Brazilian federation. By the 1960s it was also clear that national developmentalist policy was desirable but not sufficient to end Minas's dependency. Most of the products of Minas's public firms were exported to São Paulo and Rio de Janeiro to supply the raw material base for advanced consumer durable and capital goods industries.

Before the military came to power, the governorship of Magalhães Pinto (1961–65) sought ways of reversing these tendencies in Minas Gerais's development. Pinto supported the delegation of resources and authorities to a series of new developmental institutions and agencies modeled on CEMIG (Mata-Machado 1987). This faith in state-led change was reinforced by the weakness of *mineiro* entrepreneurs whose investments were deployed in agriculture and traditional industries or were dependent upon public investments in mining and steel. In the view of Minas's politicians and state technocrats, "local entrepreneurs had, by their inability to carry out a project for industrialization, in effect forfeited their claim to lead this process" (Hagopian 1996: 87).

Mineiro labor was also politically weak. Minas's labor unions lacked the strong immigrant experience that propelled the emergence of an organized worker movement in São Paulo. Minas remained a largely rural and oligarchical society for much of the 20th century. As a result, *mineiro* labor relations continued forms of oppression common to the oligarchical system of patron-client relations.[9] Repressive labor relations weakened labor unions in Minas, even in sectors where Brazilian workers made tremendous strides in São Paulo and other places. For example, of the 80,000 metalworkers in Belo Horizonte and Contagem, only 16,000 were union members in 1990, a rate far below the *paulista* levels (*Estado*

---

9. Author interview with Otávio Dulci, professor of political science, Universidade Federal de Minas Gerais (UFMG), June 24, 1996, Belo Horizonte, Minas Gerais. A 1990 study of small and medium-sized auto parts firms concluded that patron-client relations are reconstituted within the firm, compelling workers to avoid any actions that might be in conflict with the general interests of their "patron." The study was conducted by Allan Claudius Barbosa, and the results were reported in *Estado de Minas*, January 14, 1990.

de Minas January 14, 1990). Minas's clientelistic labor system was epitomized by the practices of the *mineiro* public firms, CEMIG included, which was notorious for bypassing the unions.[10] Major *mineiro* public and private firms such as Fiat, Usiminas, CEMIG, and CVRD mastered labor repression by mixing coercion with modest concessions to workers on salaries and the provision of low-cost health and education benefits. These efforts were successful in keeping strike levels well below the Brazilian average: CVRD did not suffer a major strike in 50 years and Fiat was strike-free throughout most of the 1980s and 1990s.

Given a tradition of elite accommodation both within the oligarchy and between it and the political technocracy, and lacking any significant political challenges to state government intervention in the local economy by business and labor, *mineiro* politicians had few obstacles to delegating authorities and resources to an array of new economic agencies. Political technocrats evaluated Minas's economy and launched initiatives based on a *mineiro* development mission, which ultimately did not differ much from the developmentalist principles of state planning under Kubitschek and the later military governments. The Pinto administration, with the token backing of the Federação das Indústrias do Estado de Minas Gerais (Federation of Industries of Minas Gerais State, FIEMG), the state's major business association, created the Banco de Desenvolvimento de Minas Gerais (Bank of Development of Minas Gerais, BDMG) in 1962 as a credit agency to provide finance to small- and medium-sized firms ignored by the national development banks.[11] Virtually moribund for a couple of years, the BDMG's existence took on a whole new significance after 1965. In that year, the Departamento de Estudos e Planejamento (the Department of Studies and Planning, DEP) of the BDMG, a bank department staffed by some of the best and brightest

10. Despite the firm's willingness to engage in collective bargaining with the influential Electrical Workers' Union, CEMIG was known to issue compensated dismissal plans without consulting the union and literally on the eve of contract renegotiations. At the same time, CEMIG was prone to limit union organization and activity, particularly worker participation in designing workplace responsibilities, pension policy, productivity management, and even worker access to basic financial information about the firm (*Boletim Diesse*, no. 151, October 1993). Even CEMIG's management in charge of labor relations admits: "These actions are all part of a deliberate strategy to politically weaken union representation which is seen as predatory from the perspective of the firm" (quoted in *Boletim Diesse*, no. 151, October 1993).

11. Although *mineiro* business groups had originally supported the idea of a state development bank in 1957, these actors had no real political influence to create one. Only when political elites supported the idea of building up the state government's technocratic capacity during the 1960s, was the BDMG conceived (Hagopian 1996: 86–88). For a discussion of the origins of the BDMG, see C. Diniz (1981: 138–40), Brito (1984: 243–45), Gama de Andrade (1980), and BDMG (1964).

economists from the Federal University of Minas Gerais,[12] initiated a diagnostic on Minas's economy. The report created a stir when it was published in 1968. It concluded that the dominance of agriculture and public enterprises in Minas held little hope for diversifying or developing the local economy. The report ended with a phrase that would continue to haunt *mineiro* leaders decades later: "Worse still are the expectations for Minas's future." Appropriately, the diagnostic's authors would come to be known as the "prophets of doom."

The "prophets"' warning reinforced the commitment of Minas's political class to use the state technocracy to address the backwardness of the *mineiro* economy.[13] The BDMG political technocrats expanded the developmentalist mission of the bank, creating the Instituto de Desenvolvimento Industrial (Institute of Industrial Development, INDI) in 1967 with the technical and financial support of CEMIG and the consulting experience of the Arthur D. Little Company (ADL).[14] The new agency was charged with the responsibility for conducting studies and providing consulting services to potential investors and clients for both BDMG and CEMIG (Brito 1984: 247–48). Following the military's fiscal reform, the state government implemented a new fiscal incentives law in 1969 to provide additional financial mechanisms for industrial policy.[15]

Other development agencies were created in the wake of INDI's genesis in 1968. In 1972, the state government launched the Companhia de Distritos Industriais (Company of Industrial Districts, CDI). The CDI developed industrial districts with the logistical and political support of municipal government and supplied these projects with basic infrastructure. The Fundação João Pinheiro (The João Pinheiro Foundation, FJP), named after a former early 20th century *mineiro* governor, operated as an official research organization. FJP supplied state planners with the statistics and sectoral studies they needed to plan and finish investment projects. In addition, the FJP and the Centro de Planejamento (Center of Planning, CEDEPLAR) of the economics department of the federal university of Minas Gerais played prominent roles in supplying technocrats to the state government's planning apparatus.

12. For an excellent study of the importance of the DEP in creating the *mineiro* industrial policy system during the 1960s and 1970s, see Gama de Andrade (1980).
13. This was the main subject in discussions among the *mineiro* elite during the 1960s (see BDMG 1964).
14. CEMIG paid for 75 percent of the INDI while the BDMG maintained 25 percent interest in the agency. At CEMIG's prompting, the Arthur D. Little Co. became a model for the INDI's operations (Brito 1984: 249).
15. For an analysis of the 1969 Law of Fiscal Incentives, see Duarte Filho, Carvalho, Chaves, and Silva (1979).

From their creation, the agencies were designed to work together on common projects and under the overarching direction of the state's development goals as set down in the 1968 BDMG diagnostic. This degree of plan-oriented horizontal embeddedness was reinforced through joint ownership of agencies such as INDI, which was governed by BDMG and CEMIG, and the routine circulation of technocrats among the agencies. Yet the construction of horizontal linkages was also due to political and larger logistical reasons as well. Seeking federal support for Minas's industrial policy, the architects of the development agencies argued that the creation of a specialized and connected network of agencies would remedy Minas's economic problems (Brito 1984). Following the "prophets of doom" in their conclusion that without action "Minas would be exploited by other states of the Brazilian federation," *mineiro* executives pressed central government authorities for more resources for the agencies. Within the politics of the authoritarian regime, this meant using privileged access to the generals to gain leverage in the game of intergovernmental conflict. This was crucial at the earliest stages to clear the way for the creation of the agencies. For example, Israel Pinheiro who succeeded Pinto as governor in 1965, employed his contacts with Rondon Pacheco, then Chief of Staff for the Costa e Silva military presidency, to short circuit Central Bank opposition to the creation of INDI (Brito 1984: 250). Once the agencies were created, Minas's political and technical leadership saw the forging of regular and close horizontal linkages among the agencies as crucial factors in assuring the effectiveness of the state's industrial policy (C. Diniz 1981: 142–47). The state elite, therefore, mixed technical and political arguments concerning Minas's "exploitation" by other states to create horizontal networks among the agencies. Most important, these arguments were initially directed at federal authorities who were asked to clear institutional obstacles and provide fiscal resources. As Paulo Valladares, one of the founders and original president of the INDI, remembers:

> INDI was created to rapidly industrialize Minas Gerais. When it was created it was infused with the professionalism of CEMIG and BDMG. At the time of its creation many in state government wondered if we needed yet another development agency. I was at BDMG at the time, and was among those who argued for a more sui generis entrepreneurial information agency that would help coordinate the activities of the development bank and the utility companies with greater flexibility than they could do alone. . . . At the time, I did not just have to make technical arguments in favor

of creating INDI, I also could point to how far back we were in comparison to São Paulo and Rio. These became the chief political arguments that accompanied the technical criteria [for the creation of INDI]. (Author interview, June 18, 1996, Belo Horizonte)

To be sure, the effectiveness of such arguments ultimately relied on close ties between the *mineiro* leadership and the authoritarian regime. Rondon Pacheco and his successor in 1975, Aureliano Chaves, both used their personal friendships with key military leaders such as General Ernesto Geisel (president of Brazil from 1974–78) as a means of garnering resources for development projects in Minas, including the Açominas steel mill (Schneider 1991: 125–28). During Chaves's governorship, Francelino Pereira was national president of the military's ARENA party and was a key advisor to Geisel and his closest counselor, General Golbery do Couto e Silva. Pereira assumed the *mineiro* governorship in 1979 and used his high-level connections to procure World Bank and Inter-American Development Bank loans for his government's planning projects.[16]

While political arguments for horizontal ties among the agencies were important during their creation, logistical exigencies became more important in actually defining the mission of the emerging network. CEMIG and BDMG were already dedicated to utility infrastructure and finance, respectively. Yet meeting the development goals set down in the DEP's diagnostic would require coordination among a larger array of specialized state agencies. Following the advice of ADL and the view of the CEMIG and BDMG political technocrats, political leaders agreed that the state's industrial projects would require a coordinating technical information agency (INDI) and a second firm to oversee other infrastructural needs (CDI). Most important, all of these agencies would be tied together through joint projects and would remain free of political interference (C. Diniz 1981). The latter was guaranteed by a sweeping reform of the state Secretariat of Economy during the Pinheiro and Pacheco governments that allowed the agencies to work as autonomous organizations within the state apparatus (Brito 1984: 241). In this way, both traditional elites and political technocrats agreed on the advantages of a system of horizontal linkages among Minas's industrial policy agencies.

16. In April 1980, IDB board of governors met in Rio with Brazilian president Figueiredo (1978–84). On the table for consideration were a number of multimillion-dollar planning projects, many of them *mineiro*. Pereira ceaselessly lobbied Ministry of Finance officials and Golbery, Figueiredo's powerful chief of staff, for the president's support, which he would later receive (*Estado de Minas*, April 15–18, 1980).

Once in place, the agencies pursued the expansion of the capital goods and consumer durables sector in the state. INDI employed its contacts with ADL to attract firms such as Fiat (Italian—autos), Krupp (German—machines), White Martins (American—chemicals) and a host of other industries, many directly linked to the steel and mining economies. Fiscal incentives and government ownership were used to attract investors from São Paulo and abroad. Among these, the most noteworthy case was Fiat. BDMG financing proved to be the principal factor that made Fiat's proposed investment in Betim, Minas Gerais, viable.[17] As C. Diniz argues, the BDMG-INDI system transformed Minas Gerais into a "paradise of multinationals" (1981: 194). Almost one-fourth of all FDI between 1971 and 1977 in Brazil went to Minas (Brant 1983: 322).

The activities of the *mineiro* agencies facilitated the most impressive expansion of industrialization in Minas Gerais's history. Total new investments in the state increased 20 percent and the industrial growth rate improved 17 percent between 1970 and 1977, superior to the Brazilian average during the same period. More than $7 billion in new investment and over 200,000 new industrial jobs were created during the decade.[18] The most impressive gains were made in the capital goods sector, which expanded from 7.3 percent of Minas's economy in 1970 to 19.8 percent in 1980. Mechanical industries, in particular, went from 2.4 percent of Minas's industrial production in 1968 to compose 8.7 percent by 1974 (Duarte Filho 1986: 36). The auto sector emerged *de novo* in Minas during the 1970s with the start-up of the Fiat auto-making plant in the city of Betim near Belo Horizonte. By 1980, Minas was producing 20 percent of Brazil's capital goods, whereas in 1970 it produced less than 8 percent (C. Diniz 1981: 214; BDMG 1989a: 33).

Areas of the state that had once been dedicated to agriculture became centers for industrialization. Under the leadership of Paulo Haddad, the Pereira government's secretary of planning (1978–82), the state developed the *cidades diques* ("dike cities") program in 1980. The main goal of this policy was to avoid the industrial concentration experienced by metropolitan São Paulo. *Cidades diques* allocated over $180 million ($60 million funded by the Inter-American Development Bank, and $120 million by the state and federal governments) to develop the infrastructure and

17. Author interview with José Eduardo de Lima Pereira, director of external relations, Fiat Co., April 4, 1995, Betim, Minas Gerais.
18. *Estado de Minas,* January 10, 1988. Estimates of this number vary somewhat. C. Diniz (1984: 267), perhaps the best authority on the subject, suggests that investments topped $10 billion in the 1970–74 period alone. For an understanding of the spatial dimensions of this period of high growth, see C. Diniz (1994).

administrative facilities of municipalities in the interior of the state.[19] Under the program, the western region of the so-called *triângulo mineiro* (the *mineiro* triangle) and the Sul de Minas (Southern Minas) regions evolved complex industrial structures in chemicals and auto parts, respectively.

The Crisis and Restructuring of *Mineiro* Industrial Policy in the 1980s and 1990s

The emerging economic crises of the 1980s put severe strains upon the *mineiro* development mission. The decline of public sector production, part of the more general contraction of the internal market, forced many of the capital goods producers that invested in Minas during the 1970s to downsize or close down. The share of Minas's industrial product composed by capital goods and consumer durables fell from almost 20 percent in 1980 to 17.7 percent in 1986 (BDMG 1989b: 20). Minas's GDP grew 157 percent during the 1970s but only 17 percent between 1981 and 1989 (BDMG 1989a: 28). More telling still, the formation of fixed capital as a percentage of Minas's GDP fell from 30 percent during the 1970s to 18 percent during the 1980s (*Estado de Minas* September 8, 1989).

As a result, the development agencies' client base eroded. But there was no attempt on the part of the new, democratic state government elected in 1982 to re-empower the agencies to counteract the recession in investment. The new government led by presidential aspirant Tancredo Neves was mainly concerned with playing a leading role in the transition to democracy, not the economic development of Minas (Dulci 1988).[20] Moreover, Neves and his supporters identified the development agencies with the institutions of authoritarian planning. As one promi-

19. Some of the most important projects occurred in Montes Claro, Juiz de Fora, Uberaba, Uberlândia, Patos de Minas, Unaí, Varginha, Três Corações, Poços de Caldas, Pouso Alegre, Itajubá, Coronel Fabriciano, Ipatinga, Timóteo, Governador Valadares, and Teófilo Otoni (see *Estado de Minas,* June 5, 1980). These municipalities were invariably located in the western, southern, and central sections of Minas. Their geographic proximity to the centers of *mineiro* and *paulista* industrialization made the dike cities program a mechanism that promoted the expansion of industry in Minas through agglomeration. Haddad (1985) argues that these locations were chosen based on this criteria, but Hagopian (1996) offers an important corrective by pointing to how municipal and electoral politics influenced the evolution of the dike cities program. The overall picture provided by the evidence suggests that both views are not mutually exclusive. The *mineiro* dike cities program generated important economic and political rewards, the former lasting longer and having greater implications for Minas Gerais's development well into the 1990s.

20. The new governor's official plans for Minas Gerais spelled out only minimally the roles to be played by the development agencies. The document's prescriptions were vague and inconsistent (see Estado de Minas Gerais 1982). Hagopian (1992: 262) points out that

nent observer from the period told me: "The political meaning of planning was more important at the time than the practical meaning and importance of planning."[21]

When Neves left the governorship in 1984 to assume the mantle of the Party of the Brazilian Democratic Movement (PMDB), the largest opposition party in the presidential race, he shifted Hélio Garcia into the governor's chair. Garcia, however, remained politically concerned with Neves's national candidacy. Garcia was also overburdened with his additional responsibilities as mayor of Belo Horizonte, a seat to which he unwisely clung. With only two years left on his predecessor's mandate, Garcia had little time to develop lasting institutions.

The 1986 elections produced a surprise that few had predicted—a political break in the long line of classic, traditional elites in *mineiro* politics. Newton Cardoso, a little known politician who was born in the state of Bahia, beat out the long-time *mineiro* politician and future president and governor from Juiz de Fora, Itamar Franco. Cardoso's nomination and subsequent victory generated considerable debate within the PMDB, which reluctantly sponsored his candidacy. The frictions were caused by the fact that Cardoso was an outsider in Minas's political oligarchy. Whereas recent *mineiro* governors were linked with the state's evolving political technocracy, the nature of Cardoso's electoral base made him a representative of the traditional oligarchy of the poor northern region of Minas that went almost uniformly for Cardoso, while the more developed south, west, and center backed Franco.

As a relative outsider, Cardoso had little consideration for the political technocrats who played prominent roles in the traditional politics of Minas Gerais (Brito 1988: 283).[22] Cardoso showed outright disdain for the *mineiro* agencies, appointing political supporters rather than political technocrats to head the development organizations.[23] His first appointment to the presidency of the BDMG was a businessman with no more than four years of schooling. Cardoso's secretary of planning (SEPLAN),

---

the agencies remained in technocratic hands while Neves employed the support of traditional elites in his government.

21. Author interview with Marilena Chaves, assistant secretary of planning, SEPLAN (interviewed June 14, 1996, Belo Horizonte, Minas Gerais).

22. Reportedly, Cardoso so personalized his blatant hostility toward traditional *mineiro* politicians and technocrats that his aides were instructed to formulate lists of dismissals organized by last name! (Anonymous author interviews at BDMG, June 1996).

23. Paulo Roberto Haddad, the ex-secretary of planning and key spokesman for the *mineiro* agencies, argued that Cardoso was "hollowing out" the state's planning structure for the sake of the governor's political cronies (*Estado de Minas*, September 11, 1987).

another technically unqualified appointment, gave an inaugural speech that questioned whether his own secretariat had a purpose.[24]

The few political technocrats in Cardoso's administration, such as the president of the CDI, Floriano Martins de Mello, abandoned the government after being forced to dismiss indiscriminately from their agencies.[25] The Fundação João Pinheiro was particularly hard hit as dozens of its best technocrats abandoned the agency after the governor succeeded in slashing their salaries.[26] Marilena Chaves, a technocrat at FJP recalls Cardoso's relations with the agencies as conflictual:

> Newton Cardoso deliberatively tried to dismantle the agencies. There was a lot of turnover during his government; much political instability. The secretary of planning, for example, only lasted a year. Politics, in the pejorative sense of the word, was predominant. This was the case partially because Newton Cardoso was a political outsider who had come to power and needed to reward his supporters by putting them in positions of power regardless of the consequences for Minas's development. (Author interview, June 14, 1996, Belo Horizonte)

Divisions among the political technocrats within state government translated into larger rifts among Minas Gerais's national representatives (the *bancada mineira*). Martins de Mello's forced resignation from the CDI was one of many shifts in Cardoso's handling of the *mineiro* bureaucracy that deepened greater differences among members of the governor's ruling party, the PMDB. One of the most prominent of these rifts occurred in January 1988 when a well-known PMDB politician, Hélio Costa, accused Cardoso of illegally appropriating World Bank monies for the governor's political campaign (*Estado de Minas* January 9, 1988). PMDB politicians who supported Itamar Franco rallied behind the charges. Without

---

24. Cardoso even attacked CEMIG's thirty-five-year history of being administered by highly qualified and experienced engineers. The governor succeeded in placing a number of *fazendeiros* (plantation owners) with close political ties to the governor on the power company's governing board. This cleared the way for the governor to appoint Geraldo Paulino Santana, a little-known politician from the poor town of Salinas and a man without any experience in the energy sector, to head CEMIG (*Estado de Minas*, September 4, 1987).

25. In this case, the governor's policy backfired. After being ordered to restructure his agency, Martins de Mello pursued a rational set of priorities and dismissed the most obviously redundant workers, including Geraldo Maurício Regadas, one of the governor's most celebrated benefactors. Cardoso's secretary of industry, Luiz Ricardo Goulart, was then asked to pressure Martins de Mello to resign himself (see *Estado de Minas*, October 20, 1988).

26. See *Estado de Minas*, September 6, 1987.

its traditional base in the governor's mansion in Belo Horizonte, the oligarchical *mineiro* elites of the national Congress started to divide into pro- and anti-Cardoso factions (*Estado de Minas* September 13, 1987). The national-local *mineiro* political linkages that had served the state so effectively in past decades were in jeopardy.

Faced with escalating opposition from rivals within his own party, Cardoso pursued patrimonial economic policies to strengthen his political position. The political outsider presented himself as a "man of public works" (*homem de obras*). As such, Cardoso built roads for large *fazendeiros* in the poor north, but only selectively for individuals, families, and areas that had supported him in 1986. The governor funneled millions to advertising agencies, some owned by close political friends, to promote himself.[27] The developing south, west, and parts of Belo Horizonte were almost ignored.

Cardoso's populist program was part and parcel of an attempt to centralize power in ways that would limit his opposition's influence. While unsympathetic observers have argued that the governor was antagonistic to the *mineiro* agencies, more balanced assessments suggest that Cardoso harbored no ill will toward the economic bureaucracy. Instead, the governor was compelled by political circumstances to embrace a centralization of power that was inconsistent with the model of organization used by the development agencies. As Valladares, who continued to work at INDI and BDMG during the 1980s, observes:

> Cardoso had been in the opposition for a long time. He created a party of opposition in the state. But Cardoso also created his own problems while he was in power. He was not supported or looked well upon in his own party. . . . Deep down, I believe Cardoso appreciated the work of the agencies, but he wanted to do it all personally. Cardoso wanted to centralize power, not to decentralize it. He liked to fight with his assistants. . . . So Cardoso did not really try to destroy the agencies. He tried to centralize power and that was inconsistent with empowering the agencies. (Author interview, June 18, 1996, Belo Horizonte)

The result of these tensions was a challenge to the *mineiro* agencies on two major fronts. First, the economic crisis of developmentalism had begun to erode the plan-based organization of the agencies. Second, the transition to democracy produced higher levels of elite conflict and eventually a populist government in 1986 that threatened the political

---

27. Over Cr 200 million of state money were discovered in a promotion slush fund in 1988 (*Estado de Minas,* April 5, 1988).

technocratic management of economic policy. Nonetheless, horizontal embeddedness protected the agencies from becoming politicized or losing their capacity for intervening in the economy. The absence of overarching development plans and reductions in funding caused the agencies to focus on more project-oriented strategies. More important, the continuation of frequent contact, common planning of policy goals among the agencies, and circulation of personnel kept lines of communication open, allowing for political technocrats to mobilize business constituencies in their defense and creating opportunities for reforming the development mission under a subsequent delegative government.

Several factors continued to protect the agencies from clientelism. First, the technocracy of the agencies remained professionally adept and well entrenched. Despite the economic crisis, or perhaps because of it, the Cardoso administration had no good reasons for disassembling the agencies on technical grounds. Second, none of Cardoso's advisors were neoliberals, so the governor did not represent a direct challenge to the state-led development mission. Moreover, the agencies were linked in ways that did not allow for a frontal attack on any one agency at one time. CEMIG's and BDMG's technocrats in INDI were defended by their mother agencies. Attacks on CEMIG were complicated by its role as both a power company and a partner in the development network linked to INDI and its partner, the CDI. Thus the proliferation of veto points prevented sweeping restructuring.

The agencies were also politically protected by networks of private clients and formal and informal associations with the national public firms who still wielded considerable power in the state legislature and in the governor's office.[28] Attacks on BDMG in particular were untenable in this regard. Apart from the fact that the bank's existence could not be threatened since it was self-financing, the BDMG also maintained financial resources that proved useful for mobilizing private firms, public agencies such as INDI and CEMIG, and their respective lobbies within the state government apparatus.

Cardoso's policy of benign neglect toward the agencies did produce some favorable staffing decisions that would have important implications for the reform of *mineiro* industrial policy in subsequent governments. While the potential political costs of dismantling the agencies were too high for Cardoso, the governor did take a particular interest in

---

28. One example is how business leaders, particularly José Alencar, then-president of Fiemg, convinced Cardoso in closed-door audiences, to remove BDMG president Joaquim Mariano in 1988, who had proven inept (confidential interview with BDMG officials, June 1996, Belo Horizonte, Minas Gerais).

the development of BDMG.[29] Two of the governor's appointments would help BDMG take a proactive role in redesigning development policy in Minas. The first of these was João Batista de Abril, Cardoso's secretary of the economy. A contemporary of Paulo Haddad, Abril shared many ideas with the old planning guru of Minas Gerais. Abril helped insulate the BDMG from clientelism by insisting on keeping the bank staff under professional management. The second appointment was Carlos Alberto Teixeira, president of BDMG, who made his mark after Abril left in 1988. In Cardoso's initial tendency to weaken the agencies with clientelistic appointments, he had given control of the bank to a political supporter, Joaquim Mariano. Mariano had not only proven to be a weak president but also emotionally unstable. His frequent fits of pique and hysteria culminated in his dismissal by Cardoso and his subsequent suicide. Teixeira, an ex-president of the private financial giant Safra Bank, was considered by many to be one of the most competent political technocrats in state government when he was called upon to succeed Mariano.

Teixeira's priority was to return the BDMG to its previous role as an investment bank. The new president commissioned the BDMG to conduct a second diagnostic of the *mineiro* economy. This new BDMG report would become more than a useful economic study of Minas Gerais; it became a political statement. The diagnostic argued for a proactive industrial policy to be sponsored by the state government. The new approach for intervention would be "highly selective" and would not require much public production of goods (BDMG 1989a: 25). The report reflected a sensitivity to the manner in which industry was restructuring globally, the competitiveness of the state's key sectors, eventual privatization of the national public firms, international interdependence, and the fiscal well-being of the state government. Most important, the diagnostic focused on policies that would create externalities based on Minas's proximity to São Paulo. The old concern with dependency on the *paulista* economy was jettisoned along with state-led prescriptions for development.

The BDMG's 1989 diagnostic became a vehicle for linking intellectuals and political technocrats under a new development mission. In the next

29. Some observers have suggested that Cardoso maintained a personal exception for the BDMG based on the general rule that banks must remain professional agencies (author interview with Iran Almeida Pordeus, executive advisor, BDMG, June 13, 1996, Belo Horizonte, Minas Gerais). Carlos Alberto Teixeira, president of the BDMG 1988–90, insists that Cardoso provided all the backing he needed to modernize the bank in 1989 (author interview, June 25, 1996, Belo Horizonte, Minas Gerais). See the BDMG 1989 diagnostic, (BDMG, 1989a, 1989b, and 1989c) and BDMG (1995).

few years, these elites would steward a restructuring of the *mineiro* industrial policy system under the second Hélio Garcia administration beginning in 1990. Paulo Paiva, a leader on the 1989 study, became Garcia's secretary of planning. Marilena Chaves, a future executive advisor at planning; Paulo Eduardo Rocha Brant, a future manager of the BDMG's industrial credit programs; and Iran Almeida Pordeus, an executive advisor at the BDMG, all emerged as key actors during the coming reconversion of *mineiro* planning. Each had a technical background in economics and administration and good political connections to the key political technocrats of the new Garcia administration.

Even before Garcia's second coming, Minas's industrial policy technocrats could claim some isolated successes in bringing the system back. BDMG technocrats in 1989 created Proindústria, a fiscal incentive program for new investments. Proindústria had worked based on the development of particular projects on which different agencies played specific roles and sometimes coordinated their actions with World Bank infrastructure programs. Without an overarching plan requiring continuous contacts and common goal-setting among the agencies, Proindústria's role was limited by this project-oriented form of horizontal embeddedness. In the post-1990 period, however, the financial program became one of several tools that were redesigned to form part of a plan-oriented horizontal embeddedness.

Nevertheless, other obstacles emerged to the restructuring of *mineiro* industrial policy before 1991. Reductions in financial transfers from the national development bank (BNDES) to BDMG undercut the bank's loans to private industry. By 1990, the BDMG was facing a severe liquidity shortage. During the 1970s and 1980s, the *mineiro* development bank lent millions to the national steel holding company, Siderbrás, and the national cane alcohol program, IAA. President Collor ignored these debt obligations and tried to write them off after liquidating Siderbrás and IAA in 1990. This single act placed severe financial restrictions on the BDMG. It froze $250 million of the bank's liquid capital, which effectively put a halt to all attempts to move on the prescriptions of the 1989 diagnostic.[30]

CEMIG, which had always been a model of the state's developmentalist agenda, also fell on hard times during the Collor presidency. The state power company owed millions to the federal Itaipu/Furnas project and was owed millions by Minas's state and municipal governments. A

---

30. Author interview with Iran Almeida Pordeus, executive advisor, BDMG, June 13, 1996, Belo Horizonte, Minas Gerais.

sharp drop in demand for the company's energy in 1990 strained CEMIG's capacity to honor its obligations and to exact payment on its outstanding accounts (*Dirigente Industrial* September 1991).

On the eve of Garcia's return to the governorship in 1990, the *mineiro* industrial policy system was in severe disrepair.[31] The state of the SEPLAN building in Belo Horizonte, which was suffering from serious structural decay, was emblematic of the larger condition of decadence in the institutions governing economic planning. The secretariat's offices were technically backward and the file system was chaotic. Staff members tended to have outdated training and were underpaid. These technocrats also had a nostalgic affinity for the state's developmentalist past, a factor that made them initially hesitant to restructure planning institutions. Minas Gerais's constitution, which had been ratified only two years earlier, added to the confusion. The document mandated that even the slightest reforms to the state bureaucracy first be written into law. As a result, technocrats were overburdened with the need to prepare hundreds of amendments of law in the first few months of the reform process. Even minor name changes within agencies were subject to questions of law. Eventually, state managers resorted to "Frankenstein" bills with hundreds of amendments mandating the needed changes. Valuable time was lost.

Another disruption occurred on the day Garcia was inaugurated as the new governor. Without warning, the federal government closed Minascaixa, one of Minas Gerais's public banks. The closure forced state officials to relocate over 15,000 public employees among the agencies of the state bureaucracy. After the initial confusion had settled, the dispersion of Minascaixa's relatively well-trained, professional technocrats provided solutions to some of the problems facing the *mineiro* agencies. The ex-Minascaixa technocrats injected new blood into the secretariats. In SEPLAN in particular, these highly qualified and well-remunerated ex-Minascaixa officials greatly improved the technical capacity of the secretariat and broke the hold of the nostalgia for past policy.

Unlike Cardoso, who faced intense opposition as a political outsider, Hélio Garcia's return to the Palácio da Liberdade (the governor's mansion) in 1991 represented the re-emergence of the old system of coordination between traditional elites and political technocrats. Alarmed by the Minascaixa incident and threats by neighboring states to use tax rebates to lure industries out of the state, Garcia delegated authority to a core group of political technocrats who were intent on reforming and

---

31. The following is based on an author interview with Marilena Chaves, executive advisor, SEPLAN, June 14, 1996, Belo Horizonte, Minas Gerais.

strengthening the economic policy-making apparatus of the state government. As one popular joke about Garcia stated, "Hélio does not delegate, he devolves" authority (*"Hélio não delega, ele entrega"*). This popular notion was upheld in practice, as Garcia's economic policies relied almost exclusively on three political technocrats: Garcia's secretary of planning, Paulo Paiva; (2) the secretary of the economy, Roberto Brant; and Garcia's chief of staff, Ivandro de Padua Abril. Abril focused on legal matters, making him more of a secondary actor in the process. Paiva and Brant became Garcia's point men on industrial policy.

Both political technocrats had close and common ties. Brant's chief advisor, José Afonso Bicalho da Silva, had university (CEDEPLAR) and personal ties with Paiva. Both had been prominent participants in the national campaign for direct elections for the presidency (Diretas Já) during the transition to democracy. Paiva's chief advisor, Antônio Agusto Anastasia, was also closely tied to the *mineiro* intellectual elite.

In practice, economic policy and bureaucratic reform were the result of informal agreements made among these individuals. Anastasia acted as the point man in the political and institutional process, retaining frequent contacts with key leaders in the state assembly. Paiva, Afonso, and Brant coordinated planning in all affairs of state, particularly economic policy. Hélio Garcia played the role of main political coordinator, maintaining absolute confidence in his three *secretários*. The other secretariats, including the Secretariat of State for Industry and Commerce, reported in practice directly to Paiva and Afonso.

Between 1991 and 1994, Paiva and Afonso revised the entire structure of industrial policy-making in Minas Gerais. The first and most important move was to find new sources of revenue and to rationalize the state budget in order to allow for significant industrial policies. These government leaders turned to international financial markets and multilateral agencies. The *mineiro* government accessed $200 million on European financial markets, a practice that was repeated several times, making Minas Gerais's state government the first subnational government in Latin America to directly capture funds in international capital markets. The World Bank agreed to provide $600 million for dozens of state government programs to improve the efficiency of administration and public works. Separately, a number of infrastructural programs received additional funding from the World Bank and the Inter-American Development Bank. The reformers also modernized and enforced tax collection functions, allowing Minas to recover more ICMS revenues.

The second reform focused on the "new directions" of planning. In 1992, a group of political technocrats led by Paiva and Afonso drafted goals for *mineiro* industrial policy that were eventually published as the *Plano Mineiro de Desenvolvimento Integrado* (the Mineiro Plan of Integrated Development, PMDI) in 1995 (see Estado de Minas Gerais 1995a). Consistent with the 1989 BDMG diagnostic, the new framework for planning recognized the fiscal limits of industrial policy and rejected the more costly developmentalist models used in the past.[32] According to state officials who were involved in these discussions, the state development agencies agreed to create "priority sectors" and "structural initiatives."[33] The auto parts sector, for example, clearly had a strong presence in Minas Gerais and one with excellent prospects for growth through new investments. Previously protected sectors such as textiles, however, were not priorities. Only particular textile firms actively engaged in efforts to modernize their production and become more competitive in the domestic and international market received official attention.

Based on my conversations with state officials and my review of government documents linked to these discussions, it is clear that the architects of the new *mineiro* planning were designing a pragmatic industrial policy more in line with the limited fiscal resources of the state government. These were policy ideas that sought to follow market forces and improve the market's effects on the *mineiro* economy. The essential elements were similar to those first proposed several years before in the BDMG's 1989 diagnostic. Faced with a crisis in the old developmentalist model, the new political technocracy in Minas redesigned the development mission along more market-oriented lines.

The third important reform was the empowerment of the industrial planning structure of the state government. In this regard the secretary of state for industry and commerce received special attention. Having been decimated by the Cardoso administration, it was a weak and ineffectual

32. Consider the characterization of the new role of the state described in a key industrial policy document: "The state government is committed to policies designed to structure, promote and stimulate economic activities, with a strategic and long-term vision, but within its fiscal and financial limits and conditions. Paternalistic and state-oriented models are rejected" (Estado de Minas Gerais 1995b: 8). This document was a later version of one published in 1993. As an illustration of how the state government's thinking changed during this period of time, it is noteworthy to compare the wording of the same paragraph as printed in the earlier edition: "Paternalistic and state-oriented models are rejected, except in cases in which the state government is a direct investor in situations regarded as strategic, and only as a minority interest for a finite period" (Estado de Minas Gerais 1993: 7). The later edition defines the state's role more directly while keeping the caveat about fiscal limits and the distinction between current policy and developmentalism.

33. Author interview with Cláudio de Paiva Ferreira, chief director of the superintendency of industrialization, Secretariat of State for Industry and Commerce, June 26, 1996, Belo Horizonte, Minas Gerais.

entity upon Garcia's inauguration. Paiva and Afonso strengthened the secretariat by creating the Fundo de Industrialização (Industrialization Fund—FIND), a state fund meant to finance fiscal incentives for industrial investment. The FIND supplied funding for two major tax incentive schemes. The first, the new Proindústria (the Integration and Industrial Diversification Program), was designed to attract new, mostly medium-size investment to the state by supplying venture capital as a "fiscal incentive" meant to reduce start-up costs.[34] The second program, the Induction and Modernization Program (Proim), was designed as a true venture capital fund for established firms wishing to modernize their plant and equipment and generally expand production. As firms paid back their tax "finance" through the Proindústria program, a percentage of the repayment was channeled to the Proim account to finance approved projects. As of 1996, over $550 million had been transferred into the Proim account of the FIND and over $313 million had been utilized as finance.[35] As Figure 3.1 demonstrates, the Proindústria and Proim programs expanded rapidly between 1991 and 1996, as they played a role in virtually every industrial project including the BDMG.

The Superintendência de Industrialização (Superintendency of Industrialization, SUIND) was created as a subagency of the Secretariat of Industry in order to administer the fund. In practice, though, SUIND's major decisions were taken by an "executive group" of political technocrats from different *mineiro* secretariats and agencies and some private business organizations that met in a Conselho de Industrialização (Council of Industrialization, COIND).[36] The new structure improved the capacity for

34. The program had first been proposed in 1989 by Teixeira and his technocrats at the BDMG. The initial successes of the program proved encouraging but modest due to fiscal constraints. In 1991, COIND restructured Proindústria and later provided it with additional resources under the newly approved FIND in June 1994. Proindústria requires firms to pay ICMS and then returns between 30 and 70 percent of the amount in the form of finance for a period not exceeding 5 to 8 years. The "finance" aspect of the Proindústria tax incentive served to avoid federal restrictions on tax exemptions and preserve foreign tax credits for multinational firms approved for the incentive.

35. FIND was replaced by the Fundo de Desenvolvimento de Empresas Estratégicas (Fundiest) after 1995. Proindústria and Proim continued and were even expanded in the 1995–98 period.

36. COIND had existed before as a forum for private business associations and government agencies. In its new form, COIND has 15 members who send representatives to COIND meetings. The members are the Secretariats of Planning, Economy, Industry, Science and Technology, and Environment, the state banks, BDMG, INDI, CDI, Fiemg, the Commercial Association of Minas Gerais, and the Center for Industrial Cities (a collection of *mineiro* mayors).

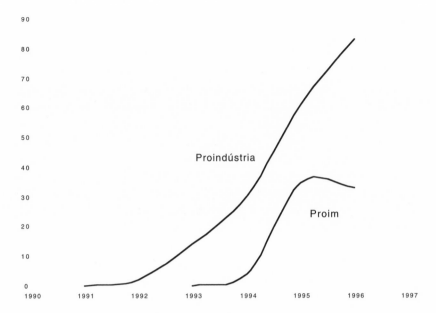

FIG 3.1   Proindústria and Proim projects, 1991–1996 (all figures in millions $ US).
SOURCE: BDMG documents.

decision-making by concentrating administration in the COIND in ways that would facilitate joint planning while maintaining horizontal account-ability. Presently, the council approves projects by a majority vote that is taken in public. BDMG does the technical analysis of each project. COIND decisions are based on BDMG's report and regional and political priorities. Academic observers of this new structure argue that regional interests of-ten assert themselves within COIND, but final decisions are almost always made exclusively on technical grounds.[37] In essence, the current structure is a formalized version of the plan-oriented horizontal embeddedness that governed the *mineiro* agencies during the developmentalist period.

Another area of industrial policy that received attention during the 1988–96 period was infrastructure. State officials reasoned that attention

37. BDMG, for one, is unlikely to approve technically and financially deficient projects since the bank's past activities have made it extremely reluctant to mire itself once again in bad debts or to continue to service the rollover of mounting debt (author interview with Carlos Maurício C. Ferreira, special advisor to the secretary of state for industry and com-merce, June 12, 1996, Belo Horizonte, Minas Gerais). Bank officials confirm Ferreira's opin-ion (author interview with Paulo Eduardo Rocha Brant, director of Credit Area One, BDMG, June 21, 1996, Belo Horizonte, Minas Gerais).

to infrastructure would be the necessary "bond" to create "packages" of incentives for new investors and sectors wishing to modernize their production.[38] CEMIG, which made attracting new industrial clients for its energy the primary means of getting the power company back on its feet, increased its investments in electricity distribution and natural gas to $400 million annually in 1995. More ambitious projects like the expansion of the Fernão Dias Highway (BR-381), which links Belo Horizonte with São Paulo, required a mix of finance from multilateral agencies, the national government, and the state government.

Governor Garcia's successor, Eduardo Azeredo of the Party of Brazilian Social Democratic (PSDB), whom Garcia ardently promoted as a candidate in 1994, consolidated and expanded the state's industrial policy menu, adding monies for larger projects. As a trained engineer with a strong political background, Azeredo was a *mineiro* political technocrat in the mold of Rondon Pacheco. His father, Renato Azeredo, had been a longtime federal deputy for the state and a close follower of the developmentalist ideas of Juscelino Kubitschek. Yet the younger Azeredo was also a pragmatist who was sensitive to the resource limitations of the federal government and concerned for the continued fiscal well-being of the state government. That made Azeredo an ideal governor for continuing the phase of delegative government initiated by Garcia that allowed for the consolidation of the new *mineiro* development mission.

Under Azeredo's government, Minas's finances improved even as the state's industrial policy system became more active. Unlike São Paulo and Rio de Janeiro, states that faced almost chaotic fiscal structures in the early 1990s, Minas Gerais enjoyed prolonged periods of revenue increases, decreasing public deficits, and a public commercial bank system that was able to recover from the debt crisis created by the public sector borrowing binge of the post-1982 period (Oliveira and Cypriano 1995; Jayme and Cerqueira 1995).

The election of Itamar Franco and the return of Newton Cardoso, this time as vice-governor, in October 1998 created a new set of political questions in Minas Gerais. Soon after taking office in January 1999, Governor Franco declared a ninety-day moratorium on debt payments to the federal government. The announcement encouraged portfolio investors to flee Brazil, putting pressure on the exchange rate band within which the Central Bank controlled the 'real's devaluation. Days later the federal government was forced to take the currency off the band and allow a

---

38. Author interview with Paulo Eduardo Rocha Brant, director of Credit Area One, BDMG, June 21, 1996, Belo Horizonte, Minas Gerais.

maxi-devaluation. By helping to precipitate the crisis of January 1999 and directly challenging Fernando Henrique Cardoso's presidency, the new *mineiro* government hurt the interests of the *bancada mineira*. In subsequent months, the governor was criticized by segments of Minas's business sector, but these conflicts did not lead to a significant reorganization of the state government's relationship with the private sector. What Itamar Franco and Newton Cardoso will do with the *mineiro* agencies is difficult to determine. Yet through 2000, the *mineiro* agencies continued to thrive. Given the ability of these entities to withstand significant political and economic change, it is likely that they will survive.

PROMOTING EXTERNALITIES: THE FIAT SYSTEM AND AUTO PARTS

The creation and persistence of the *mineiro* agencies due to horizontal ties produced a series of synergistic linkages between the state and private firms. The most impressive of these cases involved the long history of ties between the agencies and the Italian multinational automaker, Fiat. The installation of the Fiat plant in Betim was emblematic of the state's strong developmentalist push during the 1970s. For years afterwards, the presence of Fiat in Minas defined the state's private sector. Fiat became Minas Gerais's number-one exporter. Auto parts firms exclusively serving Fiat moved to Minas during the late 1970s and early 1980s to set up more efficient productive links with the car-maker.[39] Over 84 percent of the firms currently located in the state arrived after the Fiat investment in 1974 (Prates and Marques 1995: 180). By the end of the 1980s, Minas Gerais was home to the largest Fiat plant in the world.

The state government was a prominent partner of Fiat's production and investment strategy from the very beginning. The CDI and the Betim municipal government donated land and basic infrastructure to the Italian automaker in 1974. The state government became a financial partner by providing 45 percent of the capital for Fiat's initial investment, including fiscal incentives and BDMG finance (C. Diniz 1981: 194). The network of public support increasingly targeted auto parts investments linked to Fiat, as dozens of the automaker's suppliers received aid.[40]

39. In comparison to São Paulo's auto parts sector, Minas Gerais's auto parts sector is small. Whereas São Paulo was home to 86 percent of Brazil's auto parts firms in 1994, Minas Gerais, Rio de Janeiro, Rio Grande do Sul, Santa Catarina, and Pernambuco *together* maintained only 13.5 percent of the sector (Prates and Marques 1995: 181).
40. In the case of one prominent Fiat supplier, Kadron, a producer of exhaust systems (1 of 4 employed by Fiat), the firm maintained very close and constant contact with both INDI

Therefore, during the developmentalist period when the *mineiro* agencies were coordinated through a plan-oriented horizontal embeddedness, Fiat and the agencies were able to collaborate on the automaker's investment plans in ways that produced external economies, namely, an auto parts industry where there had previously been none.

The survival of the agencies due to horizontal ties in the 1980s would prove crucial to the evolution of synergistic links in this case. Given changes in the Brazilian development model and pressures to improve productivity in the global car market, both Fiat's investment and production strategy and the *mineiro* agencies' development missions required adjustment. Horizontal ties such as personnel circulation, common ownership, and frequent contacts on common projects kept the agencies going and encouraged policy innovation, creating the possibility that they would play a key role in the restructuring of Fiat's production chain during the late 1980s and in the 1990s. The timing of the agencies' move back to a plan-oriented horizontal embeddedness under the new market-oriented development mission coincided with Fiat's restructuring of production under new global technological and market pressures. This fortunate concurrence produced extraordinary externalities in Minas in the 1990s.

During the 1980s Fiat faced a highly competitive Brazilian and world car market that required profound changes in the firm's system of production. Demand in North America, Western Europe, and Japan, three areas that accounted for 85 percent of the global market, began to saturate during the decade. Meanwhile the proliferation of car-makers in Southeast Asia created competitive pressures that led many international and national firms to ruin. In Brazil, the 1980s proved to be a decade of oscillating demand in the domestic car market due to repeated bouts of inflation. The sector produced over one million automobiles in 1980, but would not reach that annual figure again until 1988, and then only briefly (E. Diniz 1994: 290).

---

and BDMG from the inception of its installation in Minas Gerais during the 1970s. According to the firm's director, the activity of the agencies at this time was crucial to starting up the firm's *mineiro* operations and establishing productive links with Fiat, which encouraged Kadron to employ the agencies. As the manager of Kadron told me: "Their help [INDI and BDMG] was considered within the firm to be quite crucial. I do not believe, and it is not popularly believed within the management of this firm, that our installation and operations in Minas Gerais would have been possible without the help of the INDI or the BDMG" (author interview with Paulo Marcucci, manager, Kadron, June 17, 1996, Belo Horizonte, Minas Gerais).

Pushed by competitive forces within and outside Brazil, the automakers were increasingly compelled to engage in the same methods of productive restructuring practiced by other global producers. Investments in research and development, quality, and inventory management and marketing increased at a frenetic pace during the decade in order to keep and expand market share. This was also true for suppliers who had to offer higher quality products to meet the automakers' standards. Producers were forced to adopt "best practice" techniques that called for eliminating management hierarchies and installing flexible management systems, establishing more cooperative labor relations, and replacing "dead time" inventory systems with "just-in-time" (JIT) links with suppliers. The reasoning behind these reforms was the same: find more flexible ways to adjust to ever-changing market conditions and consumer preferences.[41]

Fiat was no more immune to these changes than its competitors. The firm moved rapidly after 1988 to improve the productivity of its labor force and set up JIT links with suppliers.[42] Although "global sourcing"— the practice of regularly importing parts from foreign suppliers—could be employed to reduce car production costs, local content requirement laws compelled Fiat and its competitors in Brazil to produce cars for the domestic market with 90 percent locally produced auto parts and 60 to 70 percent local-content parts in exported units (Lee and Cason 1994: 299). Fiat also made a strategic decision to avoid the uncertainty associated with imports (Addis 1999: 221).

These constraints placed several limitations on Fiat's attempts to bolster its productivity. The firm's first-tier Brazilian suppliers had little capital with which to import state-of-the-art machine tools. Moreover, these firms had almost no capacity to globally source their own production. Like many of Brazil's other businesses, Fiat's suppliers were hampered by the country's decaying infrastructure and the high cost of finance. The latter was exacerbated by a contraction in BNDES funds during the 1980s. Fiat would have to use other techniques to reorganize its supply links in more efficient ways.

In order to reduce inventory costs and improve quality control, Fiat prepared just-in-time links with some first-tier suppliers and established

---

41. For a review of these changes in the automobile industry, see Deyo (1996), Thomas (1997), and Tuman and Morris (1998).

42. For a treatment of how Fiat did the same in its home country, Italy, see Locke (1995: 105–15).

a model for more fully incorporating suppliers directly within the plant. The new arrangement intended to eliminate the need to maintain an inventory of parts and shift the responsibility for improving quality to the automakers' parts suppliers.[43] The creation of a JIT system could accomplish all of this, but the new arrangement required Fiat to select a "first line" of key suppliers with which it would do business consistently. The target aimed for by the company was 100 total suppliers in 1995, down from 500 in 1988.[44]

For JIT to work, most of these firms would need to be located close to the automaker's plant in Betim. Fiat thus created a *mineirização* strategy ("Minasizing" suppliers), a policy of negotiating with suppliers and convincing them of the technical and financial rewards of relocating from São Paulo or abroad to Minas Gerais and close to the firm in Betim. To be sure, Fiat could not dictate its terms to these suppliers. As Addis (1999) has argued, after the 1970s, suppliers in the Brazilian motor vehicle industry had leverage over the strategies of the assemblers through their syndicates, specifically Sindipeças (the National Syndicate for Producers of Auto Parts and Other Similars). By forming monopolies and cartels across suppliers after production contracts were signed, auto parts firms were able to determine prices and organize production themselves.[45] In Fiat's case, 45.3 percent of its purchases were controlled by monopolies (21.3 percent) or cartels (24 percent) (Addis 1999: 151). Therefore, reorganizing these assembler-supplier relations on Fiat's terms would be tricky.

Encouraged by Fiat's commitment to locally source their production while most of Brazil's assemblers leaned toward global sourcing, many first-tier suppliers embraced *mineirização*. If only 26 percent (or 35 firms) of Fiat's suppliers were located in Minas Gerais in 1989, by 1995 that number was up to 44.3 percent (54 firms). And the majority of those 54 suppliers in 1995 were located in three proximate poles: 18 in Betim (5 kilometers from the plant), 6 in Belo Horizonte (30 kilometers), and 17 in Contagem (15 kilometers) (Fiat 1995). Many of these firms were linked by computer network to the Betim plant so that orders on JIT could be processed without unnecessary delays.[46]

43. For more on Fiat's JIT strategy, see Prates and Marques (1995: 189).

44. Author interview with José Eduardo de Lima Pereira, director of external relations, FIAT, April 4, 1995, Betim, Minas Gerais.

45. Auto parts suppliers were forced to issue competing bids on new product lines, but once contracts were established they could solve their coordination problems and keep assemblers from initiating a price war among them. See Addis (1999: 151–52).

46. Fiat depended on its computer network to link car dealerships as well as suppliers to the Betim plant (author interview with José Eduardo de Lima Pereira, director of external relations for FIAT, April 4, 1995, Betim, Minas Gerais). Also see *O Globo*, February 19, 1995.

Table 3.1 Economic performance of Fiat, 1985–1994
(all dollar figures in millions)

Years	Number of Vehicles Produced	Net Sales	Exports	Employment
1985	452,863	$750	$324.2	9,642
1986	173,283	740	249.2	12,644
1987	216,126	1,080	531.9	11,637
1988	217,482	1,230	571.0	12,007
1989	220,098	1,450	629.3	13,000
1990	219,525	1,658	547.4	12,549
1991	254,000	1,626	449.0	13,364
1992	310,176	2,215	707.0	14,001
1993	393,600	2,600	622.0	15,000
1994[a]	450,000	3,000	720.0	17,000

Source: INDI (1994: 3).

[a] Data are preliminary.

The combined restructuring of management-labor relations and Fiat's productive relations with suppliers dramatically reduced production costs, despite the persistence of macroeconomic instability, inefficient infrastructure, and suppliers with little access to finance. As a result of its restructuring, the firm saved an estimated $1 billion from 1988 to 1994 in production costs while sales increased 174 percent (*O Estado de São Paulo,* August 22, 1994).

Improvements to productivity and relations with suppliers at Fiat during the 1980s and 1990s led to significant gains in the Brazilian marketplace. Sales improved by four times and employment at the automaker expanded markedly (Table 3.1). Fiat's share of the auto market in Brazil increased impressively from 13.4 percent in 1980, to 24.5 percent in 1990, and 33.4 percent in 1994 (ahead of Volkswagen's 33.2 percent), making Fiat Brazil's number-one automaker that year. In less than three years, Fiat jumped from last place in the Brazilian market to the top spot. Fiat's suppliers also fared well. During the period of the firm's extensive restructuring of producer-supplier links, sales and employment at Fiat's suppliers improved markedly (Table 3.2).

A noteworthy point in the cases of both Fiat and its suppliers is that improvements in exports could not explain the better performance. Fiat's exports increased but not consistently enough to account for the improvement in performance, and exports by Fiat's suppliers actually *decreased* during the period. From 1996–98 only 12 percent of the sector's production was exported (INDI 1998: 14–15).

Table 3.2 Economic performance of Fiat suppliers, 1985–1994 (all dollar figures in millions)

Year	Net Sales Brazil	Net Sales Minas Gerais	MG as % of Total Sales in Brazil	% of Total MG Exports	Employment Minas Gerais
1985		232.25		18.11	10,351
1986		255.88		18.47	12,194
1987		365.11		24.97	12,762
1988		387.23		9.25	14,206
1989		544.62		36.71	18,800
1990		393.52		8.62	16,692
1991	9,800	305.00	3.1	20.00	14,500
1992	10,000	340.00	3.4	20.40	15,000
1993	11,300	600.00	5.3	17.00[a]	16,600
1994	12,800	720.00	5.6	17.00[a]	17,000

SOURCE: INDI (1994: 7).

[a] Estimated from preliminary data.

The effect on the *mineiro* economy was also pronounced, although concentrated in one area. The boost in Fiat's production contributed to the expansion of the automotive complex in and around Belo Horizonte and Betim, which housed 60 percent of the auto parts producers in Minas (41 firms in 1993). During the most intense period of *mineirização* between 1992 and 1994, Betim saw $130 million of new investment, $115 million in additional tax revenue, and 5,000 new jobs (*O Estado de São Paulo*, August 22, 1994).

Mineiro agencies such as INDI and BDMG saw Fiat's strategy of convincing suppliers to relocate from São Paulo or invest from abroad as consistent with their own strategy of improving the productivity of the auto parts sector. Fiat was well aware that the agencies shared mutual interests with the firm, and both publicly announced cooperative "partnerships" involving a mix of state fiscal incentives and financial supports to realize agreed goals. These partnerships were not only consistent with Fiat's *mineirização* strategy, they were also tied to the focus of the new *mineiro* development mission on producing external economies at low cost.

In the case of Kadron, one of Fiat's chief exhaust system suppliers, Fiat's strategy and the activity of the agencies worked in tandem. In March 1993, Kadron initiated the first phase of a three-step modernization program designed to improve its evolving just-in-time links with Fiat. In April 1994, the firm completed construction of its new plant for the JIT construction of exhaust systems and catalytic converters. Total investment in the plant exceeded $4 million and created 150 new jobs. Kadron received Proindústria tax incentives of over $4 million for the initial stages of the firm's modernization and all of its investments since 1990 (a sum that was paid back in 1996). INDI provided technical and infrastructural support (telephone lines, energy, roads), which in the opinion of Luis F. S. Machado, Kadron's general manager, accelerated the firm's modernization at a rate that "exceeded expectations."[47]

Another example of the "partnership" system between INDI and Fiat was the creation of a program to supply ready-made sheet metal to the automaker. Before 1984, Fiat prepared steel pieces internally at great cost. In that year, INDI officials organized a program to have Usiminas, then a national public steel firm, produce ready-made pieces of 300, 400, and 500 tons and make them available on timetables established by Fiat. By 1992 Usiminas was stamping body parts itself. Fiat officials note that the original partnership was made possible eight years before only because INDI officials were well-connected enough at Usiminas to implement the program. As a result, Fiat saved millions on inventory and transportation costs while Usiminas was guaranteed about $100 million in sales every year with the Fiat deal.[48]

Fiat succeeded in increasing the percentage of the firm's *mineiro* suppliers, but overall the process of *mineirizção* moved along more slowly than the company wanted. One reason suggested by Prates and Marques (1995: 190–91) was the unsophisticated nature of many of the *mineiro* and transplanted *paulista* suppliers. These auto parts firms tended to lack the organization and technical ability required to make the adjustments to JIT as quickly as Fiat demanded.[49] Many of these firms had not learned how to outsource their own operations and so they could not meet the quality standards required by Fiat. From the suppliers' perspective, this problem was tied to the inadequacy of private sources of finance and the need to focus resources on technology and worker training.[50]

47. This case is described in *INDI Informa* (1993).
48. Author interview with José Eduardo de Lima Pereira, director of external relations, FIAT, April 4, 1995, Betim, Minas Gerais. Deiter Kux, mechanical engineer in the Department of Mechanical and Electronic Industries, INDI, confirmed this story from the agency's perspective (interviewed February 22, 1995, Belo Horizonte, Minas Gerais). It should be noted that the original contracts with Usiminas were extended in 1994 to include other steel products used in Fiat's production line. The new contracts added $20 million in annual sales to Usiminas' output (see *Gazeta Mercantil*, January 28, 1994).
49. One of the key areas of concern for Fiat was the technical backwardness of local electronic parts suppliers. See the interview with the firm's chief of Brazilian operations, Pacífico Paoli, in *Jornal de Brasília*, May 15, 1994.
50. These were highlighted as the top need areas by the firms in an INDI survey of 50 percent of the auto parts sector in Minas Gerais. See INDI (1998).

Another reason for the gradual evolution of the firm's JIT strategy was the continuing uncertainty with national macroeconomic policy. As Minas Gerais's chief exporter, the firm was directly affected by changes in national macroeconomic policy. Like its competitors during the 1980s, Fiat's export strategy suffered from fluctuations in price and exchange rates resulting from repeated failures at heterodox stabilization (Lee and Cason 1994: 234–35). The firm attempted to increase its imports of auto parts for its top models (50 percent of content) as part of its global sourcing strategy at the same time that it maintained high domestic content in its popular models (about 90 percent). Yet sudden changes in import tariffs complicated the firm's global sourcing. In September 1994, tariffs were reduced from 63 percent to 20 percent, but they increased again in February 1995 to 35 percent and then to a whopping 70 percent in March 1995 in response to growing Brazilian trade deficits that threatened the Real Plan. Sudden changes like these in macroeconomic policy made it difficult for Fiat's management to determine costs for the production of top and popular models and to set targets for what supplies to organize on JIT locally and what supplies to import.[51] Finally, Mercosul, the common market of Brazil and the Southern Cone that was inaugurated in 1995, failed to improve markedly either Fiat's or the state's trade performance. By 1997, Minas's exports to Mercosul countries (11 percent of total exports) remained below the national average of 17 percent (Libânio 1998: 243).

The final reason for the gradual nature of Fiat's *mineirização* strategy was a subtle change in the firm's relationship with the state promotion agencies. From the beginning, the agencies' interests were consistent with those of the firm. As Fiat's interests became more specific in terms of where it wanted its suppliers to locate, the state government continued to support the firm's strategy, as in the case of Kadron, but it also looked to diversify the externalities produced by the car-maker's presence in the state. Long wary of making the same mistakes that São Paulo made in allowing industrialization to concentrate in one major metropolitan area, a process associated with rising labor costs, highly organized (and political) unions, pollution, and transport bottlenecks, the *mineiro* political technocratic elite was intent on spreading the effects of the large automaker's investment. And this meant subtly opposing Fiat's priorities in locating suppliers close to Betim and metropolitan Belo Hor-

51. Company officials routinely qualified their estimates on the firm's long-term restructuring and performance on the existence of import liberalization, favorable exchange rates, and flexible credit. These conditions were not consistently available during the 1990s (*Exame*, January 8, 1992).

izonte and forming synergistic ties with suppliers directly. Despite the close assembler-supplier relations *mineirização* demanded, Fiat, much like its competitors in Brazil, was not able entirely to shape the evolution of the auto parts sector. This produced an opportunity for state interests to prevail in diversifying the auto parts sector in Minas Gerais.

Following the Mineiro Plan of Integrated Development (PMDI), the *mineiro* agencies sought to relocate auto parts suppliers and their associated firms to other areas of the state where the initial wave of auto parts investments in the 1970s and 1980s did not reach and where Fiat's production system did not dominate. This angered some Fiat executives who felt that their *mineirização* strategy was being undermined. Such suspicion was inflamed by the state's insistence (to Fiat's chagrin) on attracting a second large automaker, a prospect that would be made more difficult if the auto parts sector concentrating around Betim, Contagem, and Belo Horizonte became exclusive suppliers of Fiat. Had the agencies not been able to articulate a development strategy that looked beyond the particular interests of the Italian automaker, these conflicts and their attendant results would not have occurred.

If the price of such conflicts for Fiat was a slowdown in their *mineirização* strategy, the benefit to the state's economy was a more diversified auto parts sector, a condition improved by official commitments to create infrastructure in other areas of the state and to tie existing auto parts producers to other automakers—potential new investors in Minas and those located in neighboring São Paulo and Rio de Janeiro. Pulling off the new strategy would demand a whole new level of coordination among the agencies; specifically, an ability to work through continuous horizontal contacts among the agencies and through close vertical contacts with Fiat's suppliers and other firms.

The most prominent example of the state's attempt to diversify the auto parts sector's presence in the state was the development of Sul de Minas as an alternative region for the placement of auto parts investments relocating from São Paulo. The state agencies and municipal governments conceded financial incentives under the FIND programs, land grants, and subsidized infrastructure to auto parts firms wishing to set up shop in Sul de Minas and service producers in São Paulo. Frequent plant visits by technocrats from each of the agencies coordinated mutual goal-setting at the shop-floor level with common planning across the agencies at the state level through COIND and the PMDI. The result was a widespread set of external economies in Sul de Minas that transformed the region.

Industrial policies in Sul de Minas improved the already attractive location of the region for *paulista* auto parts manufacturers, many of which maintained investments in Sul de Minas since the early 1970s. This was the case of the region's two largest auto parts producers: Mangels and Cofap. Other auto parts manufacturers, attracted by the proximity of Sul de Minas to automakers in São Paulo, the region's developing infrastructure and fiscal incentives, followed these pioneer firms in the 1980s and early 1990s to the industrial districts of Pouso Alegre (Brasinca, JPX, KTE, Sima), Três Corações (Elma Metalúrgica, TRW, Belgo Mineira, G. Lúcio), and the coffee region of Varginha (Zurich, Keiper Recaro, and Politek Tecnologia). Nearly all of these companies did their primary business with the automakers in São Paulo rather than Fiat. Of the 71 auto parts producers in Minas in 1993, 20 of them were located in Sul de Minas and only one of those served Fiat directly (Prates and Marques 1995: 179).

The state government's interests in developing Sul de Minas were purely strategic. State technocrats knew that the relocation of suppliers to Sul de Minas would promote the deconcentration of industrial investment from São Paulo to the adjacent *mineiro* region.[52] This process was seen as good for the development of the southern part of Minas Gerais, and the additional tax revenue was good for public coffers. One perhaps unintended consequence was that relocated *paulista* firms, by escaping the inefficiencies of metropolitan São Paulo's agglomerated industries, reduced their costs of production. Moreover, since over 80 percent of raw materials were imported from São Paulo,[53] the growth of the region would boost neighboring economies. Minas's politicians, however, hoped for still more: the possibility that the next big automotive investment in Brazil would locate in Sul de Minas, in the midst of all of those auto parts suppliers. Both the combined effort of *mineiro* technocrats who prepared candidate locations with infrastructure and the more public appeals of *mineiro* politicians provided the groundwork for the eventual agreement by Mercedes to build its new Brazilian facility in Juiz de Fora in 1996.

Both horizontal and vertical ties with other firms played key roles in consolidating the Mercedes investment. In 1993, INDI officials, the municipal government of Juiz de Fora, the Secretariat of Industry of Minas Gerais, and representatives from the city's two largest private firms, the steel firm Siderúrgica Mendes Júnior (SMJ) and the mining firm Com-

---

52. Carlos Alberto Teixeira de Oliveira, state secretary of industry and commerce for Minas Gerais in 1990, argued that fiscal incentives would be used to promote the industrial deconcentration of São Paulo and make Sul de Minas a magnet for electronic and auto parts firms (*Gazeta Mercantil*, July 13, 1990).

53. This observation is based on a comprehensive INDI study of the auto parts sector. See INDI (1998: 17–18).

panhia Paraibuna de Metais (CPM), signed an accord that allotted responsibilities for each actor in attracting new investment to Juiz de Fora. INDI, SMJ, and CPM were responsible for creating market studies; the municipal and state government would prepare fiscal incentives and provide additional infrastructure as needed (Silva de Mattos et al. 1995). Critical was CDI's construction of a 7-million-square-meter industrial district with complete infrastructure for potential suppliers and CEMIG's $5 million natural gas project for Juiz de Fora.[54] During the secret negotiations with Mercedes, these actors were mobilized by COIND officials while the final call on granting the "megafund" allotment was made by Governor Azeredo.[55]

The results of the Mercedes investment satisfied the *mineiro* technocracy's goals of developing an automaking platform outside the Fiat-dominated Betim–Belo Horizonte–Contagem pole that would link the diversified auto parts firms in Sul de Minas and the adjacent, under-developed Zona da Mata area in which Juiz de Fora was located. All were accomplished with the Mercedes deal (Brandão, Guimarães, Leme, and Silva 1998: 256). The initial investment of $400 million would create an estimated 6,500 new jobs in a region that accounted for only 7 percent of Minas's GDP prior to Mercedes's arrival. Future investments proposed by the company would add another $300 million through 2019 to Zona da Mata, not including the inevitable movement of auto parts producers and their suppliers to the region (*Exame*, June 5, 1996).[56]

Catalyzed by the impending arrival of Mercedes and the continued expansion of Fiat, the *mineiro* auto parts sector expanded during the mid- to late 1990s. Between 1996 and 1998, the sector expanded its investments by $800 million and sales increased from $1.2 billion to $2 billion. *Mineiro* auto parts also became more productive, generating $28,000 of sales per worker in 1996 and $42,136 in 1998 (INDI 1998).

Although laying the groundwork for attracting a rival producer

54. CEMIG's commitment to natural gas in the Zona da Mata was the product of an INDI study in the late 1980s and the BDMG's diagnostic, both of which pointed out that 70 percent of the industrial users of natural gas worked between Juiz de Fora and Belo Horizonte. Thus Juiz de Fora was a logical location for the development of natural gas distribution systems for industrial clients (see BDMG 1989a: 124).

55. The coordinating group, or "executive group," of COIND was responsible for mobilizing INDI, the municipal government, and the other agencies (author interview with Marilena Chaves, assistant to the secretary of planning and member of the "executive group," June 14, 1996, Belo Horizonte, Minas Gerais).

56. Under the terms of the financial incentive granted to the company, Mercedes agreed to fully repay the state's credit by the 2019 target date, adding to the estimated several billion dollars of additional revenue that would be generated from Mercedes's presence in the state.

raised the hackles of executives at Fiat, the agencies and the Italian multinational remained confident that their partnerships would continue despite interests that diverged on what was best for Minas Gerais. Both came to accommodations regarding Fiat suppliers that were convinced not to locate in the increasingly concentrated Betim–Belo Horizonte–Contagem pole. In some cases, the state government got Fiat's backing for developing industrial districts outside these municipalities but still sufficiently close to the automaker to satisfy its interests in establishing JIT links.

One such example was Sumiden Tokai do Brasil Indústrias Elétricas, a private multinational (Sumitomo Group) producer of electronic components employing 1,000 workers. In 1993, when Sumiden first made contact with INDI, the agency was looking to develop the industrial district of Mateus Leme, a municipality located only 32 kilometers away from the Fiat circle of suppliers in Betim. Months before, Mateus Leme had lost the Juatuba Industrial District in a redistricting controversy that stripped the municipality of its chief source of tax revenue and virtually all of its industry with the exception of a beer factory owned by the Brahma company, a Brazilian firm. In cooperation with the mayor, Francisco Rodrigues da Cunha, who had strong political interests in getting the city's district back or developing a new one quickly, INDI technocrats developed a program to attract new Fiat suppliers to Mateus Leme.[57] The municipality's land, infrastructure, and telephone system were developed by state authorities. City government donated land, water, asphalt, energy from a transformer purchased from CEMIG, over 4,000 construction workers, and ten years of local tax incentives. All the local political parties provided the mayor carte blanche to organize the city's resources.

The development of Mateus Leme was well underway when Sumiden's management was taken there by INDI officials in 1993. The agency's work convinced Sumiden's executives that Mateus Leme was a better location than Betim for the Fiat supplier's proposed 10,000-square-meter plant. According to Sumiden officials, the activities of the INDI and the local government reduced the firm's costs, increasing production and employment in the short term by freeing up resources during start-up. The result was a faster, more efficient start-up and a larger initial investment than would have been expected in Betim.[58] After Sumiden's

57. Francisco Rodrigues da Cunha told me that he turned to the INDI in 1992 out of frustration and political pressures created by the loss of the Juatuba District (author interview, June 19, 1996). Rodrigo Fiuza Costa of INDI predicted Cunha's story (author interview, June 18, 1996).

58. Author interview with Sumiden Tokai director, June 25, 1996.

initial investment, the firm's further expansion was promoted in 1995 with $1 million of BDMG finance.

Mateus Leme did not have to wait long to see the resources spent on Sumiden begin to return to the municipality. Twenty more firms followed Sumiden's investment between 1993 and 1996. These firms created over 1,700 new jobs directly and many more in commerce and services indirectly.[59] All were interested in taking advantage of Mateus Leme's resources and many of these firms were unassociated with the automotive sector.[60] Within three years, the "valley of plastics," a collection of plastics and recycling firms, developed in and around Mateus Leme. Many of these firms first appeared as subcontractors of Sumiden and other Fiat suppliers. In time, however, these firms developed their own subcontracting relations with service firms.[61] In the case of CGE, a Fiat supplier, the firm diversified and began to market its plastics products to other industrial consumers. In little more than three years, Mateus Leme, which had been without any industry but a Brahma beer factory, developed a formidable array of infrastructure that attracted Fiat suppliers like Sumiden and a host of diverse firms in plastics, services, and other sectors through backward linkage effects. Sources at Sumiden, at INDI, and in Mateus Leme's government told me that none of this could have been accomplished so quickly without a coordinated effort on the part of politicians, the state agencies, and the firms.

The global strategies of the car-makers, motivated by international competition and technological change, were the key factors affecting the investment patterns of the automobile and auto parts firms: their location, the quality of their production, and the intensity of required modernization of plant and equipment to keep up with global auto production. However, even these factors were mediated by complex horizontal linkages among INDI, BDMG, *mineiro* secretariats, and other meso- and municipal-level agencies. Through these associations, public infrastructural investments and a host of informational, financial, and fiscal resources provided by the *mineiro* agencies mediated how both the assemblers and the auto parts firms invested in Minas Gerais and how

---

59. Francisco Rodrigues da Cunha, mayor of Mateus Leme (author interview, June 19, 1996). Once again, INDI's Rodrigo Fiuza Costa's data mirrored that of Cunha (author interview, June 18, 1996).

60. Sogef, a producer of filters, and Petri, a manufacturer of plastics, among others, soon joined new Fiat suppliers Produflex (rubber parts) and CGE (plastic parts).

61. I thank Rodrigo Fiuza Costa, chemical engineer, Department of Industrial Chemicals and Nonmetallic Materials, INDI, for his careful description of how this process occurred (author interview, June 18, 1996, Belo Horizonte, Minas Gerais).

those investments generated externalities. Vertical links between the agencies and Fiat, its competitors, and its suppliers, provided the *mineiro* industrial policy system with the capacity to ascertain firm interests, increase productivity, and help shape investment strategies to suit the development goals of state policy.

Without horizontally embedded agencies, *mineiro* industrial policy would have evolved very differently. The agencies might not have been as successful as they were during the developmentalist period. Agency rivalries would have impeded investments such as Fiat's, which depended at one point on BDMG's ability to coordinate finance with CEMIG's and CDI's commitments to develop infrastructure on the Betim site. More important, they might not have survived populist government in the 1980s or the latest political challenge posed by Governor Itamar Franco and his vice governor, Newton Cardoso. The return of a plan-based horizontal embeddedness proved crucial to orienting industrial policy to innovative directions during the 1990s. The coordination of the agencies under the PMDI made possible the promotion of new externalities in the auto parts and chemical industries, in underdeveloped regions of the state, and in Fiat's plans to improve productivity. Many of these goals were satisfied in ways that sometimes opposed Fiat's interests. This is an indicator that the agencies were pursuing an overarching plan, and that not even the state's primary private-sector taxpayer could keep the agencies from their task. Minas Gerais's plan-oriented horizontal embeddedness demonstrated an extraordinary ability to generate high and complex networks of synergy in a once underdeveloped and state-dependent economy.

Designing Reindustrialization in the Principado de Asturias

Because the region was in industrial decline, economic change produced an emerging consensus among the Asturian political elite around several unifying principles. The decay of INI industries in the region and the limited nature of national programs designed to improve local economies such as the ZURs reinforced the deeply held belief among many that the Principado's economic fortunes had to stop depending on decision-makers located outside Asturias. At the national level, the central government was increasingly disposed to softening the political impact of the industrial reconversion and consolidating a formula for democracy based on a new regional structure of administration: the "state of the autonomies." Asturian efforts to build regional autonomy coincided with attempts to address the region's persisting economic problems. In order to answer the claims of the region's powerful unions, which remained fragmented sectorally and organizationally, the regional government, led during most of the 1980s by the Socialist party, forged broad political support for making national and EU resources available to Asturias. With these resources, the Socialists constructed an apparatus of technocratic development agencies to address the region's economic problems.

The Asturian PSOE's leadership and that of rival parties were agreed on their opposition to national industrial reform. For the PSOE this meant challenging their governing party's national agenda. The processes of opposing national restructuring policy, and decentralizing authorities and resources for implementing economic policy locally, created opportunities for regional leaders to assert control over Asturias's economy in unprecedented ways. By building support among the region's unions in the opposition to industrial restructuring, regional Socialist leaders were able to press Madrid for national and EU resources to fund Asturias's development agencies and industrial promotion policies. Once these agencies were constructed, they built horizontal ties that preserved them through subsequent Socialist governments that became more vulnerable to rival parties.

This chapter examines the politics of regional industrial policy in Asturias. The first section analyzes the limits of Asturian development by highlighting the dominant role of steel and mining in the region, the politics of unions linked to these sectors, and the repeated failures of national reform efforts. The second section examines the advent of an Asturian development mission during the 1980s that emerged in response to the region's experience with failed industrialization. The mission emphasized the creation of horizontally linked development agencies designed to follow evolving development plans. This section explores the ways in which political leaders navigated among union interests opposed to national industrial reconversion and built a common position in support of a plan-based horizontal embeddedness in Asturian industrial policy-making. Although these initial political compromises were threatened when rivals to PSOE rule presented a more dangerous threat in the mid-1990s, horizontal embeddedness preserved the agencies and the region's industrial reform agenda. The Socialists' plans for a new industrial policy focused on aid to small- and medium-sized firms (Asturias's most important employers), and provided new goals and expanded resources for the development agencies. Subsequent center-right politicians produced no new initiatives but did little to reduce the range of activities of the industrial policy agencies. Horizontal embeddedness became more project-based, without the kind of delegative government that prevailed during the network's creation. The final section analyzes how cooperative exchanges of information and resources between the agencies and small and medium-sized firms promoted productivity during this transition from plan-based to project-based horizontal embeddedness.

CRISIS AND CHANGE IN ASTURIAN INDUSTRIALIZATION

The industrialization of the Principado de Asturias was emblematic of the travails of Spanish industrialization. The dominance of public steel and mining in the region from the late nineteenth century and throughout the twentieth century reflected the important role of extractive and heavy industry in the Spanish economy through the end of the 1970s.[1] The largest public steel firm, Empresa Nacional Siderúrgica (ENSIDESA), established in 1956, and the largest public mining firm, Hulleras del Norte (HUNOSA), established in 1967, remained among the most important firms within the INI. They dominated the Asturian economy. HUNOSA and ENSIDESA were responsible for 87 percent of public sector employment in the region (CREP 1992: 11; SADEI 1990a). Asturians composed one-fourth of all employees in INI firms and the public sector was responsible for up to 45 percent of all Asturian industrial production.[2]

By the end of the 1970s, the crisis of the Spanish public sector was magnified into a crisis of deindustrialization in Asturias. Between 1976 and 1985, the Asturian economy grew a paltry 0.6 percent while the Spanish economy maintained a 1.8 percent rate of growth. From 1986 to 1992, regional growth improved to 2.8 percent but remained well below the national average of 4.4 percent, the highest national growth rate in Europe for the period (Castells and Vázquez 1994: 84). Industrial employment fell from 116,961 workers in 1980 to 81,244 in 1992 and the unemployment rate increased from 8.6 percent in 1980 to 20 percent in 1987 (Castells and Vázquez 1994: 74, 701; CREP 1992: 22).[3]

One of the main causes of Asturias's poor performance during the 1980s was the restructuring of ENSIDESA and HUNOSA by the national Socialist government. Reconversion policy caused total employment at ENSIDESA to fall from 21,012 in 1984 to 14,161 in 1992. Total employment at HUNOSA fell from 21,018 in 1984 to 14,341 in 1992 (Fernández 1994: 888). These adjustments had a significant effect on the region's overall industrial performance. In the years following Solchaga's phase of reconversion (1986–92), Asturian industry grew only 0.8 percent, 2.5 percent less than the national average; 18,100 jobs were lost in industry (over 16,000 in the public sector), 18 percent of all industrial employment

1. For more on the industrial history of Asturias and its importance in the economic history of Spain, see Ojeda and Vázquez (1988), Benito del Pozo (1995), and Anes Alvarez (1990).

2. The literature on the presence of the public sector in Asturias is large and repetitive. Among the most noteworthy works are the studies by CREP (1987, 1992), SADEI (1974, 1983, 1990), and the scholarship of Ojeda and Vázquez (1990) and Fernández and Vázquez (1990).

3. Asturias's industrial crisis was repeated in other Spanish regions along the northern coast, the Cornisa Cantábrica (Cantabrian Coast). There is an extensive economic and historical literature on this process. See Castillo (1987), Fernández de Pinedo and Hernández Marco (1988), Castillo and Rivas (1988), and Vázquez (1988).

in 1986 (Castells and Vázquez 1994: 87, 89; CREP 1992: 24). The shrinking of the workforce at HUNOSA and ENSIDESA catalyzed a chain reaction of deindustrialization as their local suppliers were forced to "flexibilize" production by downsizing and contracting out. One of the best global estimates provided thus far suggests that between 1980 and 1992, 24 percent of all industrial jobs were phased out, with 55 percent of those losses occurring in the public sector (CREP 1992: 21).

The decline of Asturias's core industries revealed deeper problems with the region's remaining industrial firms. After decades of being overshadowed by public steel and mining, private entrepreneurs in Asturias were unprepared for these profound economic changes. Most firms remained highly dependent upon mining and steel. Few private firms operated in high-demand sectors such as electronics, computers, or mechanical tools. Moreover, the average scale of production was inelastic to demand. Well over 90 percent of Asturian industrial firms remained small and medium-sized producers with little access to capital, without the means to integrate new technologies and administrative reforms, and oriented toward the internal market (Castells and Vázquez 1994: 76–77). These obstacles severely hindered the ability of Asturian firms to develop viable investments outside of the steel and mining sectors. Asturian unemployment, which was already high due to the restructuring of mining and steel, was made significantly worse by the inability of most young prospects in the labor market to find work. By 1991 over 60 percent of Asturias's unemployed were first-time job-seekers.[4]

INI's practices in Asturias only served to exacerbate the region's problems. The national holding company's investments failed by themselves to diversify the Asturian industrial structure. Despite stated objectives during the 1960s to create industrial districts called "poles of regional development," INI officials did little to promote the Asturian economy (Aceña and Comín 1990: 394–95). During the 1970s, the Franco government established a Pole of Development around Oviedo, the Asturian capital, that persisted until 1988. The Oviedo Pole supplied subsidies to 383 firm projects, generating an estimated $1 billion in investment between 1971 and 1983, and creating 17,281 jobs. Yet the vast majority of these projects were concentrated in food processing and metallurgy, the latter a sector that underwent significant downsizing during the reconversion period. There is little independent (nongovernmental) analysis

4. For more on the structure of Asturian unemployment, see Vázquez (1988: 779–84), Benito del Pozo (1995: 125–27), and *El País*, October 23, 1991.

of the Oviedo Pole, but what does exist suggests that the experience only exacerbated the dependencies of Asturian development.[5]

The question of Asturian regional development emerged again in national politics only with the Socialists' industrial reconversion during the 1980s. The national PSOE made the ZURs in Asturias, along with the Nervión region in Vizcaya (the Basque Country), priority areas. These two depressed steel regions easily fulfilled the EC's criteria for application of structural funds for restructuring declining industries. As a result, Asturias became a top priority for ERDF structural funding in addition to benefiting from loan programs subsidized by the European Coal and Steel Community (ECSC).[6] The Asturian ZUR approved 123 firm projects, generating investments of $215 million and 2,154 jobs (Arias Fernández 1989: 123–24).

Beyond the aggregate numbers, though, the performance of the Asturian ZUR was disappointing. The zone was burdened by excessive evaluative procedures and redundant levels of administration involving national and local agencies. Firm projects often sat on the shelf for two to three years waiting for final approval.[7] More important, since the ZUR was programmed to expire in 1989, it could not provide the basis for a more enduring industrial policy.

In 1988, the Spanish government implemented the Law of Regional Incentives, which sought to replace the ZURs with Zonas de Promoción Económica (Zones of Economic Promotion, ZPEs) and Zonas Industrializadas en Declive (Zones in Industrial Decline, ZIDs). Unlike the ZURs, the ZPEs and the ZIDs channeled EC monies directly to the regional government, which then had the responsibility for evaluating firm projects and apportioning EC, national, and regional funds.[8] The Law of

5. The Asturian regional government criticized the Polo de Oviedo for years. Numerous regional studies during the 1970s condemned the Polo as poorly administered and conceived (see SADEI 1972, 1974). During the 1980s, the regional government's "development plans" repeated these criticisms (see Consejería de Hacienda y Economía 1986: 83). Academics such as the respected Asturian economic historian Benito del Pozo mirrored these assessments (1995: 143).

6. These funds produced some noteworthy results, including the establishment of an investment by the Vesuvius Crucible Company, an Italian refractories producer. The $7.7 million investment, which started up in 1988, created 70 jobs. Suzuki's Asturian installation, a $5 million project, was also guaranteed by ZUR activities in 1988. For a more complete analysis of the performance of the Asturian ZUR, see Arias Fernández and Vázquez (1986: 134–37).

7. See the interview with José Sánchez Junco, general director of industry, MINER, *El País*, January 14, 1990.

8. In 1989, the ZPEs and ZIDs were supplemented with additional EC monies funneled through the National Plans of Regional Development and Reconstruction that supplied

Regional Incentives provided Asturias with valuable resources (about $110 million in 1989), yet the effectiveness of these policies depended upon the capacity of the regional government to evaluate and monitor firm projects.

One factor that severely complicated national industrial reform programs in Asturias was the role of the Asturian Communist and Socialist unions. While Fishman (1990) is correct to argue that Spain's unions are the weakest in Europe, the Asturian unions, and particularly the UGT and CCOO unions in the steel and mining sectors, were the strongest in Spain and the most influential in national politics.[9] Despite high and growing unemployment in these sectors, total union affiliation remained stable into the 1990s.

The mining unions proved throughout the 1980s to be the most powerful political actors in Asturias, and particularly in the crucial mining sector. José Angel Fernández Villa, the fiery leader of the UGT's Sindicato de Obreros Mineros de Asturias (Union of Asturian Mining Workers, SOMA-UGT), the most influential mining union in the region, often threatened strikes and demonstrations in response to Madrid's proposed downsizing of HUNOSA's workforce. As a result, substantial overhaul of HUNOSA was delayed several years. In 1981, Fernández Villa's defense of the mining giant became a thorn in the side of national UCD leaders as they sought to restructure the public firm. SOMA-UGT proved skillful in limiting the number of layoffs and in maintaining national subsidies for mining in the face of efforts by the Ministry of the Economy to restrain spending. In 1984, Fernández Villa's lobbying proved crucial in the approval of the Plan Trienal, which funneled millions in national subsidies to HUNOSA and guaranteed salary increases indexed to productivity targets. Yet coal output never satisfied the plan's official goals (Servén 1989). Strikes reduced the firm's output by 320,000 tons and al-

---

funds for infrastructure and environmental projects in regions designated Objective 1 and 2 by the EC. Based on an elaborate criteria that cannot be reproduced here, Objective 1 regions were defined by the EC as priority areas experiencing "severe" industrial decline. Normally these regions had per capita GDPs that were less than 75 percent of the EC average. Objective 2 were defined as regions affected by industrial decline where unemployment was above the EC (later the EU) average, but did not require funds from all structural accounts. The ZIDs were allocated to Objective 2 regions in Spain, which included areas in Madrid, Catalonia, and the Basque Country among others. Some Objective 1 regions, such as Asturias, also received a share of ZID financing.

9. In 1985, union workers in steel and mining accounted for 64 percent of CCOO's and 54 percent of UGT's total affiliation in the region (Gutiérrez 1994: 955). These numbers were significant nationally. UGT's unions in HUNOSA and ENSIDESA alone accounted for 37 percent of all UGT unions in Spain. CCOO had 44 percent of its unions in Asturias (García Blanco and Gutiérrez 1990: 18).

lowed for only 10 days of management-labor peace during the critical reconversion year of 1985.[10]

SOMA-UGT and Fernández Villa were particularly influential in Socialist organizations. Representatives from the mining districts maintained a majority within the Federación Socialista Asturiana (Asturian
Socialist Federation, FSA-PSOE), the coordinating body of Asturian So-
cialism. Fernández Villa was also outspoken at the national level as the
only Asturian member of the Federal Executive Council of the PSOE, the
party's administrative assembly. From that position the SOMA-UGT
boss lobbied Carlos Solchaga, and INI president, Luis Carlos Croisser, to
preserve the public firms in Asturias.[11] SOMA-UGT also exerted influence through Luis Martínez Noval, the head of FSA-PSOE. From his position as minister of labor, Noval operated as a voice for the mining
unions within the national party and the economic bureaucracy. These
connections allowed Fernández Villa to make use of political divisions
emerging between the PSOE's two key leaders, Felipe González and Alfonso Guerra, to bolster the leverage of SOMA-UGT. The expanding
public rift between González's plans for HUNOSA's reconversion and
Guerra's opposition provided Fernández Villa with a clear ally. Union
support of Guerra against the perceived "neoliberal tendencies" of
González became a key tactic for acquiring *guerrista* support within the
national PSOE for a delayed reconversion of HUNOSA, a position that
González and Solchaga both opposed.[12]

Asturian unions operating in the region's steel industry also proved to
be stalwart contenders for national resources. Like the mining unions,
the steel unions succeeded in asserting their interests in slowing the
downsizing of ENSIDESA. In 1981, Ignacio Bayón, the last UCD minister
of industry, was unable to fully restructure ENSIDESA due to persistent
union opposition.[13] Later, under the national Socialist administration,

10. For more details on this episode, see *El País*, August 28, 1986.

11. This was particularly evident in 1985 during high profile discussions among the
SOMA-UGT, Solchaga, and top INI officials (see *El País* June 17, 1985).

12. As one UGT spokesperson argued: "Regarding the restructuring of mining we are
seeing the creation of a rift between sensitivity and insensitivity. . . . It is not that Guerra has
changed his position. What has actually occurred is that Solchaga and Felipe González
have displaced themselves to the right." Observers would claim at the time that "the horse
Guerra [had] chosen to ride [was] not a bad horse to have." See *El País*, October 22, 1991.
This view was confirmed by Gonzalo Martín Pascual, coordinator of the Secretariat of Organization, UGT, in an author interview, May 9, 1996, Madrid.

13. Union opposition eventually led Bayón to threaten to reform the steel mills through
executive decrees. See *El País*, January 15, 1981, and February 1, 1981. Eventually, Bayón
failed to complete the reconversion of the steel mills due to the victory of the PSOE in 1982
(author interview, July 7, 1994, Madrid).

UGT and CCOO were successful in gaining concessions on retirement, pensions, and retraining programs for laid-off workers that avoided what they called "Thatcherite solutions."[14] The metallurgy unions of UGT, led by Manuel Fernández Lito, proved to be the most vocal advocates for Asturian steelworkers. Yet by following their own interests within the UGT, the steel unions often stepped on the toes of the SOMA-UGT. Since both unions competed for the same national resources for their respective areas, conflicts between SOMA-UGT and the UGT steel unions were frequent. These conflicts were personified by a reported animosity between Fernández Villa and Lito.

Conflicts between the most powerful unions in Asturias might well have produced serious obstacles to a regional industrial policy if it had not been for the continued weakening of these organizations over time. As sectoral reconversion policy was phased out during the late 1980s and early 1990s and replaced by more modest "horizontal policy" (promotion of technology, research, and so on), the unions became more vulnerable in their efforts to change government economic policy. SOMA-UGT's position suffered from the fact that the central government, pressured by Brussels to abandon costly subsidies to a perennially deficit-ridden public mining firm, was reluctant to resuscitate HUNOSA. Union opposition in this sector was successful in extracting limited compensatory measures from Madrid during the 1980s, but it failed to preserve jobs at HUNOSA or make the mining firm profitable for the long haul.[15]

In 1991, the Asturian CCOO and UGT asked Claudio Aranzadi, minister of industry, to begin the process of negotiating a "second reconversion" specifically for Asturias. These calls went unheeded as the national government refused to reconsider its earlier abandonment of sectoral policy.[16] As a result, central government leaders moved ahead with sig-

---

14. The 1984–86 period of reconversion of steel was particularly well negotiated between the Socialist administration and the unions. In response to general strikes in Asturias by workers in the steel sector in May 1984, the national government negotiated a series of agreements with the unions that regulated the downsizing of the metalworks giant. Negotiations between the central government and the unions tended to break down during the latter half of the decade. For more on this experience, see Navarro Arancegui (1988) and Smith (1995).

15. For an illuminating account of how union demands succeeded in producing only limited political concessions without lasting national government commitments to producing new jobs in the mining districts, see the interview with Eduardo Abellan, president of HUNOSA, in *El Mundo*, November 1, 1994.

16. Aranzadi's response in July of 1991 was that "state interventionism" in firms should be reduced, excepting "horizontal policies" meant to promote technology and liberalization of the economy (*El País*, July 20, 1991). Without additional negotiation between the unions and government, Asturian workers went on a general strike in October 1991.

nificant cost-cutting reforms at INI without the compensatory mechanisms hoped for by labor's call for a "second reconversion."[17]

In the steel sector, ENSIDESA and Altos Hornos Vizcaya, the private Basque steel giant, were merged as the Corporación de la Siderurgia Integral (Integrated Steel Corporation, CSI), effectively concluding the official restructuring process. The union role in this case became limited to negotiating severance salary percentages for laid-off workers. Labor's calls for fewer layoffs than the number envisioned in the national plan for CSI were given short shrift.[18]

The political link SOMA-UGT had forged with the *guerristas* in the national PSOE failed to fundamentally change the parameters of reconversion policy first established by Boyer and then Solchaga. In part, the much-publicized "split" between the PSOE and UGT in 1985 and 1986 freed González to maintain the reconversion schedule. After 1990, HUNOSA's miners were laid off at an accelerated rate. National subsidies to the firm were slashed despite heightened union opposition. As HUNOSA's losses became more burdensome on national accounts, political support within the party for a more thorough restructuring of the mining giant shifted in favor of the *solchaguistas*, weakening Fernández Villa's *guerrista* allies. Fernández Villa would later admit that the 1991 restructuring of HUNOSA was the "decisive battle for the *comarcas mineras*,"[19] but one clearly lost by the unions. Despite a last-minute explosion of labor militancy, national compensation declined, and with it, so did labor militancy (see Table 4.1).

Contributing to Asturian labor's eroding position was its inability to forge an alliance on Asturian concerns with the region's business groups, who were, by contrast, politically more anemic than the unions. Although Asturian business was highly organized sectorally

González's response was that "little battles here and there" would not change national policy (*El País*, October 24, 1991).

17. These "compensatory mechanisms" included retraining programs and more robust pension allotments. Although workers received severance and pensions for workers 65 and older ("normal retirement") and some slightly under the age of 55 and between 55 and 65 (so-called "pre-retirement"), these mechanisms failed to compensate for job losses. They certainly failed to allay the suspicions of younger workers that they would receive much less when their jobs were shaved from the payrolls.

18. Although UGT agreed on a pact with the government in January 1993 that would guarantee laid-off workers 79 percent of their salaries and the retirement of workers of 65 years of age, Lito and the union remained adamantly opposed to the total number of layoffs and annual production targets under 5 million tons envisioned by the CSI plan (*El País*, January 3, 1993).

19. See the SOMA-UGT leader's comments in "Valles sombríos," special report, *El País*, September 22, 1991.

Table 4.1 Labor militancy, industrial downsizing, and national compensation during the reconversion in Asturias, 1987–1993

Year	Number of Firms Affected	Number of Workers Affected	Number of Hours Lost	Number of Workers Laid Off in Industry	Number of Workers Compensated
1987	205	220,786	3,839	1,127	NA
1988	3,071	85,728	2,183	1,267	NA
1989	3,311	63,151	1,102	1,408	1,312
1990	842	80,256	1,322	865	1,504
1991	1,500	560,314	5,436	1,877	797
1992	6,085	381,615	6,618	2,046	1,266
1993	1,840	125,933	1,335	1,392	504
1st quarter	31	65,076	540		
2nd quarter	1,770	33,105	393		
3rd quarter	10	5,373	195		
4th quarter	29	22,379	207		

SOURCE: SADEI (1993: 157, 161, and 166).

and territorially and well represented by the Federación Asturiana de Empresários (Federation of Asturian Business, FADE) and the Cámara de Comercio (Chamber of Commerce), these organizations had little command over the region's economic policy. FADE did not speak for ENSIDESA, HUNOSA, and Asturias's other public firms, by far the most powerful entrepreneurial actors in the region. The most influential labor unions in Asturias negotiated directly with INI. Although INI policy affected the hundreds of small and medium-sized firms that composed FADE and the Chamber of Commerce, these associations had little say in the holding company's activities. The largest private and multinational firms in Asturias avoided FADE altogether. As a result, Asturian business organizations were often unwilling and incapable of restructuring capital-labor relations through collective bargaining with labor or political activities in Oviedo or Madrid (Gutiérrez 1994: 956).

The failure of national industrial policies to address Asturias's problems and the failure of the unions to preserve jobs in public mining and steel opened the way for a third strategy. The chief articulator of this development alternative would be the newly autonomous regional government of Asturias.

THE POLITICS OF REMAKING ASTURIAN INDUSTRIAL POLICY

The complex shifts of political interests and influence in Asturias during the 1980s created a minefield for regional government leaders. On the one hand, the Asturian PSOE, which maintained control over the regional government from 1983 to 1995, could not identify too closely with the national government for fear of being grouped with INI and industrial reconversion policy; a favorite target of labor opposition. On the other hand, regional leaders could not embrace CCOO's belligerent opposition and risk agitating the politically influential SOMA-UGT. While Asturian PSOE leaders tended to put up a united front with the UGT, internally the Socialists were divided. Fernández Villa rallied a loyal segment of the Asturian Socialists to his side, particularly in defense of mining jobs at HUNOSA, while Lito maintained a separate base of support within the FSA-PSOE.

Yet a common project united the Asturian Socialists and allowed them to overcome these initial cleavages. The PSOE hierarchy, led by the regional president Pedro de Silva Cienfuegos-Jovellanos (1983–91), and the region's political technocracy forged ties with opposition parties, unions, and national elites in an effort to create an Asturian industrial policy designed to respond to the region's problematic industrial experience. During the initial phases, the new development mission was boosted by its connection to the process of building Asturian autonomy. Later, it was supported by the PSOE's absolute majority in the regional parliament (the Junta). When political fortunes changed after 1987 and the Socialists lost their absolute majority, Silva's successors attempted to reinforce their political support by currying favor with the mining and steel unions. The agencies, however, continued to function. Horizontal ties protected the agencies from political influences during the 1990s, allowing them to produce new sources of support among the unions and government leaders, including the center-right Partido Popular, which came to power in the Junta in 1995.

From the beginning of its rule in Asturias, the regional PSOE sought to build a coordinated response among the unions and parties on the industrial reconversion. In part this was the result of a previous experience with coalition formation in Asturian politics. The Asturian Statute of Autonomy, the first to be processed through Article 143, was the product of a virtually even representation in the national Cortes between UCD (4 deputies) and PSOE (4 deputies).[20] As the process of negotiating Asturian

20. AP had one representative and the Communists had another one. The roughly even balance between UCD and PSOE did not mean that both parties agreed on the Statute of

autonomy proceeded, the regional political parties shared common interests in pressing the national government to devolve authorities governing the development of the mining and energy sectors in the *vía 143*.[21] In the area of national industrial policy, the parties agreed on the need to soften the social impact of reconversion policy. In April 1981, the PSOE led the other major political parties of Asturias in support of an economic plan that demanded "compensatory" measures from the central government designed to assuage the economic and social effects of the reconversion.

In May 1983, the Asturian PSOE won an absolute majority in the Junta due to the strong performance of the national PSOE in the October 1982 elections.[22] The new Junta gave the PSOE 26 of 45 seats; the center-right Alianza Popular (and forerunner of the Partido Popular) and its coalition partners held 14 seats, with the remaining 5 falling under the control of the Communists. Important municipal governments also went to the Socialists, including the key industrial areas of Oviedo, Langreo, Avilés, Gijón, Siero, and Mieres. Although it was no longer necessary to forge strong cross-party alliances, Asturian politicians still agreed on the basic principles of Asturian autonomy and the need to react to national policy.

All of the regional parties, and particularly the PSOE, showed solidarity with the Asturian unions in their respective political strategies on national reconversion policy.[23] For example, UGT and CCOO opposition to INI's restructuring of ENSIDESA in the critical reconversion years of 1984 and 1985 received the backing of all of the regional parties.[24] In the reconversion of shipbuilding, a predominantly private industrial sector

---

Autonomy. UCD advocated a more limited interpretation of Article 143, while the Asturian PSOE, which had initially defended Asturian autonomy by way of Article 151, embraced an expanded base of authorities for the regional government under 143. For more on this, see Barrio Alonso and Suárez Cortina (1989: 148–49).

21. The major Asturian parties presented a common front on these issues during the pre-autonomy process. See *El País*, November 13, 1981.

22. Reminiscent of what happened to the UCD after the October 1982 national elections, the UCD in Asturias dwindled.

23. It should be noted that Socialist support of the unions was not entirely shared to the same degree by all other political parties or every segment of the PSOE. IU maintained a more fanatical embrace of union interests, particularly those of CCOO, than the PSOE did of UGT. SOMA-UGT's activities often were followed up with significant support by the regional Socialists, yet particularly Socialist representatives of the mining districts. Socialist politicians in the steel areas around Avilés and Gijón, were often suspicious of SOMA-UGT and more likely to support Lito and the metallurgical unions of UGT when their interests were in conflict with those of the powerful Fernández Villa. AP/PP maintained more of an arms-length relationship with the unions, a position that allowed the PP to advance their support of privatization of public firms after 1995.

24. For example, Socialist Junta members participated in the general strikes held by UGT and CCOO in 1984 (*El País*, June 29, 1984).

in Asturias, the regional government often mediated negotiations among central government actors and sectoral business and labor groups.[25] The regional government also supported SOMA-UGT's defense of HUNOSA and used its most boisterous language in favor of the mining giant during SOMA-UGT and CCOO strikes.[26] Junta politicians in the mining districts and in the coastal cities of Avilés and Gijón depended on their defense of mining and steel, respectively, for their political survival, so their actions in this regard were understandable.

The political importance of shared interests between PSOE and the unions in the face of national reconversion policy proved even more important after the 1987 regional elections. The Socialists lost their absolute majority in the Junta, forcing them to form a coalition with the leftist Izquierda Unida (United Left, IU), which had emerged, as it did in other regions, from the vestiges of the Spanish Communist Party. One of the preconditions IU placed on a coalition with the PSOE was that the Socialists support stable levels of employment at HUNOSA. The Socialists' vulnerability in this area was worsened by the fact that the PSOE had also lost its absolute majority on the municipal councils of key industrial cities, including Gijón and Avilés, and the mining districts of Siero and Langreo. The Socialists made a virtue out of political necessity by reinforcing their ties to union interests and forging an alliance with IU.

Despite these common political ties among regional parties and Asturian labor and the regional government's strong interests in softening the economic impact of industrial restructuring, this was only the first level of Asturias's official response to industrial change. The regional presidency and the economic bureaucracy of the Principado constructed a more subtle response during the 1980s. This response was founded on the emergence of a new development mission based on the prior experiences of key members of the Asturian PSOE's hierarchy and the political technocracy. These experiences led these actors to advocate a regional industrial policy that sought to minimize Asturias's dependence upon the public sector. While the PSOE held its absolute majority in the Junta, this development mission and the agencies created to implement it thrived

25. Although CCOO opposed the final accords, UGT leaders saw the negotiations mediated by the regional government as the best recourse (*El País*, August 27, 1986).

26. The most noteworthy example was the lobbying of Alfonso Guerra during the summer of 1986 by both the regional PSOE president, Pedro de Silva, and the SOMA-UGT chief, Fernández Villa. The Asturians wanted the government to guarantee the survival of HUNOSA past the year 2000, a commitment they finally received from the government in 1987 (*El País*, May 30, 1987). In the area of more public demonstrations, the regional government supported 48-hour strikes by SOMA-UGT and CCOO in 1987 (*El País*, February 9, 1987).

by creating horizontal embeddedness governed by regional development plans. After the PSOE lost its absolute majority, and even after it
lost control of the regional government to the PP in 1995, horizontal embeddedness allowed the agencies to stay the course on industrial restructuring, and even innovate under a more project-based pattern of
policy-making.

Soon after the PSOE gained its absolute majority in the Junta in 1983,
Pedro de Silva Cienfuegos-Jovellanos, a former Socialist deputy for Asturias who was known for his periodic attacks on INI, UCD steel policy,
and his attempts to create a "territorial" industrial policy for the PSOE,
gained control of the government. Silva was the classic political juggler,
particularly with regard to the sensitive subject of the industrial reconversion. The new regional president often took up the causes of both Fernández Villa and Lito, HUNOSA and ENSIDESA, but was wary of
becoming their government spokesperson. By subtly playing Fernández
Villa against Lito and vice versa, Silva avoided becoming politically dependent upon mining or steel union support. Instead, Silva skillfully
leveraged the Asturian unions' political power and negotiated through
political party squabbles to extract national resources for long-term development policies conceived by his staff of political technocrats.

Silva's political portfolio had been molded by his own experiences
within the PSOE and as a politician in Asturias during the industrial reconversion and the early phase of negotiating the region's autonomy. Before gaining power in 1983, Pedro de Silva had been one of the national
PSOE's most spirited advocates for reorienting industrial policy. Specifically, Silva supported a set of policy proposals in 1981 that were organized into a Plan Nacional de Industria (National Industrial Plan, PNI). Of
particular importance to Silva was the PNI's sensitivity to the territorial
dimension of industrial restructuring, and especially the social and economic impact of national policy. The PNI argued on behalf of long-term
"reindustrialization" policy that would create new industrial activity in
depressed regions.[27] During a private meeting in early 1982 at the Hotel
Real in Madrid, Silva met with PSOE leaders, including Miguel Boyer
(the PSOE's future minister of economy), Javier Solana, and the UGT's
Carmen Mestres. The PNI became the subject of intense debate at this
meeting. Boyer's concerns with macroeconomic stability were pitted
against the unions' and regional leaders' proposals for state-sponsored
industrial promotion. In the end, the meeting produced a stalemate, one

27. Author interview with Pedro de Silva Cienfuegos-Jovellanos, June 26, 1995, Gijón,
Asturias. Also see the press account in *El País*, October 3, 1981.

that, according to Silva, would free Boyer to implement an industrial reconversion program that would almost completely ignore the priorities
of the PNI:

> I wasn't able to present my views because the document we con-
> ceived was too "controversial." When Calvo-Sotelo presented the
> UCD law of reconversion, I collected articles of my law and used
> them as amendments to the UCD document. But the dominant
> politics of the day was not in favor of a real industrial policy.
> There was no serious attempt to face up to the problems of Span-
> ish industry. The PNI attempted to do this but was shot down by
> the snob liberalism that had afflicted the party. (Author interview,
> June 26, 1995, Gijón, Asturias)

The Hotel Real meeting convinced Silva that the PSOE would soon dismantle the public firms with little regard for the social and economic
consequences to Spain's regions. The Asturian president would later
claim that the Hotel Real meeting was the first indication that the responsibility for development policy initiatives would become that of the
regional government of Asturias.

During the early years of Silva's presidency of the Principado and the
PSOE's sectoral reconversion of steel and shipbuilding in the region, a
second experience would move Silva to advocate Asturian industrial
policy: the ZURs. Although the ZUR experience in Asturias had produced some noteworthy successes, Silva became increasingly frustrated
with their administration and business complaints. The Asturian president resented the minimal role that the regional government maintained
in the administration of the ZURs. In November 1986, Silva campaigned
publicly to have the ZUR administration decentralized to the regional
government. His efforts met with little success. The regional president's
frustration grew as businesses complained about the slow approval
process in Madrid and the unwillingness shown by the ZUR's national
administration to follow through with their agreements to firms:

> The management of the ZURs would promise a certain amount of
> money according to objective limits. Theoretical amounts were ne-
> gotiated with the firms but the central government and particu-
> larly the Ministry of Economy had to approve the allotment. And it
> was *always less* than what was previously negotiated with the firm!
> How could such a policy be credible to businesses? (Author inter-
> view, June 26, 1995, Gijón, Asturias; emphasis established by Silva)

Silva's thinking was guided by his own political interests. The Asturian president was concerned that the very "industrial identity" of Asturias was being dismantled with nothing to take its place. This process threatened the core of the region's, and Silva's, most important political concern: the building of Asturian autonomy. As a uniprovincial and *vía lenta* ("slow track") region, Asturias's claims to autonomy had always been based on a weak foundation. Regional leaders could not refer to a previous history of having a "special regime" (*régimen foral*) as was the case in the Basque Country and Navarra or a national identity with a distinctive regional language as in Catalonia and the Basque Country.[28] Silva himself had articulated these concerns earlier in a book (Cienfuegos-Jovellanos 1977). Lacking both a strong juridical and ethnic basis for autonomy, Silva increasingly spoke of the regional government's role in implementing industrial policy as a key legitimating pillar of regional autonomy. Regional development plans designed by the economic bureaucracy reflected the perceived need to expand autonomy in order to enhance the capacity of the regional government to intervene in the economy.[29] But the expansion of Asturias's autonomy also came to depend on the justification produced by the economic crisis and the regional administration's emerging network of development agencies. These arguments became crucial in 1983–85 when Silva successfully concluded a series of negotiations with Alfonso Guerra and the national PSOE that expanded the Asturian Statute of Autonomy's authorities in economic policy under the aegis of "organic laws" delegated to the Junta. This was an exceptional achievement at the time, since Asturias remained a *vía lenta* autonomy with relatively limited authorities. In 1988, Silva, backed by the regional PSOE and IU, began the process of expanding the powers of the Asturian Statute of Autonomy despite opposition to fundamental changes from the national government. As a result, revenues increased by a factor of 10 and spending by a factor of 13 (Monasterio Escudero 1994: 268–69).

The building of Asturian autonomy was, in essence, the creation of an expanded subnational bureaucratic apparatus with extensive authorities. In 1981 Asturias had been the first uniprovincial region to campaign for autonomy. Its well-organized campaign at that time translated into the construction of a highly professional, regional bureaucracy well before

28. Asturians speak dialects of Spanish known as Asturian and Bable, but few regional inhabitants converse in these dialects today. More important, in comparison to the Catalans and the Basque, Asturians do not make any claims to be a "nation." For a historical perspective on Asturian regionalism, see Barrio Alonso and Suárez Cortina (1989: 148).

29. Author interview with Pedro de Silva, June 26, 1995, Gijón, Asturias. One noteworthy example is the region's first development plan. See Consejería de Hacienda y Economía (1986: 135).

that was possible in other Spanish regions. More than 44 percent of the regional budget went to personnel, well above the average for succeeding years, and more than 40 percent of bureaucratic positions were given to career professionals, not civil service employees (*El País* April 18, 1988). These developments coincided in 1981 with negotiations over the pending Statute of Asturian Autonomy, in which industrial policy as a political concern of the Principado became one of the main shibboleths in the regional government's campaign for autonomy and the prime mover in building the capacity of the official apparatus. At this time, the regional government called for the establishment of a regional institute of industrial promotion, based on the view that previous experiences with national industrial policy in the region (Franco's Poles of Development) were failures.[30]

As Asturias's economic problems worsened and other regions competed for shares of national and EC resources, the regional government justified the further devolution of authority over economic policy by pointing to an array of development agencies run by the government of the Principado. Among the most important were the Instituto de Fomento Regional (Institute of Regional Promotion—IFR) created in 1983, the Servicio de Asesoramiento y Promoción Empresarial (Service of Assistance and Entrepreneurial Promotion, SAYPE) initiated in 1988 (and replacing the Programa de Actuaciones Urgentes de Reindustrialización or Urgent Activities for Reindustrialization Program, PAUR), and the Sociedad Regional de Promoción (Regional Society of Promotion, SRP) created in 1984.

The thinking of these agencies was conditioned by key political technocrats in the Chancelleries of Economy and Industry and the Asturian statistical and research agency, Sociedad Asturiana de Estudios Económicos e Industriales (Asturian Society of Economic and Industrial Studies, SADEI), which had been developing the groundwork for an Asturian industrial policy for several years prior to the transition to democracy. Rosa Corujedo, one of these key political technocrats, had earlier championed the creation of regional mechanisms to develop the Asturian economy in the 1970s. As a chief researcher for SADEI during the late 1960s and 1970s, Corujedo had participated in a series of studies of the Asturian economy that argued for an administrative decentralization of economic policy among other alternative development strategies. Reflecting on the experience, Corujedo would argue that SADEI and its staff had been motivated by the foreseeable decline of mining and steel and the failure of national planning to deal with these problems. Conse-

30. See *El País*, February 11, 1981, May 17, 1981, and May 2, 1981. Later, a similar perception of the Asturian ZURs would justify demands for national resources to fund Asturian development agencies.

quently, these studies pioneered an advocacy for devolving planning functions to local administrations years before the "state of the autonomies" would become a reality.[31]

SADEI was especially critical of the INI, which was viewed as a central state agency that had "taken advantage of Asturias without any conscience for the social problems it caused in the region."[32] Moreover, SADEI's studies argued that the most virulent aspect of Asturias's dependency on the INI was the elimination of all possibilities for the creation of a "pressure group capable of defending the economic/industrial interests of the region before the central state" (SADEI 1974: 73). Consequently, these early SADEI studies evinced not only a suspicion of central government industrial policy, but a strong willingness to empower local administration to engage in industrial policy as an advocate for Asturias's regional interests vis-à-vis INI. These principles became the defining points for the Silva government's first major industrial policy statement, which was conceived as a comprehensive development plan authored by SADEI in 1983 (see SADEI 1983). Between 1985 and 1994, three "regional development plans" were issued by the Principado. Each embraced the criticisms of Asturian industrial development first articulated by SADEI and set out goals and priorities for long-term regional policy.[33]

Like the *mineiro* BDMG diagnostic of 1989 and the PMDI, the Asturian development plans and the earlier SADEI studies upon which they were based argued for a pragmatic market-oriented industrial policy; one that would prepare the region's firms for more competitive domestic and foreign markets. The Asturian plans emphasized the need to make small and medium-sized firms in particular more productive by enhancing their access to finance, information, and skilled labor. Unlike the state planning of old, the new Asturian industrial policy called for "strategic intervention," not public ownership or production. Given both the poor performance of the national public sector and the region's reliance on mining and steel, the plans emphasized the need to "diversify" the re-

---

31. National planning had failed to develop a "regional dimension." As one study argued: "Without a true administrative decentralization of planning in favor of local administration, the possibilities for promoting a harmonic development of all the regions of Spain becomes an abstract notion lacking effective mechanisms for executing much-needed economic policies" (SADEI 1970: 137). The Pole of Industrial Development of Oviedo was frequently singled out for criticism. SADEI argued in cryptic prose that the Pole was too limited in geographical scope and too dominated by a concern for public steel (SADEI 1972: 128–29). The Pole lacked all understanding of Asturias as an integrated region.

32. Author interview with Rosa Corujedo, May 31, 1995, Oviedo, Asturias.

33. The last development plan is the most comprehensive and analytical. See Consejería de Hacienda y Economía (1994).

gion's industrial and service sectors through externalities that would increase employment and break Asturias's traditional dependencies.

Another watershed in the evolution of the regional government's thinking about industrial policy occurred in 1988. The Comisión de Representantes del Principado en la Empresa Pública (Commission of Principado Representatives in the Public Firms, CREP), a multiparty (PSOE, IU, AP) organization formed to evaluate the effects of the INI's decay on the Asturian economy, completed an extensive study. Besides sharing the PNI's advocacy for a regional rather than sectoral set of criteria, the CREP condemned INI for failing to live up to its obligations in compensating Asturias for expected job losses. For regional government leaders the CREP's conclusions reaffirmed their view that national reconversion policy would not lead to the reindustrialization of the region. Rather, the government of the Principado needed to tackle that question itself.[34] As the director of the CREP told me:

Only with the rise of an autonomous regional government in 1983 did Asturias begin to forge a new industrial policy. While organizations such as the CREP and the unions were important interlocutors of what needed to be done in Asturias, it was the economic bureaucracy and Silva himself who created a strategy for dealing with the region's deindustrialization. The parties disagreed on specific approaches, but all agreed on the principle that the national government was no longer going to fight for Asturias and that only regional solutions were possible. This gave Silva and SADEI the opportunity to pursue specific policies to diversify the regional economy. (Author interview with Javier Fernández, May 31, 1995, Oviedo, Asturias)

Other key political technocrats in the Silva government shared the views of SADEI, Corujedo, and the CREP. Pedro Piñero, the head of SADEI and former chancellor of public works, became Silva's most influential advocate for preparing regional development plans and funding them with central government and, eventually, EC resources.[35]

---

34. For a definitive statement of the CREP's analysis, see CREP (1992).

35. Author interview with Pedro de Silva Cienfuegos-Jovellanos, June 26, 1995, Gijón, Asturias. Policy statements by other key members of Silva's economic team reflected the earlier thinking of the SADEI studies that the regional government had to mount its own industrial policy in order to counteract the economic problems of the region. In this regard, see comments by Felipe Fernández Fernández (regional director of economy and planning) and Francisco Macías Mateo (chief of service, Consejería de Hacienda y Economía) in Fernández Fernández and Macías Mateo (1986).

Nieves Carasco, a young technocrat from the Chancellery of Industry, would become Silva's regional director of industry in 1988 and the administration's point person on attracting foreign direct investment to Asturias. Dozens of economists, engineers, and administrators were added to the staffs of the regional development agencies. The Pedro de Silva administration created an economic bureaucracy for industrial policy-making, composed development plans based on earlier SADEI studies, staffed the bureaucracy with SADEI political technocrats and young technocrats dedicated to market-oriented industrial policies, delegated policy-making authorities to these actors, and used the building of this apparatus to justify extensions of Asturian autonomy in the face of competition from other regions claiming the same privileges from the same pool of resources (Cienfuegos-Jovellanos 1994). In the absence of significant levels of elite conflict among the major parties or with the labor unions, delegative government created opportunities for a new Asturian development mission to take root inside the region's industrial policy agencies.

BUILDING HORIZONTAL EMBEDDEDNESS AND PRESERVING THE AGENCIES IN THE FACE OF SHIFTING INTERESTS

Although regional government leaders advocated a more aggressive strategy of reindustrialization in Asturias, they were not able to implement it all at once. The unions demanded action on the reconversion sectors first. Reconversion was also the priority for the national PSOE government, which dealt only indirectly with the question of diversifying Asturian industrialization through the ZURs. Moreover, by the early 1990s, the national PSOE's top regional political concern became placating the mining unions.[36]

At no time did the regional government believe that it was capable of reversing the overwhelming economic crisis of the region on its own.[37] If the region's development agencies were to become significant actors in Asturias's economy, the regional government would have to be skillful

36. In 1991, the minister of labor, Luís Martínez Noval, asserted before 30,000 mining workers that the government's priority was the issue of "salaries and organization of production" in Asturian mining (*El País*, September 2, 1991). Noval, it will be remembered, was also the head of the FSA-PSOE, which was heavily influenced by the Asturian mining unions.

37. For example, the regional government's first "development plan" argued that "Asturias' current situation of industrial decline cannot be reversed based on the region's own resources" (Consejería de Hacienda y Economía 1986: 88).

in extracting resources for development policy from other sources, and this it did with the help of the Asturian unions.

Initially, the regional government's coordinated response among political parties and unions to national reconversion policy produced a solid basis for demanding additional fiscal and infrastructural resources from Madrid. In 1987, during negotiations between the regional government, the Asturian mining unions, HUNOSA, and INI, the Asturian government backed a SOMA-UGT proposal requiring the creation of a venture capital society under the regional government's control. The proposed society would reinvest proceeds from HUNOSA's cost-cutting in the mining districts. The regional government employed SOMA-UGT's political leverage with INI to extract a financial commitment from HUNOSA to create the Sociedad para el Desarrollo de las Comarcas Mineras (Society for the Development of the Mining Districts, SODECO), a venture capital society designed to provide subsidies, low-interest loans, and collateral to investors in the mining districts. SODECO would eventually prove to be a strong political symbol for the regional government that it was doing all it could to rejuvenate the deteriorating economy of the *comarcas mineras*. In turn, this symbolic effect served to reinforce the regional government's political support within SOMA-UGT, which represented the mining districts that were to gain from SODECO's activities.[38]

Maintaining an influential position vis-à-vis the national government gave Asturias unprecedented access to EC resources. In 1987, Madrid made Asturias the first region of Spain to receive monies for infrastructural projects under the proposed Programa Nacional de Interés Comunitario (National Program of Community Interests, PNIC). The program provided $500 million during the 1988–92 period to the region's infrastructure and industrial promotion programs, including $167 million in EC structural funds. A crucial factor in having Asturias approved was the region's economic crisis, a requirement for EC backing. More important to the PNIC's creation was the ability of Asturian regional leaders to convince José Borrell and Carlos Solchaga of the plan's usefulness and the regional government's capacity for generating significant economic change based on these monies.[39] This would not be easy, as Solchaga, the

38. SODECO's emphasis on aiding the mining districts was politically significant for SOMA-UGT, because the union saw itself not just as a defender of the HUNOSA workers and other mining employees, but of the mining districts themselves, their culture, and social structure (interview with Rodolfo Gutiérrez Palacios, a sociologist who was present during the HUNOSA-SOMA-UGT negotiations in 1987, July 26, 1994, Oviedo, Asturias). For more on the politics of reconverting HUNOSA, see Gutiérrez and Vázquez (1991).

39. Author interview with Pedro de Silva, June 26, 1995, Gijón, Asturias; author interview with Nieves Carasco, director of industry 1988–93, June 28, 1995, Llanera, Asturias.

minister of economy, had little faith in the ability of the regions to spend money in efficient or constructive ways. He complained generally about the deficit-bloating, spendthrift ways of regional governments (see Solchaga 1997: 315–20).

Despite these obstacles, Madrid eventually succumbed to prodding by the Asturian Socialists and secured EC backing for declaring the region a top priority for structural funds in January 1988. Asturias received an additional $28 million for infrastructure, environmental, and industrial programs from ERDF's steel reconversion fund, making Asturias the first Spanish region to have two major sources of funding from Brussels. The influx of EC funds expanded the size of the Asturian development agencies. For example, the IFR's operational budget doubled between 1987 and 1988 due to the PNIC (Consejería de Hacienda y Economía 1989: 150–51).

The political leverage of the Asturian mining regions proved particularly propitious for building the economic policy-making capacity of the regional government. Despite the stated intentions of national leaders to gradually phase out industrial subsidies for reconversion sectors such as mining and steel, national PSOE leaders led by Solchaga advocated devolving resources and the authority to allocate them under the umbrella of "reindustrialization policy" to the Asturian government. Only a couple of days after the Asturian general strike of 1991, Solchaga reaffirmed his commitment to place industrial promotion policies in the hands of the regional government. In January 1992 during the height of negotiations between Asturian unions and the national government over the final restructuring of HUNOSA, the national budget made Asturias the highest priority region for infrastructural investment. The national government approved the Plan de Dinamización Económica de Asturias (Economic Dynamization Plan of Asturias, PDEA), which funneled $820 million to the region in the form of infrastructural investments. The PDEA was approved only one day after the Asturian unions and the national government had begun to make headway on the restructuring of HUNOSA. Both the timing and the political context of the plan suggested that the Asturians had successfully exerted political leverage for compensatory measures for HUNOSA's reconversion.[40]

---

40. The importance of Asturian politics for the genesis of the PDEA are evident if the plan is placed in the context of national political economy at the time. Despite significant political attention to keeping the national public deficit low for monetary union, the significant spending levels of PDEA were approved by the central administration and subsequently okayed by Brussels (see Esteban and Velasco 1996: 293). For the details of the PDEA, see MINER (1995) and Principado de Asturias (1994).

Acquiring resources from Madrid and Brussels became only the first step to providing the Asturian regional government with the resources it needed to pursue its own development policy. By themselves these funds were insufficient for dealing with the long-term problems of Asturian industries. National infrastructure, social, agricultural, and environmental projects, which represented the lion's share of EC and national funds, could be managed directly by national officials in cooperation with regional leaders. Many of these projects simply cofinanced national infrastructure projects. However, funds for more specific firm-level and sectoral projects outside the domain of the public firms and their national restructuring programs required the activity of the development agencies. The agencies' own resources became more important after 1992 when EC structural funds to Asturias fell by 50 percent (Table 4.2).

IFR, SAYPE, SRP, and SODECO increasingly took on more tasks and coordinated their efforts to maximize their resources. The agencies evaluated firm proposals for national and regional subsidies and venture capital; they supplied technical and investment information, and they funneled national infrastructural programs to areas of the region considered critical to the Asturian economy. The Asturian development policy apparatus matured during the course of the 1980s, in terms of size, range of activities, and institutional complexity.[41] The IFR and SAYPE both implemented an increasing array of financing programs for small and medium-sized firms. In addition, IFR developed infrastructural, technological, and retraining programs. SRP and SODECO, both venture capital societies that fell under IFR's administration, attracted some large noteworthy investments such as Thyssen (elevators) and DuPont (chemicals) to the region.

The regional government used national and EC resources to provide administrative cohesion among the development agencies. For example, the PNIC financed the construction of Asturias's only "technology park" in Llanera, just off the highway linking Gijón, Avilés, and Oviedo. The park would become the headquarters of the IFR, SAYPE, SRP and a number of other development agencies of the Principado. Although the technology park would not attract any firms for several years, it served its most important role in coordinating the activities of the public agencies. Both the founding document of the technology park and development

---

41. This section is based on numerous author interviews: María Rosa González Corujedo, May 31, 1995, Oviedo, Asturias; Encarna Rodríguez Cañes, Chancellery of Economy and Planning, July 26, 1994, Oviedo, Asturias; José Manuel Suárez, Metallurgical Federation, UGT, March 26, 1996, Madrid; Rodolfo Gutiérrez Palacios, sociologist, July 26, 1994, Oviedo, Asturias.

Table 4.2 European structural funding to Asturias, 1988–1993 (all figures reported in millions of dollars)

Fund	1988	1989	1990	1991	1992	1993	Total
ERDF[a]	6.8	24.2	35.0	46.0	55.7	22.0	189.7
ESF[b]	3.5	.4	2.2	4.6	5.0	6.0	21.7
EAGGF[c]	.4	2.2	6.9	12.0	7.7	3.6	32.8
Total	10.7	26.8	44.1	62.6	68.4	31.6	244.2

SOURCE: Consejería de Hacienda y Economía (1994: 375); Monasterio Escudero (1994: 275).

[a] European Regional Development Fund
[b] European Social Fund
[c] European Agricultural Guidance and Guarantee Fund

agency staff emphasized that the physical proximity of the agencies greatly enhanced the efficiency of administering joint projects. Both SAYPE and SRP were placed inside the IFR's main building and that center was surrounded by more specialized working groups located in separate buildings. Under these circumstances the agencies increasingly worked as one, emphasizing joint planning and encouraging daily meetings among agency directors.[42]

After the agencies were able to develop a high level of horizontal embeddedness, their political fortunes changed. By 1990, the unions' diminishing and limited campaign against national policy and labor's ill-fated focus on the possibilities for a "second reconversion" convinced Silva and his staff that the unions could be allies in principle, particularly in the task of acquiring resources for "reindustrialization" projects, but workers would not organize those projects themselves. The regional unions were generally supportive of the agencies, but frequently criticized them as insufficient. Labor tended to view the agencies through the lens of the process of industrial restructuring. But as union efforts to slow or stop industrial restructuring weakened, the UGT and CCOO began to champion and participate in the agencies' governance of industrial projects. This was not only a result of labor's failure fundamentally to alter the path of national reconversion policy; it was also a result of new political alliances between the regional government of the Principado and the unions that were based on the pursuit of "reindustrialization." Even CCOO participated, as Dario Díaz, an organizer of the regional CCOO, told me:

42. See *El País*, August 8, 1987 and author interviews at IFR, SAYPE, SRP and ITMA, 1994, 1995.

Concertation between the unions and the Principado was easy because we agreed that Asturias was in crisis. We agreed on the causes of the crisis. We agreed also on what had to be emphasized to get us out of the crisis—new public investments in infrastructure, in promoting small- and medium-sized firms, the provision of investment information, finance—all of this could be organized through collaborative efforts among firms, the government, and the unions. The problem actor was the national state. INI was national and industrial policy, particularly the reconversion, was national. All actors in the Principado clearly disagreed with INI. They argued that INI was acting exclusively in sectoral terms and ignoring territorial concerns. Ironically, the Principado and the unions, even the Communists, were more in tune than the Principado and the central government, although they belonged to the same party! There were disagreements between the Principado and CCOO during the 1980s, but now we are fundamentally in agreement. The Principado began to include us and we began to listen after around 1988 and 1989. (Author interview, June 27, 1995, Oviedo, Asturias)

José Manuel Suárez, a director in the Metallurgy Federation of UGT in Asturias added:

The regional government became the primary actor behind industrial policy in Asturias. UGT and CCOO were always too busy focusing on the reconversion and criticizing macroeconomic policy, while Pedro de Silva and the agencies, and particularly IFR, pursued more long-term strategies led by clear ideas. . . . We were late in joining the effort but it was clear by the end of the decade that only the regional government was dedicated to a transformative project; the central government was simply not going to be the protagonist. (Author interview, March 26, 1996, Madrid)

While labor support became more available, the regional PSOE became less reliable as a political base for articulating long-term development policy. As particular union demands in mining, steel, and shipbuilding became more desperate in the face of additional waves of official layoffs, underlying cleavages within the Asturian PSOE that separated pro-SOMA-UGT and pro-Lito factions boiled to the surface. More Socialist politicians made combating the reconversion a political priority over long-term development goals. As a result, Silva and the regional economic bureaucracy could not turn to local party leaders to provide sufficient political support for the agencies. The immediate interests of these politicians lay with the short-term effects of the industrial reconversion on their local constituencies.[43]

Considering the increasing isolation of the Silva government and its relationship with the agencies, Asturian industrial policy might well have encountered a severe organizational crisis in July 1991 when Silva retired from the regional presidency. Silva's Socialist successor, Juan Luis Rodríguez Vigil, showed none of the first president's concern for expanding the agencies. Faced with increased tensions due to the restructuring of HUNOSA and related criticisms from PSOE's alliance partner, the IU, the new regional president's chief political concern became currying the support of the mining unions and the FSA-PSOE, which continued to be dominated by Fernández Villa.[44] The new president became more concerned with the restructuring of HUNOSA than with long-term development policy.[45] Almost immediately, Rodríguez Vigil used his political capital in Madrid to soften the Ministry of Industry's proposed dismantling of one-third of HUNOSA's workforce. The Asturian president's efforts, however, came at a time when significant fiscal and EC pressures were compelling national industrial policy to shave HUNOSA's workforce more thoroughly and swiftly.[46] As a result, Rodríguez Vigil's protests tended to fall on deaf ears.[47]

43. Indicative of this point was the consistent articulation of local interests in the Junta as opposed to more regional interests. Mayors in the mining districts took a leading role in negotiating the final restructuring plan for HUNOSA in 1991 and 1992. The political pressure these local politicians placed on national elites was second only to that of the SOMA-UGT itself (see various issues of El País in October 1991–February 1992). Local leaders also played a significant role in negotiating the restructuring of steel (see various issues of El País in April–June 1992). Historically, the Junta was always more responsive to local demands than it was an articulator of a more unified Asturian set of interests. On this last point, see Barrio Alonso and Suárez Cortina (1989: 147).

44. Rodríguez Vigil had strong personal ties to Noval, the secretary general of the FSE, and to Fernández Villa. The Asturian president's chancellor of industry, Víctor Zapico, was also very close to Fernández Villa. See the respected Asturian historian Germán Ojeda's editorial, "Asturias: la transición al capitalismo," in El País, January 20, 1992; and El País, September 22, 1991.

45. One noteworthy demonstration of that fact came in a major interview with Rodríguez Vigil in El País, January 19, 1992, at the height of the HUNOSA crisis. The Asturian president concentrated his comments on the mining sector and made no mention of the Principado's development agencies or concrete examples of longterm industrial policy.

46. Through much of 1991, Rodríguez Vigil met with Aranzadi only to be told that EC standards were forcing Aranzadi's hand (for example, see El País, September 24, 1991).

47. The regional president increasingly viewed the INI's and Industry's plans as threatening to both his political base and the ability of the regional government to attract future investments. The conflict reached a fever pitch when Rodríguez Vigil, days after coming to power, accused the INI in July 1991 of attempting to dismantle the Asturian economy. For

In the months to come, Rodríguez Vigil would become the object of criticism for his inability to improve the Asturian economy. Having embraced the interests of the mining unions so visibly, the regional president was attacked for his passivity toward the national PSOE's restructuring of the steel sector. In March of 1993, the Asturian Junta publicly chided Rodríguez Vigil for his acquiescent stance on the creation of the CSI. Perhaps this and the political pressures created by HUNOSA's restructuring led the regional president to the desperate gamble that would mark his downfall. In May of 1993, the regional president announced that a Saudi oil group was interested in the construction of a pharaonic petroleum refinery outside the port city of Gijón. The deal turned out to be part of a fraudulent international scheme to capture public subsidies. After issuing strong denials that he or his staff were involved, Rodríguez Vigil resigned from office in disgrace only weeks after the initial announcement of the phantom deal.

The failure of the opposition to form a coalition government allowed PSOE and IU to retain control of the Junta following Rodríguez Vigil's resignation, but many of the internal cleavages within the governing coalition that had been subdued under Pedro de Silva's administration began to flare up. This caused Rodríguez Vigil's immediate successor, Antonio Trevín, to cultivate a base of solid support among the mining districts, but this moved the regional president into the SOMA-UGT camp and exacerbated tensions with its rivals. This also forced Trevín to narrow his approach to industrial policy by adopting the untenable position of the unions in the restructuring of HUNOSA. Unlike Rodríguez Vigil, however, Trevín became involved in bitter disputes with Fernández Villa that divided the PSOE further. The Socialists' fortunes worsened later when IU abandoned the PSOE in the Junta, accusing the Socialists of having converted Asturias into an "industrial desert."[48] Despite equally incendiary attacks on the PP's leader, Sérgio Marqués, who one IU official unscrupulously called a "Nazi" for his alleged insensitivity to the social dislocation produced by industrial restructuring, IU's defection from the government allowed Marqués to rise to power following the May 28, 1995, regional elections.[49] The new PP government embraced the privatization of CSI and the rapid restructuring of HUNOSA.

---

more on Rodríguez Vigil's position on the reconversion of the mining districts, see his editorial "Futuro para Asturias," *El País*, September 20, 1991.

48. This comment was made by Gaspar Llamazares, head of the Asturian IU, during his public statement renouncing the party's coalition with the PSOE (see *El Mundo*, June 7, 1995).

49. The author of these attacks was IU European deputy Laura González (see *El Mundo*, June 5, 1995). González reluctantly apologized for the statement a few days later.

With regional politics so divided and distracted away from the "reindustrialization" mission of the agencies during the post-Silva governments, the industrial policy system tended to stagnate somewhat from 1991 to 1993. The agencies continued to function, however, and they were even able to find additional resources for new industrial policies. The continuity and innovation of the Asturian development agencies was due to the fact that the political technocracy first created under the Silva administration continued to evolve under weaker, succeeding governments. Key technocrats, such as Nieves Carasco, circulated from executive positions in the Chancellery of Industry to agency directorates, preserving important sources of experience from the previous period of activity.[50] This experienced core of political technocrats utilized existing close contacts among IFR, SAYPE, the chancelleries and other agencies to refocus industrial policy on the promotion of small and medium-sized firms. In part the new focus emerged from the experience these officials had with the problems of promoting large public and foreign investments in a secondary region with poor infrastructure. They agreed based on experience and the fact that national outlays for regional industrial policy were finite that the promotion of small and medium-sized firms was the most feasible function for the development agencies.[51]

Nevertheless, the new direction in policy manifested itself only in the redirection of resources and agency planning to the promotion of small and medium-sized firms and away from the goal of attracting large investors such as DuPont. The agencies developed experience in projects on which they cooperated, but contacts among the agencies became less regular in the absence of a regional development plan for small and medium-sized firms.[52]

Another important factor that explains the preservation of the agencies was that the Principado did not face strong fiscal pressures to disassemble them. The regional government's budget remained relatively healthy during the period. While other Spanish regions such as Catalo-

50. In Carasco's case, she continued as director of industry until 1993 when she became director of the Instituto Tecnológico de Materiales (Technical Institute of Materials), a public technological institute for the metallurgical industry in Asturias (author interview with Nieves Carasco, June 28, 1995, Technology Park of Asturias, Llanera, Asturias).

51. Author interviews with María José Suárez Puente, IFR, July 26, 1994, Llanera, Asturias; Nieves Carasco, director of industry (1988–93), June 28, 1995, Llanera, Asturias; and Encarna Rodríguez Cañes, Chancellery of Economy and Planning, July 26, 1994.

52. Author interview with Carasco.

nia and Andalusia were overwhelmed with debt, Asturias maintained a debt level equivalent to 5.4 percent of current revenues, well below the 25 percent legal limit. Indeed, Asturias was one of the few regions that consistently respected national fiscal laws (Monasterio Escudero 1994: 273). By the early 1990s, Asturian debt levels increased, forcing the regional governments of the period to propose zero-growth budgets, but the rate of debt growth did not justify more radical action.[53] In comparison to the other Spanish regions, Asturian debt levels grew slowly. More important, the agencies did not consume large portions of the regional budget.

In 1994, the agencies, and the IFR and SAYPE in particular, resuscitated their resources and functions with an ambitious Plan de Apoyo a las PYMES 1994–96 (Support Plan for Small and Medium-Sized Firms 1994–96). The improvement in the agencies' activities was possible only because new sources of political support appeared. By this time, the unions and the Asturian technocracy first assembled during the Silva government, were agreed on the priorities of regional industrial policy. Defeated in their attempts to change national policy, UGT and CCOO organizers increasingly turned to supporting the Asturian technocracy's strategy of promoting small and medium-sized firms as a mechanism for preserving and increasing employment.[54] Union representatives sat on the Board of Directors of the IFR and attended the board meetings of other agencies. The advent of significant union support for the work of the agencies provided political protection from any attempts by the post-Silva governments, and particularly the PP government, to disassemble the economic technocracy. More important, in the political vacuum left by intra-PSOE conflicts over the reconversion of mining and steel, the political technocracy was able to take advantage of close horizontal ties among the agencies to find resources for small projects. Without alternatives in the face of national restructuring policy, the Principado's government placed its bets on the policies that the IFR and SAYPE had been designing for years.

53. One prominent cause for the rise of Asturian debt levels was the fact that after 1991 approval of the regional budget required cross-party coalitions in the Junta. Monasterio Escudero (1994: 273) explains that public spending increased sharply during this period in order to cement these temporary coalitions.

54. Based on author interviews with José Manuel Suárez, UGT, March 26, 1996, Madrid; Dario Díaz, CCOO, June 27, 1995, Oviedo, Asturias; María José Suárez Puente, IFR, July 26, 1994, Llanera, Asturias; and Nieves Carasco, director of industry (1988–93), June 28, 1995, Llanera, Asturias. Also see the language in the agreement affirmed by both UGT and CCOO in January 1994 in Principado de Asturias (1994).

PROMOTING SMALL AND MEDIUM-SIZED FIRMS:
THE PROJECTS OF THE IFR AND SAYPE

The activities of the Instituto de Fomento Regional (Institute of Regional Promotion, IFR) and the Servicio de Asesoramiento y Promoción Empresarial (Service of Assistance and Entrepreneurial Promotion, SAYPE) in the promotion of small and medium-sized firms developed persisting responses to Asturias's chronic problems with dependency on public mining and steel. The creation of the Zones of Economic Promotion (ZPEs) and Zones in Industrial Decline (ZIDs) in Asturias devolved significant resources to the IFR in 1988, allowing it and its sister agency, SAYPE, to operate in diverse sectors and policy areas. Yet even when these resources began to dry up during the early 1990s, IFR and SAYPE retained enough administrative and political flexibility to engineer a renewed campaign for the promotion of small and medium-sized firms under the *Plan de Apoyo a las PYMES* in 1994.

The political battles of the 1980s between organized Asturian interests and those of the central government opened the door to the decentralization of an entire array of resources for regional industrial policy. Many of these resources were decentralized in the form of fiscal outlays, national infrastructure programs with EU funding, and subsidy programs. National guidelines for allocating these monies were often open-ended, allowing for regional interests to articulate a wide range of priorities in order to garner these resources. The IFR made use of all of them. Institute managers presented funding proposals to the Ministry of Infrastructure and lobbied Ministry of Industry officials for the inclusion of Asturian firms in national subsidy and innovation programs.[55]

Since their arguments were based on technical criteria, IFR personnel had to be technically adept as well as politically skillful. Over the course of the 1980s, IFR officials diversified and developed the agency's institutions and the skills of its technocracy. Despite the autonomy and open-ended authorities the IFR gained upon its creation in 1983, the agency's small staff initially tended to concentrate on efforts to attract foreign capital and provide venture capital through the SRP. Both were responses meant to reverse Asturias's declining industrial performance in real and symbolic ways. However, neither provided strong results or long-term options during this period. After 1986, the IFR's staff took up the study

---

55. Author interviews with Belen Menéndez Bañuelos and Encarna Rodriguez Cañes, Regional Directorate of Economy and Planning, Chancellery of the Economy and Planning, July 26, 1994, Oviedo, Asturias.

of the region's infrastructure and it listened to the demands of small and medium-sized firms (San Miguel Cela 1994: 662–63). As a result, the IFR's staff expanded in size and interest, developing specific programs to promote innovation, quality, infrastructure, and technology in small and medium-sized firms. By 1988, the year the Law of Regional Incentives was passed, the IFR's staff was already highly diversified, larger, and more technically competent than it had been during its first few years.[56]

One significant aspect of the IFR's evolution was its ability to increasingly coordinate its activities with other Asturian development agencies. The IFR's partial ownership of SRP and SODECO already gave the agency's directorate considerable access to the information, personnel, and other resources of the venture capital societies. Yet IFR, which was governed by the Chancellery of Industry, also developed relationships with SAYPE, the development agency for small and medium-sized firms under the command of the Chancellery of Economy and Planning. On paper the two agencies seemed to duplicate each other's functions. SAYPE subsidized interest on loans for small and medium-sized firms, but like IFR, it also granted investment subsidies to firms. Nonetheless, in practice, the two agencies increasingly coordinated their activities. SAYPE's programs were designed to operate in collaboration with the IFR's Service of Regional Economic Incentives (the institute office that administered regional and national subsidies).[57] In regular practice most SAYPE allocations were evaluated by a technocratic commission that maintained regular contact with IFR personnel and the venture capital societies, and coordinated final funding with these agencies.[58] More important, the construction of the technology park in Llanera in 1987 effectively placed IFR, SRP, and SAYPE in the same building, allowing agency officials to meet regularly to coordinate their efforts. This proximity allowed the agencies to function increasingly as branches of the same entity. Each brought a particular experience and know-how to common projects, enhancing administration with interdisciplinary knowledge and additional links across the chancelleries of Industry and Economy

56. Author interviews with María Rosa González Corujedo, Principado de Asturias, May 31, 1995, Oviedo, Asturias; Encarna Rodriguez Cañes, Chancellery of Economy and Planning, July 26, 1994, Oviedo, Asturias; Javier González-Rico Herrero, assistant director, SAYPE, June 26, 1995, Llanera, Asturias; María José Suárez Puente, director of technical services, IFR, July 26, 1994, Llanera, Asturias.

57. For more on how the regional government assigned responsibilities for the design and implementation of industrial promotion programs, see Consejería de Hacienda y Economía (1993: 247).

58. Author interview with Javier González-Rico Herrero, assistant director, SAYPE, June 26, 1995, Llanera, Asturias.

and Planning. As a result, the largest promotion program in Asturias in recent years, the Plan de Apoyo a las PYMES 1994–96 (Support Plan for Small and Medium-Sized Firms 1994–96), was implemented by IFR in cooperation with SAYPE and it received the broad support of the two main economic chancelleries, SADEI, and the unions. This represented the most mature example of plan-based horizontal embeddedness in Asturias.

Another significant aspect of the IFR's activities was the increasing ability of the organization and its sister agency, SAYPE, to maintain close contact with Asturian firms. Both IFR and SAYPE evolved monitoring functions capable of evaluating firm proposals for funding, coordinating with other agencies and banks, and supervising the execution of official resources in private entrepreneurial projects. IFR officials, for example, would meet with firm managers at the technology park and arrange plant visits to supervise the progress of ongoing projects or to provide follow-through monitoring on completed jobs. Since the agencies were most interested in entrepreneurial projects with the greatest potential for improving the quality of production and employment, continual monitoring became an essential practice for evaluating firm needs and adapting limited resources to the areas where they would have the most substantial effect. These practices were informed by the earlier trial-and-error experiences of political technocrats at IFR and SRP during the 1980s.[59]

The IFR's improved institutional and technocratic capacity proved essential in conceiving and implementing industrial policy, but it was not sufficient for guaranteeing the system a sizable and constant influx of resources. Table 4.3 summarizes the subsidy programs of the IFR and the amounts provided through national industrial promotion funds. As the figures indicate, total national funding for subsidy programs *decreased* in Asturias from the high represented in 1990 by the resources used to attract DuPont to the region. The IFR's own subsidy programs, however, remained relatively stable. The figures reflect the fact that the agency's institutional capacity continued to keep regional industrial policy afloat, but the decline of Asturias's political capacity in extracting national resources led to some deterioration in levels of national industrial subsidies in the region between 1991 and 1994.

The recession in resources for the promotion of industrial investment

59. Severino García Fernández, administrative director of the SRP, recalled how SRP personnel in the mid-1980s would drive throughout the region to visit entrepreneurs, evaluate their production processes, and then return to SRP's offices to discuss potential solutions (author interview, June 26, 1995, Llanera, Asturias).

Table 4.3 Subsidies administered by the IFR 1990–1994 (all figures reported in millions of dollars)

Years	ZPE[a]	ZID[b]	CDTI[c]	R&D[d]	ATI[e]	PIT[f]	PITMA[g]	Quality[h]	IFR	Total
1990	272	6.9	2.0	.5	-	-	-	-	.7	282.1
1991	8	32.5	3.3	-	.4	.15	1.9	.1	1.1	47.5
1992	8	1.2	6.6	-	.5	-	1.8	.6	.9	19.6
1993	7.1	-	3.7	-	1.2	-	4.0	.3	.9	17.2
1994	3.7	-	7.5		.9		.2	.1	1.6	14.0

Sources: IFR (1994 & 1995); Castells and Vázquez (1994: 306 & 308).

[a] Zone of Economic Promotion
[b] Zone of Declining Industry
[c] Center for Industrial Technology Development
[d] Ministry of Industry R&D Support Program
[e] Industrial Technology Activation Plan
[f] Technological Infrastructure Plan
[g] Environmental Plan for Industry and Technology
[h] National Plan of Quality

shifted political and technocratic interests even more strongly away from big-ticket investments and in favor of small and medium-sized firm projects. During the height of the industrial reconversion years in the 1980s, the IFR could maintain a dual strategy of promoting large foreign investments and more modest firm projects. In addition to significant allocations for large projects, the national government, through national agencies responsible for aiding small and medium-sized firms, maintained specific programs for these investments. Yet by 1995, Asturias was far down on the list of Spanish regions being considered for this specialized funding (see Table 2.3). This fact, in addition to the other dwindling sources of national funding for industrial promotion in the region, placed even more emphasis on the policies and resources of the IFR and its affiliated agencies.

In January 1993, the regional government began negotiating the terms of the Plan de Apoyo a las PYMES 1994–96 with the Asturian labor unions and the regional business association, FADE. Battered as they were by the national reconversion of steel and mining, the Asturian unions backed the regional agencies as they had never done before, allowing IFR and SAYPE access to political resources that exerted leverage on the regional executive and Junta to provide support for the 1993 plan. As a result, the negotiations produced significant commitments of resources by the regional government to an array of policies designed to promote small and medium-sized firms in Asturias (Table 4.4). According to the regional laws that codified the agreement (Decreto 39/94, May 5,

Table 4.4   Financing of support plan for small- and medium-sized firms,
1994–1996 (all figures reported in millions of dollars)

Financial Programs	1994	1995	1996	Total
Project finance	$22.6	$20.3	$18.8	$61.7
Quality control	1.5	3.1	3.8	8.4
Innovation and technology	1.8	1.7	1.9	5.4
Internationalization	.8	1.1	1.2	3.1
Infrastructure	2.7	4.3	4.5	11.5
Total	29.4	30.5	30.2	90.1

SOURCE: IFR (1994).

and Decreto 60/95, April 27), most of these resources went to financial subsidies to be administered by the IFR and SAYPE. The agencies offered direct subsidies to proposed investments, subsidies on the interest of short-term loans, subsidies to firms seeking leasing arrangements, and access to subsidized collateral in Asturgar, S.G.R., the Asturian mutual collateral society.[60] The IFR coordinated its daily activities under the plan with SAYPE, and in November 1994 the IFR sponsored a series of conferences that informed local offices of SAYPE, municipalities, and firms about the mechanisms of the Plan de Apoyo a las PYMES.[61] By 1998, IFR and the SAYPE had more than doubled their regular activities in the promotion of small and medium-sized firms under the plan (IFR 1995, 1997, 1998; SAYPE 1998, 1997).[62] Agency officials reported a marked increase in business consultations, project proposals, and approvals (although final approval remained relatively competitive). In the view of some agency

60. For the details of these and other mechanisms under the *Plan de Apoyo a las Pymes,* see Principado de Asturias (1994); *Boletín Oficial del Principado de Asturias y de la Provincía,* Decreto 39/94, May 5, June 9, 1994 and Decreto 60/95, April 27, June 1, 1995; and *Boletín de Información del IFR,* no. 9, June 1994.

61. For more on these meetings, see IFR (1995).

62. Global figures for the activity of the agencies demonstrate an increasing preoccupation with small and medium-sized firms. This is particularly true of SAYPE. Over 80 percent of the agency's projects were directed at firms employing between 1 and 25 workers. For the IFR, indicators are more scarce in the pre-1994 period, however, the turnover rate—the time from first hearing to final approval of a firm project—increasingly became less than one year. While most ZPE projects for 1992 were first proposed in 1990 and 1991, the overwhelming majority of ZPE projects for 1993 and 1994 were concluded in the same years that they were proposed. These trends underline statements by IFR officials that the political and technical priority of the post-1993 period became the promotion of small and medium-sized firms whose projects could be completed in the year they were first proposed. It appears that the IFR was moving in that direction in the years prior to the consecration of the *Plan de Apoyo a las PYMES.*

technocrats, this was evidence that despite political turnover in Oviedo the industrial policy network was well-grounded, thereby inspiring business confidence.[63]

The measures of the IFR's and SAYPE's effectiveness are both general and specific. General figures for the performance of the IFR's financial programs under the Law of Regional Incentives show that between 1988 and 1997, 172 firm projects were rejected, 339 were approved, and half of these had been completed by 1998. The average firm project received a subsidy equal to 24 percent of the firm's initial investment. Approved projects generated $1.5 billion in new investments, created 5,121 new jobs, and maintained 11,508 old jobs (IFR 1998: 73). In 1991, SAYPE approved 364 small and medium-sized firm projects, which generated $75 million in new investments and 1,332 jobs. By 1998, SAYPE was organizing over 1,000 such projects per year and generating an average of $210 million in investment and 1,927 jobs per annum.[64]

Although industrial manufacturing and affiliated service industries represented the priorities of IFR and SAYPE programs, agency mechanisms evinced a high level of sectoral diversity. Manufacturing, metallurgy, and hostelry received 85 percent of ZPE monies. Between 40 and 60 percent of SAYPE funding went to industry and services linked to manufacturing. In their study of all IFR subsidies, Castells and Vázquez (1994: 309) found that although metal-mechanical and chemical industries make up a significant portion of IFR programs, there does not seem to be a larger sectoral strategy. Rather, IFR subsidies went to a variety of different manufacturing endeavors, including metallurgy, electronics, ceramics, chemicals, food processing, construction, manufacturing, and industrial services, but most important, almost all of these projects occurred in small and medium-sized enterprises.

SAYPE's activities confirmed the growing financial importance of the Caja de Ahorros de Asturias and Asturgar, S.G.R., for small and medium-sized firms. Caja de Ahorros de Asturias handled over 50 percent of SAYPE's financial operations between 1991 and 1993. No other bank approached even 8 percent of total projects and loans.[65] The mutual

63. Author interview with Rosendo Rojas Sánchez, director of the Area of Business Information and Research, December 11, 1998, Madrid. Also see the testimony of a director of the IFR, San Miguel Cela (1994: 658–59).

64. These figures are official figures from SAYPE (1992, 1993, 1994, 1997, 1998).

65. These figures do not include financial operations handled through the ICO system. Annually these programs represent only a handful of projects and a relatively negligible amount of financing (about $1.6 million in 1993). Banco Central Hispanoamericano is the largest lender under this system in Asturias.

collateral society, Asturgar, saw an increase in its financial activities between 1991 and 1994, but its total liquidity remained small (about $4 million). However, over 66 percent of Asturgar's subsidized collateral projects were processed through the Cajas de Ahorros, thus reinforcing the importance of the Asturian savings bank as the key financier of small and medium-sized firms in the region (Asturgar 1995: 33).

These global figures for IFR and SAYPE performance do not reveal the true effectiveness of these policies. In order to analyze the performance of the agencies, particularly their monitoring and follow-through functions, I conducted a small-n study of small and medium-sized firms in Asturias. The firms contacted in this study were chosen randomly from numerous directories of Asturian enterprises that had initiated projects with the development agencies. With only the most general information about the nature of the selected projects but without any prior knowledge about the outcome of these projects, I arranged for interviews with the managers of these firms to acquire details about their contacts with the Asturian agencies.

Table 4.5 summarizes the eleven small and medium-sized firms contacted in this study. All dealt directly with the IFR, although a couple also had direct contact with SRP, SAYPE, and SODECO. Subsequent inquiries at the IFR revealed that firms that listed "IFR" as their contact agency tended to think of SAYPE and SRP as IFR subunits rather than as separate agencies. The fact that firm managers often attended conferences at the IFR building that also houses these two other agencies probably added to the confusion. This problem in coding complicates an assessment of IFR's activities versus those of SAYPE, but this impediment was partially redressed in open-ended interviews in which firm managers were asked to comment on the coordination and preparation of "the agencies," allowing for discussion of whether problems of collaboration among the agencies emerged and affected cooperation with the firm.

The dominant form of industrial promotion in the sample is subsidization, although information accompanies a few firm projects. The selection is sectorally diverse, reflective of the universe of firm projects administered by the agencies. There are variations in size ranging from the small firms with 8–20 employees to the medium-sized firms of 100 and 300 employees. The selection is also diverse in export orientation.

The specifics of each firm's project and the agency's role are difficult to determine due to the resistance of firm managers to revealing the details of confidential financial arrangements and production processes. Based on firm interviews and data provided by the agencies, however, it is possible to get a glimpse into these projects. This information shows

Table 4.5 Selected small and medium-sized Asturian firms

Firm	Sector	Number of Employees	Export Rate	Promotion Type	Promotion Agency Contacted
Aguas de Fuensanta	Food processing	104	2%	Subsidies	IFR, SODECO, SAYPE
Arcillas Refractarias	Construction	29	10%	Subsidies	IFR
Astur Calco	Graphic Arts/ Design	8	0%	Subsidies	IFR
Asturpharma	Pharmaceuticals	44	90%	Subsidies, Venture capital	IFR, SRP
Auxquimía	Chemicals	10	<5%	Information, Trade show	IFR
Compañia Electrometalica Asturiana	Steel/ Metallurgy	15	0%	Subsidies	IFR
Construcciones Metalicas Joama	Steel/ Metallurgy	60	0%	Subsidies, Information	IFR
Electro Materiales KLK	Electrical equipment	75	20/25%	Information	IFR
Juan Roces	Engineering	30	.8%	Subsidies	IFR
Muebles Campa	Furniture	20	10%	Subsidies, Information	IFR
Seresco Asturiana	Computers	380	5%	Subsidies	IFR

SOURCE: IFR (various annual reports) and author's interviews, March–May 1996.

that the nature of firm projects was often decided by short-term production needs, particularly efforts to improve the productivity of current operations. For example, the small firm, Arcillas Refractarias, required financing for automation that would greatly improve its quality control operations. Asturpharma used its financing to design and construct a hydrogenation plant and purchase quality control equipment that was crucial for the firm's plans to improve productivity. Compañia Electrometálica Asturiana used regional subsidies to finance the purchase of painting and oven equipment and a numeric control system that firm managers considered vital to current operations. Similarly, Juan Roces and Muebles Campa used public support to finance the development of quality control and automated systems that became crucial to the efficiency of important segments of current production. Perhaps the most intriguing case is that of Seresco Asturiana, which used an array of national technology subsidies administered by IFR to aid in the financing of AIDA, a computerized data control and management system that allowed Seresco to improve productivity for some of its key operations. In all of these cases, projects were concluded within a year or little over a year.

Would these investments and others like them have been possible without the aid of the Asturian agencies? The firms were asked this general question and then asked to elaborate on the specific effects of public support on production and employment. Astur Calco and Asturpharma argued that public assistance was essential for both improvements in production and increases in employment. Compañia Electrometalica Asturiana noted that the IFR's assistance was key to improvements in production, but had a limited or negligible effect on employment. For Juan Roces, the effect was important for some operations but not all, and the effects on employment were negligible. Aguas de Fuensanta, Arcillas Refractarias, Muebles Campa and Seresco Asturiana owed some productivity improvements to IFR support, which was deemed as one key source of financing. These three firms also reported a moderate increase in employment as a result. The three remaining firms, Auxquimía, Construcciones Metalicas Joama, and Electro Materiales KLK, reported no effects on production or employment as a result of agency activities. Therefore, eight of the eleven firms reported that IFR subsidies were important to improvements in the quality of production and/or employment.[66] Managers of the eight firms that viewed IFR activities as positive complained that Asturias suffered from a lack of finance for small and medium-sized firms and that the regional agencies provided important sources of finance that made firm projects designed to improve productivity possible where they might otherwise have been impossible.

Based on interview data a couple of explanations emerge for the partial disparate performances of these firm projects. The first reason is frequency of contact between firm and agency. The firms that reported the

66. Macroeconomic factors such as the liberalization of the Spanish economy do not explain the performance of the selected small and medium-sized firm projects. Only one of the selected enterprises had a substantive export orientation (Asturpharma, a successful project), and this firm was the only one in the sample that operated in a sector with a meaningful export component (chemicals, 5.4 percent of Asturian exports).

best results for agency activities also had the most frequent contact with the agencies. Astur Calco, Asturpharma, Compañia Electrometalica Asturiana, Juan Roces, Aguas de Fuensanta, and Seresco Asturiana reported constant or very frequent contact with agency personnel. In most cases, this contact took the form of routine plant visits and follow-up consultation. Arcillas Refractarias and Muebles Campa reported less frequent, yet still substantive contact during and after the duration of their respective projects. Auxquimía and Construcciones Metalicas Joama, the least successful projects, reported little contact with the agencies. Respondents claimed that contact was associated with the ability of the official agency to "understand" the firm's problems and to shape support programs in ways that addressed these concerns. These responses are concrete indicators of the role of frequency of contact and mutual planning and goal-setting in vertically embedded ties between the agencies and the firms.

The second reason for the diverse results of agency activities in the selected cases is the nature of promotional mechanisms. Auxquimía and Electro Materiales KLK, reported almost no effects on production and employment; these firms were supplied mostly with information in the form of access to European and Spanish business databases and trade shows. In these cases, information alone was a weak mechanism for promoting investment. Construcciones Metalicas Joama received both information and subsidies and reported no effects on production and employment, but the firm was unwilling to reveal the size of the subsidy or the relative importance of information. All of the more successful projects received subsidies and assistance in the use of these monies to have the most effect on productivity, suggesting that this is a more powerful mechanism for promoting investment.[67]

Despite differences in performance, the firms agreed on the high quality of agency personnel. Unlike frequency of contact and nature of promotional mechanisms, overall quality is a much more difficult factor to measure. Firm managers were asked for their view based on past experience and their willingness to employ the official agencies again in the future. All of the selected firms reported that they considered agency personnel who had contact with them to be highly professional and knowledgeable about the operations and demands of their industry. Nine of the eleven selected firms reported that they viewed the activities of the agencies, and particularly the IFR, as positive for the Asturian

---

67. Asturpharma received venture capital from the SRP, but firm officials were unable (or unwilling) to say which was more important.

economy and they noted that they would employ the agencies in the future. That number included the three firms that previously reported few substantive effects from past agency activities on production or employment. The two remaining firms had no answer to the question. These numbers are demonstrative of more than an overall satisfaction with the performance of the agencies; they are indicative of a more diffuse confidence in agency mechanisms and their availability over time.

How do the experiences of this selected group of firms reflect the larger experiences of small- and medium-sized firms in Asturias? The first point of comparison is the widespread view among this sample of firms that the agencies performed a crucial financial function that the market did not provide. Castells and Vázquez (1994: 652–53) found in their survey of 198 Asturian firms that the three most important policy mechanisms for promoting entrepreneurial activity were: 1) subsidized interest on credit; 2) official subsidies with technocratic oversight of firm projects; and 3) collateral on finance. All three are financial mechanisms administered by IFR and SAYPE. These results underscore the finding that the Asturian development agencies provide a financial function that is essential for entrepreneurial investment, particularly among small and medium-sized firms.

It is also clear that the region's entrepreneurs generally view the agencies as professional. In their survey of 198 firms, the Castells and Vázquez (1994: 649) working group found that 77 percent of responding firms knew about the region's incentive programs and 54 percent thought that they had been well-informed about them by the official apparatus (26 percent disagreed and 20 percent had no answer). Over 68 percent of respondents viewed these incentives positively and sought to use them in the future, 22 percent were uninterested, and 10 percent had no answer. Over 44 percent reported that they had already been included in incentive programs in the past. As in our small-n study, most responding firms reported that they viewed the activities of the agencies as positive for the Asturian economy and that they would employ the agencies in the future.

Our small-n study, however, also reveals qualifications among firm managers that are not detectable in the Castells and Vázquez survey. Several firm administrators admitted that agency personnel had initially misunderstood the way that proposed projects would increase productivity. Some firm managers argued that their projects were initially delayed by administrative differences among the agencies. Yet, in all of these cases, these initial problems were resolved with additional contacts and follow-up by agency personnel. Plant visits by agency professionals were often cited as useful mechanisms for resolving initial disputes. These indicators suggest that "mutual understanding" developed between the agencies and the firms through periodic, if not continual, follow-up; this factor is closely associated with high levels of vertical embeddedness. Moreover, administrative differences were worked out in all cases, an indicator that horizontal embeddedness reinforced synergy.

The case of IFR and SAYPE activities illustrates the importance of both *horizontal* and *vertical embeddedness* for building and maintaining synergy between these public agencies and Asturian firms. Without horizontal embeddedness, the Asturian agencies' structure and their performance would have been very different. They might have not developed beyond the Pedro de Silva administration; a factor that would have made conceiving and implementing the Plan de Apoyo a las PYMES impossible. These links helped the agencies to coordinate a change in strategy away from big-ticket investments to small and medium-sized firms, and they made possible the maintenance of synergistic vertical ties (vertical embeddedness) between the agencies and Asturian firms. These actors were able to mold particular projects according to agency goals under the Plan de Apoyo a las PYMES and specific firm needs. Improvements in production and the favorable view of the agencies registered by firm respondents reflected how these cooperative exchanges of information produced and maintained high levels of synergy in a region that many feared could only become an industrial desert.

CHAPTER

5

Populist Government and Industrial Policy-Making in Rio de Janeiro and Andalusia

Policy scholars attracted to the study of "decentralization" in developing countries during the 1990s became easily enamored with the possibilities for equating this process with the spread of efficient government (for instance,World Bank 1997; IDB 1994). For these observers, decentralized government, being "closer to the people," is more accountable, more accessible, more innovative, and generally more effective than centralized government. Our observations in Minas Gerais and Asturias suggest that this general conclusion is not without merit. However, the generalization that a common national process such as decentralization can produce the uniform spread of "good government" within Brazil and Spain is baseless. The qualities that produce synergy are themselves contingent upon subnational politics, and in the political context of Rio de Janeiro and Andalusia, the roots of synergy would find fallow ground.

In both cases patterns of populist government undermined synergy. Subnational politicians were persistently threatened by rivals or they became embroiled in conflicts with regional business groups. Elites found greater utility in the use of industrial policies that could strengthen electoral and clientelistic support in the face of these rivalries. Consequently, these populist governments centralized their control over development policy and subjugated the interests of their regions' development missions and political technocracy to the short-term concerns of preserving their own political power. Horizontal embeddedness evolved in Andalusia along the hierarchical-functional type while in Rio it became nonfunctional.

By impeding the development of either plan-oriented or project-oriented horizontal embeddedness, these governments created institutions that would reinforce the populist pattern. Even in the face of eroding economic conditions and intergovernmental competition with both national and rival subnational governments, political elites had incentives to manipulate industrial policies to build and safeguard their constituency support. As a result, synergy was poorly conceived. Public agencies were disconnected from the problems of regional economies, unable to alter, even partially, problematic patterns of development.

POLITICIZING DEVELOPMENT: THE POPULIST MANAGEMENT OF INDUSTRIAL POLICY IN RIO DE JANEIRO

Like Minas Gerais, the state of Rio de Janeiro played a prominent role in national Brazilian politics. Guanabara (the contemporary city of Rio de Janeiro) was the capital of Brazil from 1763 to 1960. In 1960 Guanabara remained a federal district separated from the old province of Rio de Janeiro while the administrative capital of the country was moved to the planned city of Brasília. In 1975 Guanabara was incorporated into the surrounding area, creating the state of Rio de Janeiro.[1] This division of Rio de Janeiro was both a cause and a reflection of larger divisions within the state government's ruling political elite. Unlike Minas, Rio never enjoyed the degree of elite accommodation evident among segments of the *mineiro* political oligarchy and the political technocracy. In Rio, from at least the second half of the Old Republic, state politics were driven by conflicts among populist politicians with clientelistic bases of support. Even when these personalities faded, they were replaced by another populist-clientelistic alliance.

The persistence of populist leadership did not remove development policy from the agenda of the state government's economic policy repertoire. On the contrary, successive state leaders pursued elaborate industrial policies. Unlike the developmentalist and later market-oriented policies of the *mineiro* agencies, however, Rio's industrial policies were designed primarily to strengthen the clientelistic base of their political

---

1. For the purposes of my analysis, the statistics and arguments in this section will apply to the contemporary state of Rio de Janeiro and I will use the adjective *fluminense* to refer to the entire state of Rio de Janeiro. All figures dating back before the incorporation into Guanabara include statistics for both the federal district and the state *as if* they had been a single administrative entity. For more on how the consolidated figures are calculated, see Pereira de Melo and Considera (1986).

benefactors. Politicians exerted direct control over developmental organizations. By centralizing political administration over these agencies, Rio's politicians severely hindered the emergence of horizontal and vertical embeddedness including multiple agencies and private firms. As a result, industrial policy in Rio was inconsistently maintained and largely ineffective.

The failures of industrial policy in the state of Rio de Janeiro had little to do with the demand for these initiatives. Like Minas Gerais, Rio developed during the twentieth century as an economic satellite of São Paulo. Business leaders and some members of the political elite at times voiced concerns for this dependency and called on state governments to take the reins of development.[2] As the crisis of the 1970s and 1980s caused the state to deindustrialize, these demands became more vocal, but they were overshadowed by the populist programs of governors such as Antônio de Pádua Chagas Freitas, Leonel Brizola, and Wellington Moreira Franco. These leaders were interested in using economic policy as a means of weakening their political enemies and strengthening their own clientelistic base. Machine politics became the overarching logic governing industrial policy.

The Deindustrialization of Rio de Janeiro

Unlike Minas Gerais, Rio was not an underdeveloped state that sought to develop. It was already highly developed when the state government created industrial policy agencies during the 1970s. In 1929, Rio de Janeiro commanded 28 percent of Brazil's industrial production, second only to São Paulo with 35 percent. Minas Gerais, at the time, accounted for only 7.5 percent. But Rio's relative importance in Brazil's industrial economy eroded thereafter. The state's share of national industrial production fell to 20 percent in 1949, 17 percent in 1959, and 15.6 percent in 1970 (Pereira de Melo and Considera 1986: 113). During the 1970s and 1980s, Rio de Janeiro's decline became even more precipitous. Boosted temporarily during the 1970s with annual industrial growth rates of 10 percent, the state's industry stagnated between 1980–85, growing only 1.98 percent.[3] Indicative of Rio's loss of industrial development was its

---

2. Both private sector and government documents illustrate the history of these concerns. See Estado do Rio (1979, 1983, 1987), Secretaria de Estado de Indústria, Comércio, Ciência e Tecnologia (1991), Magalhães (1983), and Light (1985).

3. Neither agriculture nor services did much better. Agriculture's annual growth rates fell from 8 percent during the 1970–75 period to 1.28 percent during the 1980–85 period. Services dropped from 8.76 percent to 0.9 percent during the same time frame.

growth rate during the 1970–85 period (5.48). Compared to São Paulo's 6.73 percent, Minas Gerais's 8.64 percent, and the growth rates of smaller states such as Espirito Santo (9.87 percent), Rio grew slowly. Rio de Janeiro was particularly hard hit by the slowdown of the early 1980s. The *fluminense* GDP grew a paltry 0.2 percent during this time. Rio de Janeiro state had the lowest growth rate of all the Brazilian states for the period 1970–85 (C. Diniz and Teixeira dos Santos 1994: Table 2) and economic performance continued to flag after 1985. Generally, Rio's share of the Brazilian GDP dropped from 16.7 percent in 1970 to 11 percent in 1990 (C. Diniz and Teixeira dos Santos 1994: 33).

As Table 5.1 illustrates, the poor economic performance of the state caused its share of national industrial activity to decline precipitously in comparison to the other three states in the southeast region. Evaluated by sector (Table 5.2), Rio de Janeiro lost its relative share in industrial production across the board, from consumer durables and intermediary goods to advanced capital goods such as mechanical and transport equipment. Some of the state's key sectors—textiles (its first major industry), steel (dominated by the CSN complex), transport industry (primarily the huge shipbuilding sector, which was Brazil's largest), and pharmaceuticals—withered. Between 1980 and 1984, these four sectors in particular lost 53 percent, 19 percent, 62 percent, and 24 percent of their productive capacity, respectively (Pereira de Melo and Considera 1986: 118). Many observers would conclude based on this data that Rio de Janeiro was suffering from an acute crisis of deindustrialization.

The causes of Rio de Janeiro's crisis of deindustrialization were not difficult for observers to fathom. First, the contemporary state of Rio de Janeiro only became a reality in 1975. Prior to this time, the presence of the administrative capital in the metropolitan area competed with industry for space and resources. More important, the expansion of public administration during the 1960s and 1970s increased average salaries to the highest levels in Brazil, encouraging private businesses to abandon the city for other states (Cano 1977). Meanwhile, the interior regions remained poor and underdeveloped, accounting for less than 30 percent of the state's GDP. The lack of infrastructure and basic sanitation outside of the metropolitan area created few incentives for industrial firms to move to the interior (Pereira de Melo and Considera 1986: 120; Ryff 1995). As the economic crises of the 1980s worsened and Rio's social problems increased along with them, industrial firms and banks abandoned Rio for São Paulo, Minas Gerais, and the developing southern region.

Another cause of Rio's economic decline was the state's inflexible industrial structure. Rio de Janeiro's industries were poorly integrated.

Table 5.1 Rio de Janeiro's share of national GDP, in comparative perspective, 1970–1985

Region/State	1970	1975	1980	1985
Rio de Janeiro	15.26	12.99	11.80	11.76
São Paulo	56.45	55.01	46.97	43.92
Minas Gerais	6.87	6.60	8.93	8.67
Espirito Santo	0.51	0.67	1.29	1.38
Southeast	79.09	75.27	68.99	65.74
Brazil	100	100	100	100

SOURCE: Based on Diniz and Teixeira (1994: Table 7).

The CSN steel complex in Volta Redonda operated largely as an enclave, independent of any of the state's other industries. CSN's major industrial customers were located in São Paulo, Minas Gerais, and the states of the south. The shipbuilding industry might have produced important linkages, but competition from South Korea and the decline of federal protection and subsidies throughout the 1980s kept it anemic (C. Diniz and Teixeira dos Santos 1994: 32). The federal informatics law created another opportunity for fostering linkages during the 1970s by placing Brazil's number-one computer software and hardware producer, Cobra, in Rio de Janeiro. However, the state did little to promote the sector or encourage the growth of secondary effects on the local economy (Pereira de Melo and Considera 1986: 120).

While these structural problems in Rio's economy worsened, the state government appeared powerless to act. In contrast to Minas's political oligarchy and its developmentalist political technocracy, Rio de Janeiro's politics were deeply divided by competing factions of clientelistic political machines led by populist leaders.

Populist Leadership and Clientelistic Cleavages in Rio de Janeiro

Rio de Janeiro's political class was never a coherent group.[4] In the period of modern urban politics that dominated the late Old Republic period (the 1920s), rival "grand figures" (*figurões*)—populist leaders with personal followings (often bolstered by their ownership of the city's major news-

---

4. Numerous studies of politics in Rio de Janeiro depict the role of populist elite rivalries and patronage in the state and city's twentieth-century history. Among the most prominent works are Conniff (1981), Gay (1988), and E. Diniz (1982). For a study that contests class-based interpretations of politics in Rio, see Souza (1972), and Soares and Silva (1985).

Table 5.2   Composition of national industry: selected states and sectors, 1970–1985

	São Paulo			Rio de Janeiro			Minas Gerais		
Sector	1970	1980	1985	1970	1980	1985	1970	1980	1985
Textiles	61.65	53.70	50.04	11.68	7.75	7.15	6.51	8.09	10.13
Food processsing	43.95	39.46	37.37	11.34	7.64	6.02	8.82	8.69	7.08
Metallurgy	52.72	54.04	46.85	17.51	12.30	12.29	18.73	18.38	22.22
Mining	49.88	39.84	42.58	13.45	9.64	6.80	11.83	15.58	13.11
Paper	65.21	53.37	57.53	12.58	8.16	5.10	2.58	6.08	5.49
Chemicals	54.12	54.22	51.52	22.50	9.93	11.88	3.41	4.66	6.77
Mechanical	68.48	66.39	64.67	14.37	8.78	6.52	5.45	7.03	5.89
Transport	81.07	68.48	71.61	11.87	13.87	8.87	1.27	6.78	7.15
Electric goods	78.91	64.59	64.00	11.96	8.37	7.25	1.55	3.27	2.52

SOURCE: Based upon Diniz and Teixeira (1994: Table 13).

papers)—stood above Rio's political firmament. These elites expanded Rio's politics beyond the narrow clientelism of the Old Republic by constructing a mass base of support. The *figurões* depended upon the continued support of patrimonial bosses (*chefes políticos*) who could muster votes for local politicians and control elections (Conniff 1981: chap. 4). During the 1930s, the link between populism and clientelism was solidified in the person of mayor Pedro Ernesto, who registered civil servants and workers to vote, enacted social policies, and distributed patronage to cultivate the support of the *chefes políticos*. Rival elites within Ernesto's party, the Autonomist Party of the Federal District (Partido Autonomista do Distrito Federal, PADF), who competed for the same bases of clientelistic support, soon split the popular base the political boss had created.

Similar divisions among populist rivals continued in Rio after Vargas's *Estado Novo* (1937–45). In the pluralist, multiparty system of the 1945–64 period, the three national parties—União Democrática Nacional (UDN), Partido Trabalhista Brasileiro (PTB), and Partido Social Democrático (PSD)—competed in Rio along with the Progressive Social Party (Partido Social Progressista, PSP). At the state level, these parties were dominated by the personalities of their chiefs and often divided by rival leaders (Schmitt 1997: 140).[5]

5. During the 1960s, Carlos Lacerda led a fractious group within the UDN that depended for its cohesion on the Guanabara governor's following and his anti-*getulista* credentials. The PSD in Guanabara did not have notable leadership until Chagas Freitas joined the party in 1962. In the old state of Rio de Janeiro, the PSD's undisputed master was Ernâni do Amaral Peixoto. The PTB was dominated by various *getulista* leaders who had some tie to Vargas's or João Goulart's government. The most important of these included Leonel Brizola and Lutero Vargas. During military rule, these personalities would dominate state party politics, even, as in the case of Brizola, from exile. See Motta (1998: chap. 3).

Emblematic of Rio's populist leadership was the career of Antônio de Pádua Chagas Freitas. During the 1950s, Chagas Freitas was a prominent figure within the PSP, becoming its biggest vote-getter in the 1958 elections for federal deputy. Personalist leadership within the party led to the organization's fragmentation. Chagas Freitas's rivalry with PSP leader Ademar de Barros caused the former to switch to the PSD in 1962 to run again for federal deputy. Other smaller parties emerged from the PSP, further dividing Rio's polity. Yet even as party organizations withered and memberships shifted, Chagas Freitas, like Rio's other *chefes políticos*, remained a nucleus around which allied politicians could flock. As owner of Rio's sensationalist newspaper, *O Dia*, and as a politician with close ties to gangs running the numbers racket in the state, Chagas Freitas perfected the use of clientelism and populism to put together a formidable political machine.[6]

During the subsequent period of military authoritarianism, rivalries within Rio's political class continued to dominate the state's politics. Based on the military's Institutional Act No. 2 of October 27, 1965, extant parties were eliminated and, under Complementary Act No. 4 of November 20, 1965, members were reassembled into a two-party system closely monitored by the authoritarian regime. Opponents of military rule organized within the Brazilian Democratic Movement (Movimento Democrático Brasileiro, MDB), the official party of the opposition. After 1966 the MDB continued to poll higher than the military's Alliance for National Renovation (Aliança Nacional Renovadora, ARENA), but despite the MDB's persistent opposition to military rule, the party remained deeply divided by factions of competing elites in Rio de Janeiro.

In Eli Diniz's (1982) classic study of this period of Rio's state politics, the author focuses on two major factions within the MDB. The first faction was affiliated with the urban political machine of Chagas Freitas. This segment was not associated with leftist opponents of the authoritarian regime and was therefore more acceptable to Brazil's military rulers (Skidmore 1988: 112). Chagas Freitas considered himself "a man of the MDB at the service of the Revolution of 1964" (Diniz 1982: 56 n. 27; Motta 1998). He maintained close ties to key figures in the military government. The most prominent of these was Orlando Geisel, minister of the army under the Emílio Médici military government (1969–73).

The second faction was a mix of politicians known as *autênticos* ("authentics"). These were leftists who challenged military rule but the group also included independents. Also within this second faction were mem-

---

6. A useful personal account of this process is told by Chagas Freitas's vice governor, Erasmo Martins Pedro, in a series of interviews. See Motta (1998). The classic academic study of Chagas Freitas remains E. Diniz (1982).

bers of the political machine of ex-governor Ernâni do Amaral Peixoto (the so-called *amaralistas*), who were based in the old province of Rio de Janeiro and headquartered in the capital city of Niteroi. The *autênticos* and the *amaralistas* operated as an anti-Chagas force, opposed to both military rule and the political machine of the newspaper publisher who favored collaboration with the authoritarian regime.

Turf battles between the *chaguistas* and their opponents were played out within and outside of the MDB. After the military issued Institutional Act No. 5 (AI-5) in 1968, which purged key *autêntico* leaders in the federal chamber of deputies and closed down the Congress for almost a year, Chagas Freitas reorganized the MDB in Guanabara by cultivating local loyalists and excluding opponents.[7] While the *chaguistas* organized around nonideological populist politics and clientelism, the anti-*chaguistas*, and particularly the *autênticos*, formed an ideological opposition of the left. But this also made them vulnerable to AI-5, thereby strengthening the *chaguistas* and reinforcing the collaborationist logic of Chagas Freitas's version of "opposition" to the "revolution of 1964." Nevertheless, *autêntico* leaders such as J. G. de Araújo Jorge, Edson Khair, and Lisâneas Maciel continued to oppose Chagas Freitas's control over the party. In April 1975 they led a group of 82 MDB members in a campaign to oust the *chefe político*. Although the rebels were unsuccessful, their opposition continued to threaten Chagas Freitas's command over the MDB and favor that of his chief rival, Amaral Peixoto (Motta 1998: 161–62).

The fusion of Guanabara and Rio de Janeiro joined the battle between the *amaralistas* and the *chaguistas* in 1975. The union challenged Amaral Peixoto's machine by inviting Chagas Freitas to extend his dominance over the electoral territory once under the command of the *amaralistas*. At the MDB convention in January 1976, the party directorate was split into the two groups, with the *chaguistas* securing a slim majority of one. The new post-fusion political order would emerge over time through a continued process of conflict between the machines of the two *chefes políticos*.[8]

In addition to the *autênticos* and the *amaralistas*, members of the ARENA party competed for state office. These politicians proved to be a persistent opposition to Chagas Freitas's political machine. After Chagas Freitas's rise to the governorship of Guanabara in 1970 the efforts of these anti-Chagas forces intensified. Wilmar Palis, an ARENA state

---

7. The activities of the MDB and ARENA were suspended during this period, even on the state level. The reorganization of the MDB in Rio is detailed by Chagas Freitas's vice governor, Erasmo Martins Pedro. See his interviews in Motta (1998).

8. This process is described in detail by Hamilton Xavier, former federal deputy and close advisor to Amaral Peixoto, in a series of interviews. See Ferreira (1999).

deputy, even attempted (unsuccessfully) to have the governor impeached for failure to report his assets before the 1970 elections. The fusion of the states in 1975 was another attempt to undermine Chagas Freitas's machine. Key supporters of union included ARENA politicians such as Célio Borja, who believed that uniting the states would divide the MDB further (Motta 1998: 155–56). Despite these attempts, the *chaguistas* retained a fragile advantage within the MDB at the state level and Chagas Freitas captured the governorship of the consolidated state of Rio de Janeiro in September 1978 by virtue of his holding an absolute majority within the state electoral college.

Yet persisting divisions within the MDB weakened the state party's ability to represent Rio's interests in the federal legislature. While the state legislature increasingly became dominated by the pro-Chagas forces, Rio's federal representatives were anti-Chagas and opposed to military rule. Both conditions severely enfeebled the Rio MDB. Continuing divisions within the MDB hurt the party's programmatic mission. Without a disciplined party at either the federal or state levels, Rio's politics during the authoritarian period continued to be dominated by contentious rivalries and the persistence of populism and clientelism. Given also the pro-military inclinations of the *chaguista* wing of the MDB, the continuation of these legacies hindered the rise of any political coalition able and willing to represent the state's economic interests (Gondim 1986).

The weakness of local development coalitions was magnified further by the separation of Guanabara and Rio de Janeiro. As a result of this division, *cariocas* (the citizens of Guanabara) and *fluminenses* (the citizens of the old state of Rio de Janeiro) never developed a united and powerful political lobby (a *bancada fluminense*) at the national level in favor of regional interests (Pereira de Melo and Considera 1986: 120–21). Yet it was the political divisions outlined above that kept the state from expressing or defending its development concerns. Even when Guanabara and Rio de Janeiro were united in 1975, no significant attempt was made on the part of state government to promote industrial investment in either the metropolitan or the interior regions. For example, Rio's politicians proved weak even when the possibilities emerged during the 1970s to extract significant royalties from federal oil refining activities in the poor Duque de Caxias region.[9]

9. In this case, powerful conservative groups in the northeastern states were able to muffle the divided *fluminenses* and gain their own refineries despite the fact that Rio de Janeiro had more petroleum reserves than the northeast (author interview with Carlos Alberto Monteiro Rego, economic development director, IPLAN-Rio, former chemical engineer for IPEA, June 5, 1996, Rio de Janeiro).

During and after the transition to democracy, this legacy of populist government continued. Having had his political rights restored in 1979, Leonel Brizola, a former governor of Rio Grande do Sul and federal deputy from Guanabara who had opposed the military coup of 1964 and directly tried to thwart it to keep his brother-in-law, João Goulart, in office, returned from exile to Rio de Janeiro. Like Chagas Freitas, Brizola faced rival leaders within his party, the PTB, which reemerged after an electoral reform permitted a multiparty system in 1979. Challenged by two of Getúlio Vargas's relatives, Lutero and Ivete Vargas, for command of the PTB, Brizola created his own party, the Partido Democrático Trabalhista (Democratic Worker Party, PDT) in 1980.[10]

While the PDT was modeled on a unique mixture of European social democracy and Getúlio Vargas's labor corporatism, in reality it was a personal vehicle for its leader's candidacy to Rio's governorship and, later, for successive presidential campaigns in the 1980s and 1990s and his return to the governorship of Rio in 1990. The PDT expanded its following in states outside of Rio, particularly Rio Grande do Sul and Paraná, but it remained a highly top-down party, dominated by Brizola. As a personalist party of increasing national stature, the PDT pursued pragmatic political interests and avoided programmatic concerns.

Brizolismo added yet another current to the widest array of competing political interests in any state of Brazil. In the 1982 elections for governor, the first direct elections since the 1964 coup, Brizola's PDT competed against the *chaguistas* represented by federal deputy Miro Teixeira and reassembled within a new party created by Chagas Freitas, the Partido Popular (Popular Party, PP).[11] The *amaralistas* were led by Niteroi mayor Wellington Moreira Franco who affiliated himself initially with the Partido Democrático Social (PDS) (formerly the ARENA) but later joined the successor of the MDB, the Partido do Movimento Democrático Brasileiro (Party of the Brazilian Democratic Movement, PMDB). Others opposed to Brizola included Ivete Vargas and Sandra Cavalcanti of the PTB and former ARENA members in the PDS. Without recourse to their command of the state electoral college, the *chaguista* hold on power eroded precipitously. Under the military's requirement in the 1982 elections that voters could not cross party lines but would have to elect candidates from the same party on their ballot, Brizola's popularity led him to a victory based on 34.2 percent of the vote, just ahead of Moreira Franco (30.6 percent), and

10. The formation of the PDT and the conflicts within the PTB that led up to it are described by former Brizola adviser and federal deputy José Talarico in a series of interviews. See Freire (1998: chap. 6).

11. Teixeira, due in part to a falling out with Chagas Freitas, would lead the *chaguista* wing of the PMDB in the 1982 gubernatorial race.

Miro Teixeira (21.5 percent).[12] With the victory, Rio became the only state in Brazil to be run by an opposition party other than the PMDB in 1982.

The advent of Brizola's government (1983–87) was a surprise to the *chaguistas*, who found themselves out of power. Nevertheless, Brizola represented a continuation in populist government. First, his margin of victory was smaller than those of other opposition governors such as Tancredo Neves in Minas Gerais and Franco Montoro in São Paulo, who both captured close to 50 percent of the vote in their states. Brizola's base was comparatively flimsy, so reinforcing it became the top political priority of the new governor. Second, Brizola could not rely on ideology to buttress his base. Following the election, many of the intellectuals and leftists that had supported Brizola abandoned the PDT due to widespread disillusionment with the party's personalism. Under these conditions, Brizola remained encircled by opposition, just as Chagas Freitas had been (Soares 1984: chap. 8).

Once the transition to civilian rule was completed nationally, the evolution of the party system gave Rio's leadership further incentives to cultivate personal followings based on populism and clientelism. First, the transition to democracy in Brazil led to a proliferation of parties. In Rio this expansion of parties was diverse ideologically and organizationally (Schmitt 1997). Rival politicians within the PMDB, which contained ex-*chaguistas* and ex-*amaralistas*, and politicians with ties to new parties such as the Party of Brazilian Social Democracy (PSDB) and the emerging leftist Workers' Party (PT) of Luiz Inácio "Lula" da Silva, gave Brizola and his successors plenty of cause to use clientelistic exchange to bolster his political base (Gay 1988). Second, the ability of politicians to switch parties and the weakness of party labels created additional incentives for political leaders to forge populist-clientelistic coalitions that were highly unstable and contributed to elite conflict. Schmitt (1997: 148) reports that forty-three distinct party organizations competed in the four major state races held between 1982 and 1994. As an indicator of the personalism undergirding these organizations, twenty-one of them disappeared from the political stage after disputing one contest. Although these tendencies

12. Unlike the new center-right governors elected in 1982 in São Paulo (Franco Montoro) and Minas Gerais (Tancredo Neves), Brizola was a denizen of the old Brazilian left who, as a vocal opponent of military rule, was forced into exile. Exile moderated Brizola, turning him away from the militant nationalism that he entertained in the 1960s, to a more sedate form of populism in the 1980s (Skidmore 1988: 218–20 and 233–35). Nevertheless, his return to Brazilian politics in 1982 was not welcomed by segments of the military government who still saw him as a threat to the state. Some members of the military's intelligence community conspired to rig the vote-counting of the 1982 gubernatorial elections in Rio de Janeiro. The scheme failed when the Regional Electoral Tribunal intervened, allowing for a recount that gave Brizola the victory. For useful assessments of the 1982 election, see Souza, Lima Júnior, and Figueiredo (1985) and Soares and Silva (1985).

of ephemeral populist-clientelist alliances and party fragmentation were bolstered by the transition to democracy throughout Brazil (Hagopian 1992; Mainwaring 1993), they also represented patterns that had been part of the political landscape in Rio de Janeiro for decades. Unlike the cohesion that existed among the *mineiro* political oligarchy, the factional nature of populist-clientelist alliances in Rio would provide few incentives for delegative management of industrial policy.

The Failures of Industrial Policy-Making in Rio de Janeiro

Given deeply rooted traditions of populist government in state politics and an overarching high level of elite conflict, Rio's development policy was either neglected or manipulated for political purposes. The latter was possible only through the concentration of political control over development agencies that hindered any attempt to forge the horizontal ties that were crucial to industrial policy-making in Minas Gerais and Asturias. Apart from being subservient to the whims of the state's *chefes políticos*, Rio's agencies developed intense rivalries. The persistence of these problems acted against repeated attempts by political technocrats to define a coherent set of policies and a division of labor within the state's economic bureaucracy. The result was a nonfunctional form of horizontal embeddedness with few interagency contacts and poor relations with private firms.

Centralization emerged directly from the political logic of populist government. The *chaguistas* during the 1970s and the *brizolistas* during the 1980s and early 1990s attempted to control their clients and weaken their rivals by centralizing the administration of social and economic policy (Diniz 1982: 114–15; Gondim 1986; Gay 1988: 98). In industrial policy the most important example is the experience of the Companhia de Desenvolvimento Industrial of Rio de Janeiro (Company of Industrial Development, CODIN).[13]

CODIN was created in 1969 to promote industrial growth in the state of Rio.[14] During the 1970s, the organization's tasks were limited to creat-

13. CODIN was originally known as the Companhia de Distritos Industriais (Company of Industrial Districts—CODIN). In 1982 the name was changed to the Company of Industrial Development (CODIN).

14. Before 1975, Guanabara maintained the Companhia Progresso do Estado da Guanabara (Company for the Progress of the State of Guanabara—COPEG) as its main agent for industrial promotion. The old state of Rio de Janeiro had the CODERJ, a similar agency in function to the COPEG. After 1975, CODIN became the sole agency with the responsibility of managing and promoting industrial investment in Rio's industrial districts. See CODIN (1987).

ing and selling industrial districts around poor municipalities in the interior of the state. Its official concerns were promoting the industrial deconcentration of the metropolitan area of Rio and developing the interior regions (CODIN 1987: 9). To achieve these ends, CODIN was staffed by professionals, but in reality was run by political appointees who manipulated the agency's resources for political purposes and allowed the technocratic staff's skills to erode. As a result, CODIN remained unprepared to deal with the state's ongoing economic problems.

During its first few years of operation, CODIN sold none of its properties. During the late 1970s and early 1980s, the few firms that did purchase in the industrial districts at subsidized prices failed to develop their operations. In practice, the state government led by the *chaguistas* employed CODIN to sell off large parcels of land at artificially low rates to political supporters but the agency provided no follow-up.[15] Chagas Freitas required direct and centralized control over the state's development agencies.[16] Political appointees loyal to Chagas Freitas employed the agency as part of their campaigns to cultivate clientelistic bases of support for the *chefe político.*

Despite repeated attempts by the agency's staff and some state politicians to remake CODIN into a full-fledged industrial development agency following the INDI model, the industrial development company remained an industrial districts company throughout the 1980s.[17] The lack of a state-level industrial policy under Brizola's government kept the agency in its old, useless rut (CODIN 1987: 16). The first Brizola government designed an "industrial policy" meant to shift small and medium-sized firms operating in the informal market to the formal market (Estado do Rio de Janeiro 1983: 109). But the state government's fiscal incentives and financial programs failed to attract enough economic activity to CODIN's industrial districts to make them viable. The agency's budget was also cut drastically from 8.6 percent of the 1982 state budget (the highest amount ever allotted to the agency) to .008 percent in 1987 (CODIN 1987: 31). The skill levels of CODIN's staff soon eroded and became outdated.[18] Stripped of resources, burdened by staff

15. Based on author interviews with CODIN officials, May 1996, Rio de Janeiro.

16. This is apparent in the Chagas Freitas government's only development plan. See Estado do Rio de Janeiro (1979: 3–5).

17. One independent study done in the early 1980s concluded that the state of Rio de Janeiro lacked adequate public agencies for promoting industrial investment. The study specifically contrasted Rio's poor performance with the experience of Minas Gerais. See Magalhães (1983: 38).

18. For example, agency staff working on developing Rio's petrochemical growth pole could not read English, a requirement for simply keeping up with the sector's major jour-

members who were not even conversant with the essential concepts of their tasks, and generally aimless, CODIN was helpless to attract firm after firm that considered Rio de Janeiro and then moved on to São Paulo, Minas, or other states.

CODIN's task became more complex during the early 1980s after the creation of a rival: the Agência de Desenvolvimento do Rio (Development Agency of Rio, AD-Rio), a public-private mixed society that, like CODIN, fell under the command of the Secretariat of Industry and Commerce but unlike CODIN was administered by local business groups that favored the creation of a second development agency. While AD-Rio was designed to promote industrial investment in the state, it uselessly duplicated CODIN's functions and even competed with the industrial districts company for fiscal resources and recruits.[19] The agencies communicated infrequently and seldom collaborated on the same projects. Moreover, AD-Rio was weakened by incompetent leadership and poor resources. Brizola who, as a populist, was no friend of Rio's business associations and had some disdain for technocracy, gutted the public staff of the agency.

Brizola's successor as governor in 1987, Moreira Franco of the PMDB, appointed political cronies to oversee AD-Rio. Moreira Franco shared with his predecessor some distrust of technocrats. The governor was fond of saying, *"desenvolvimento econômico não precisa de Ph.D."* ("economic development does not require a Ph.D."). One of these non-Ph.D. types was José Augusto Asunção Britto, who had strong links to the president of the Federação das Indústrias do Estado do Rio de Janeiro (Federation of Industries of the State of Rio de Janeiro, FIRJAN). Under Britto's administration, AD-Rio became dominated by FIRJAN. Soon afterwards, technocrats abandoned the agency to find employment in the private sector, leaving AD-Rio to function as a propaganda wing of the business association.

The mismanagement at CODIN and AD-Rio was reflected in Rio de Janeiro's development bank (BDRIO), which remained underfunded throughout the 1980s. It also suffered from the same duplication of effort that confounded CODIN and AD-Rio. Given the poor state of human resources at the agencies and the directionless pattern of the state's indus-

---

nal, *Chemical Engineering.* Author interview with Carlos Alberto Monteiro Rego, Economic Development Director, IPLAN-Rio (Institute of Planning, Municipality of Rio de Janeiro), former chemical engineer for IPEA, June 5, 1996, Rio de Janeiro.

19. Author interview with Carlos Alberto Monteiro Rego, Economic Development Director, IPLAN-Rio, June 5, 1996, Rio de Janeiro. Also author interviews with CODIN managers, July 1999.

trial policy, BDRIO could not coordinate a strategy with the development agencies and it could not produce a sustained effort to promote the development of local industry. Although Brizola's administration spoke of creating and strengthening a BDRIO as a true development agency (for instance, Estado do Rio de Janeiro 1983), Moreira Franco hardly gave a second thought to developing BDRIO (Estado do Rio de Janeiro 1987).

The *political use* of the agencies, and particularly CODIN, was more important. Moreira Franco became interested in using CODIN as another mechanism of populist politics. Like his predecessor (and his successor as governor, Brizola), Moreira Franco viewed CODIN as simply an organization that sold land, not a development agency.[20] Motivated more by a desire to use industrial policy to garner support in areas heavily disputed by the *brizolistas*, Moreira Franco attempted to use CODIN's industrial districts as part of a populist campaign to capture the votes of informal sector workers.[21]

Between 1986 and 1990, the state government created additional industrial districts and moved to sell them off. Moreira Franco's major projects were industrial districts for fashion design, the production of optical equipment, footwear, and computers. All were smashing failures. The fashion firms needed capital, something well beyond the domain of the CODIN. The lense- and frame-producing firms of the optical district were largely small artesanal operations and, like the fashion designers, lacked capital. The footwear firms were poor, artesanal, and operated primarily in the informal sector. Not only did they not have the money to transport their machinery to the site of the industrial district, but they

20. Author interview with former CODIN president during the Moreira Franco and second Brizola governments, Jorge Fernandes da Cunha Filho, August 2, 1999, Rio de Janeiro. The next few observations are also based on this interview as well as a series done earlier at CODIN in June and July 1996 and with an outside observer, Carlos Alberto Monteiro Rego, director of economic development, Institute of Planning of Rio de Janeiro, June 5, 1996, Rio de Janeiro.

21. No doubt Moreira Franco was motivated by the success that Brizola had with a similar experiment in social policy. During his first term, Brizola had achieved national attention for the creation of prefabricated schools and community centers (Centros Integrados de Educação Popular, or Integrated Centers of Popular Education) known as CIEPs. The CIEPs would provide basic meals, showers, and other amenities to Rio's poorest children. The idea strengthened the governor's support among the mass of uneducated poor in Rio de Janeiro's interior regions and in the metropolitan *favelas* (shantytowns). Whether the CIEPs were actually completed was not important for Brizola's politics; the governor would have their votes nonetheless (Gay 1988). Brizola built 500 CIEPs during his governorships, but fewer than half were eventually completed (*Veja*, March and April 1993). Despite that, Brizola was overwhelmingly supported in the governor's elections of 1990 and the presidential elections of 1994 by Rio de Janeiro's poorest. Moreira Franco and Britto would take a page from Brizola's populist strategies in fashioning industrial policy.

feared that the state would prosecute them for working without a license if they were to set up shop in the government's industrial districts. The computer growth pole was the greatest flop. The policy depended upon the continuity of the national informatics law that protected domestic producers. When the Collor administration eliminated the policy in 1990, just two years after the inauguration of the industrial district, the project collapsed.

CODIN officials claimed, inexplicably, that they had compiled a history of success by selling off these industrial districts to firms. But a second look would show that although the land had been sold (again, at subsidized prices), no new industrial activity had been initiated in these areas. As one observer claimed: "The state government (through CODIN) was subsidizing land speculation, not industrial development."[22] In all of these cases, policy was formulated with the primary goal of extending the governor's populist and clientelistic base. By exerting direct, top-down control over the agency and encouraging its politicization and that of rivals such as AD-Rio, successive state governments replaced the economic rationale for industrial policy with the primacy of politics.

Centralization of political control also had the effect of undercutting the flow of information within CODIN and between the agency and the industrial districts and firms. Current CODIN employees who worked for the agency during the 1980s report that politically appointed administrators in the Secretariats of Planning and Industry and Commerce seldom communicated with CODIN's staff during the four gubernatorial administrations of Chagas, Brizola (two terms), or Moreira Franco.[23] Directives were often implemented in an ad hoc and opportunistic manner that denied the importance of planning.[24] Centralized control also hindered the creation of continuous communicative links with state and municipal utility companies and AD-Rio. As a result, the horizontal ties that connected COIND, INDI, BDMG, CDI, and CEMIG in Minas Gerais failed to emerge in Rio.

22. Author interviews at CODIN, May 1996, Rio de Janeiro. Also, author interviews with Paulo Peregrino, marketing chief, CODIN, July 20, 1999, Rio de Janeiro; and Jorge Fernandes da Cunha Filho, ex-CODIN president, August 2, 1999, Rio de Janeiro.

23. Author interviews with CODIN staff, May 1996, Rio de Janeiro, and interview with former presidents of CODIN, Jorge Fernandes da Cunha Filho and Marco Antonio de Araujo Lima, president of CODIN during the Marcello Alencar government, June 5, 1996, Rio de Janeiro.

24. Gondim (1986) finds that the same was true in the administration of the Foundation for the Development of the Metropolitan Region of Rio de Janeiro (FUNDREM), a municipal and regional planning agency staffed by technocrats. This observation provides further proof that the problems of CODIN had political/systemic origins.

During the second Brizola government (1991–95), CODIN's activities were subsumed by the "Plano Paraiso," an ambitious but poorly financed social project meant to create jobs and move informal sector workers into the formal sector.[25] Like Brizola's first-term industrial policy, the focus on informal small and medium-sized firms ignored the real problems of formal sector firms in industry. Brizola also rewarded political supporters in the PDT with the post of secretary of industry. The governor's third such secretary, Jorge Cordeiro Leite, had particularly ambitious political goals. Leite used the agency to support the electoral interests of family members.[26]

The legacy of Rio's industrial policy began to change only in 1994 with the election of Marcello Alencar as governor. Alencar was a former member of Brizola's PDT and a populist in the *brizolista* tradition who switched to the PSDB to advance his own career. But the new governor was also facing deteriorating economic and social conditions in the metropolitan and rural areas of Rio that could not be redressed by populism alone. Alencar's Secretary of Industry and Commerce, Renaldo César Coelho, a well-known PSDB senator, argued that the state needed professional help. Coelho took three concrete steps to restructure CODIN. First, he appointed an ex-BNDES technocrat, Marco Antonio de Araújo Lima, president of the agency. Second, Coelho added other technocrats, some from Petrobrás, the state oil company, in the upper echelon of the development agency to assist Lima. Finally, the secretary recruited dozens of young economists, engineers, and administrators from the federal university system. Within two years, CODIN's structure and activities changed from those of an industrial districts company to a development agency.

Despite these improvements, the role of CODIN in forging an industrial policy in Rio continued to be very limited by politics. First, the political motivations behind Alencar and Coelho's support were ephemeral. Alencar and Coelho were concerned chiefly with reversing the bad press created by Rio's social problems. Their thinking was that a flashy, symbolic improvement in the state's economic prospects would help separate them in the minds of *fluminense* voters from what were generally perceived to be the economically disastrous policies of

25. Details on the "Plano Paraiso" are scarce due to the inconsistent implementation of the program. My survey of the plan's documents found no reference to CODIN, which continued to be the only bona fide industrial policy agency in the state. The agency is not even mentioned in the only official statement on industrial policy during the second Brizola government (this statement remains unpublished). See Secretaria de Estado de Indústria, Comércio, Ciência e Tecnologia (1991).

26. Author interviews at CODIN, 1999, Rio de Janeiro.

Brizola.[27] By continuing the primacy of the political in CODIN's functions, however, the new administration failed to sufficiently reorganize Rio's developmental apparatus.

Alencar's successor in 1999, Anthony Garotinho (PDT), argued that CODIN should be transformed into a true development agency capable of providing financial and technical services to firms. Yet current advisors to the secretary of industry admit that the continued centralization of functions in an agency such as CODIN would deepen the incentives politicians and political technocrats have for manipulating the agency's resources.[28] In mid-1999, Garotinho proposed the creation of Regional Development Agencies in select municipalities, but the governor also insisted that his party, the PDT, directly administer these agencies. The plan does not envision any link to CODIN.

CODIN continues as a marketing arm of the Rio state government with almost no practical functions in enhancing productivity or promoting new investment. Part of the agency's functions now include the composition of studies for firm projects that apply for fiscal incentive funds under the Fundo de Desenvolvimento Econômico e Social (FUNDES). CODIN, however, plays no role in actually deciding which projects should be funded or in coordinating funding with other industrial policies involving infrastructure, labor training, and information. As a result, even agency personnel note that CODIN's activities are seen by businesses as limited due to the agency's inability to work on all aspects of proposed projects and its inability to escape from the vagaries of political turnover and manipulation.[29]

THE POLITICIZATION OF "ENDOGENOUS DEVELOPMENT": INDUSTRIAL POLICY IN ANDALUSIA

Andalusia is the largest of the Spanish regions and, while it is not the least developed, it is one of the least industrialized in Spain. Notwithstanding its status as a "poor region," Andalusia's political leadership during and after the transition to democracy argued that it could redress

27. Author interview with Marco Antonio de Araújo Lima, president of CODIN during the Marcello Alencar government, June 5, 1996, Rio de Janeiro.

28. Author interview with Jorge Fernandes da Cunha Filho, chief of staff, Secretariat of State for Economic Development and Tourism, Government of the State of Rio de Janeiro, August 2, 1999, Rio de Janeiro; and CODIN interviews, June-July 1996 and July 1999.

29. Author interviews at CODIN, June-July 1996 and July 1999. This view was verified by Charles Rossi, chief of the Department of Industrial Promotion and New Investments, FIRJAN, May 29, 1996, Rio de Janeiro.

its economic backwardness. Their reasoning, however, was couched in a contentious political context in which rival socialist, center-right, and leftist parties competed for control over the regional government. The formula for gaining power at that time was populist. In 1982, the PSOE succeeded in using populism to gain an absolute majority in the regional parliament. While they would control the regional government through the remainder of the century, opposition parties, labor unrest sparked by rising unemployment, and the antagonism of Andalusia's most powerful business association continually threatened Socialist rule. PSOE leaders responded to these challenges through the same populist tactics that were already a part of the regional political landscape. Consequently, PSOE leaders centralized their control over the region's development agencies and manipulated their resources and staff to buttress the party's political base. The result was a hierarchical-functional horizontal embeddedness in which finance and other goods were distributed by industrial policy agencies that had dwindling command over the process or goals of strategic planning. Without plan-oriented or project-oriented horizontal embeddedness, development agencies were powerless to design and follow a coherent development mission. The logic of populist government guided industrial policy with costly outcomes.

The Disarticulation of Andalusian Industrialization

For decades Andalusia was the face of the "other Spain"—an underdeveloped, underindustrialized agricultural and "traditional" society. Even when it grew, it did not develop. Between 1964 and 1973, the years of the so-called Spanish miracle, Andalusia experienced impressive rates of industrial growth (over 8 percent per year). The splendid numbers, however, hid severe costs. Over 265,200 jobs were lost during the "Spanish miracle" in Andalusia. Rapid modernization of the region's economy during this period wiped out 60 percent of all artesanal employment, previously one of the principal sources of economic activity.[30] Despite the emergence of large chemical, ceramic, cement, and paper sectors, the "Spanish miracle" did not elevate the importance of Andalusian industry as an alternative source of employment. The region's industrial firms were unproductive and operated in basic and raw materials that supplied more advanced industries located beyond the borders of Andalusia.

30. Certain artesanal sectors weathered the crisis well, surviving into the 1990s as moderately productive. This was the experience of marble in Macael, the food processing industry in Sierra de Huelva, leather goods in Ubrique, and furniture and footwear in Valverde del Camino.

Production was also concentrated in a small number of large manufacturers. In 1975, 45 firms represented 72.5 percent of the region's industrial investment (Delgado Cabeza 1993: 88). The most advanced of these firms operated as enclaves, furnishing basic chemicals and paper goods to producers in the core economies of Spain. The weakness of Andalusian industry was also reflected in the region's dependency on imported industrial, intermediate goods. Over 36 percent of Andalusia's demand was satisfied by suppliers outside the region and 78 percent of these imports were industrial intermediates (Caravaca Barroso 1995: 389). The region's distance from Spain's major markets in Madrid and Catalonia and its inadequate infrastructure reinforced the worst aspects of this poorly articulated, inflexible pattern of industrialization.

Given Andalusia's disarticulated productive structure, the region was to suffer extensively from the economic adjustments of the 1980s. The disruption of the national market for raw materials and intermediate goods slowed the growth of Andalusian industry. Only six of the region's twenty-five major industrial sectors grew above the national average during the decade. The contraction in production led to increased unemployment. While Catalonia shaved 11.6 percent of its employment, Andalusia lost over 17 percent, about 341,900 jobs (Delgado Cabeza 1993: 92). By 1985, Andalusia faced an unemployment rate over 30 percent, the highest in Spain and higher than any Western European region. Worse still, the decade saw no major changes in the inflexible composition of Andalusian industry. The region remained greatly dependent upon the same unproductive basic industries that dominated Andalusian development during the "Spanish miracle" years. The pattern of industrial investment in Andalusia between 1985 and 1990 showed no signs of significant diversification.[31] During this time, only six sectors accounted for 66 percent of total accumulated investment in the region (Pajuelo Gallego and Villena Peña 1993: 369).[32] The rest of Andalusia's firms remained mostly unproductive small firms. Overall, Andalusia contin-

31. The growth of the region's key sectors exceeded the national average during this time (5.3 percent for Andalusia, 4.7 percent for Spain as a whole). However, this rate of growth was inadequate to increase overall employment for the region's large population (17 percent of Spain's total population) and it did not address the unproductive nature of Andalusian firms. See José Ruiz Navarro, "Economía, tecnología, y competitividad," editorial in El País, February 28, 1991.

32. After some improvement in the regional investment rate between 1985 and 1989, the performance of this new investment did not weather the recession of the early 1990s well. Industrial production fell 5 percent between 1990–91 alone, and industrial employment plummeted by 34,000 jobs. The effect was felt on Andalusia's national percentage of industrial production, which fell to 8.4 percent, the lowest in the region's history.

ued to be underindustrialized. While industry composed over 24 percent and agriculture 4.5 percent of Spain's GDP, industry represented 16 percent and agriculture 9 percent of Andalusia's GDP in 1991 (Caravaca Barroso 1995: 389).

Despite the obstacles to the region's development, the national government poured significant resources into promoting Andalusia's industries during the authoritarian and democratic periods alike. Through the Poles of Development and other regional incentive schemes in operation during the 1970s, the Spanish government promoted the creation of industrial enclaves: shipbuilding in the port of Cádiz, basic chemicals in Huelva, and an auto assembly industry in Linares. These poles were dominated by large firms, supported by national subsidies and protection, and surrounded by, but unconnected to, the vestiges of decaying artesanal and unproductive small manufacturing and agriculture (Pajuelo Gallego and Villena Peña 1993). Their development and growth depended upon the performance of the national economy and the export sector. The commercial growth of these large firm sectors, however, did little to promote the regional economy. Andalusia's demand for imported manufactured goods offset the region's export growth, creating a perennial trade deficit. The agglomerated poles promoted by the national government failed to generate much new employment while they added considerably to the region's pollution. As a whole, the region's poles became symbols of unsuccessful national industrial policy and Andalusian underdevelopment (Barzelay and O'Kean 1989).

The performance of national industrial policy under democratic leadership, and particularly under the Socialists, was not successful in improving Andalusia's economic problems. The ZUR in Andalusia was concentrated in the shipbuilding enclave of Cádiz, which only succeeded in reducing its production and employment, with few positive secondary effects on the regional economy. The Andalusian SODI, SODIAN, a predecessor program to the Socialists' ZURs, also showed modest results. Established in 1978, SODIAN provided finance to 161 firms through 1986. After 1983, however, the society's capital shrank due to fiscal cuts. Its affiliated firms continually lost money, further justifying national efforts to cut back SODIAN's activities. By 1990, SODIAN could boast of projects in 77 firms, but its total financial transactions in these firms represented only $7 million (Martín Rodríguez and Martín Mesa 1993: 491).

Nevertheless, Socialist policy did not fail to finance the building of Andalusia's own public sector for industrial promotion. As in Asturias, all of Andalusia was classified as an Economic Promotion Zone (ZPE). Andalusia eventually edged out Asturias as the top Spanish region in receipt of EU structural funding. Between 1986 and 1994, over 40 percent of EU cohesion funds went to Andalusia.[33] Most of these monies were spent on infrastructural projects. But extensive EU financing did not assure that regional industrial policy would be implemented as well as it was in Asturias. Performance depended on the building of a combination of political and institutional associations at the subnational level.

The Populist Bases of Industrial Policy in Andalusia

The regional government that negotiated the first steps of Andalusian autonomy proved to be a divided source of support for a more aggressive regional industrial policy.[34] Although political technocrats in the Chancellery of Economy and the Instituto de Promoción Industrial de Andalucía (Andalusian Institute of Industrial Promotion, IPIA), which was created in 1983, attempted to redress the underdevelopment of the region by allocating more resources to the economic bureaucracy, politicians preferred the manipulation of these resources to prop up their emerging political bases.

The Andalusian political leadership that emerged from the pre-autonomy process did not make technocratic solutions to the region's economic problems a priority. In part this was due to the peculiar way in which Andalusian politicians viewed the region's autonomy and its political significance. Like Asturian autonomy, Andalusian autonomy was based on weak foundations. It lacked the distinctive cultural and linguistic components of the autonomy arguments of the Basque Country and Catalonia. The latter two could refer to a common history of political oppression under Franco that Andalusians did not know. These same factors, which created a weak case for Andalusian nationalism, also presented regional politicians with strong reasons to articulate an alternative common experience that would link Andalusians in this, Spain's largest region, around a unified political project. Combating underdevelopment became the unifying theme of the new political message, but the economic rationale for it would be overshadowed by political and strategic exigencies.

During the first regional elections of the democratic transition in 1977, the Partido Socialista de Andalucía (Andalusian Socialist Party, PSA), a party that maintained itself independent of the more powerful PSOE,

---

33. El País, November 30, 1987, and March 31, 1990.
34. The following is based heavily upon the extensive study of the IPIA and the Andalusian industrial policy system of the early 1980s in Barzelay and O'Kean (1989) and one published later by Marquez Guerrero (1997).

experienced tremendous electoral success with its campaign against "economic oppression." Following the example of nationalist parties in Catalonia and the Basque Country, the PSA argued that Andalusians were commonly oppressed. Unlike the Catalonians or the Basque, whose oppression had historical, ethnic, and linguistic components, however, Andalusians' source of oppression was economic. Accordingly the PSA articulated a nationalist message that highlighted the exploitative center-periphery relations between Madrid, Catalonia, and the Basque Country (the economic core) on the one hand, and the peripheral Andalusian region on the other. PSA leaders argued that the core economies of Spain lived off of the riches of the region without redistributing the industrial wealth created by Andalusia's raw materials. With arguments such as these, the PSA stole significant levels of leftist support away from the PSOE's base. In the 1977 regional elections the PSOE won but only by the barest of margins over the UCD: 33,000 votes. In the parliamentary elections of 1979, the PSA's electoral performance improved markedly at the expense of the PSOE, which kept its lead over the UCD but, again, it remained small (50,000 votes). These events jolted the PSOE's leadership to develop a response or face a declining electoral base in the birthplace of the new PSOE.

Rafael Escudero, a rising star within the Andalusian PSOE, provided a response by adopting the PSA's message and mixing in a populist style that stood well with Communists and Socialists. Partly as a result of these efforts, the Andalusian PSOE soon gained an absolute majority in the regional legislature in the October 1982 elections. Despite the new dominant position of the regional PSOE, Escudero did not abandon populist nationalism for a rational, bureaucratic model of addressing the region's economic problems. Rather, Escudero skillfully manipulated the symbols of underdevelopment and "economic oppression" to demand additional autonomy for Andalusia and expand his own political base within the PSOE. Since populism had already become the dominant political method for gaining and keeping political power, the Socialists were loath to change direction.

Political technocrats in Escudero's government were among the chief beneficiaries of this campaign. Julio Rodríguez, a former economist for the Bank of Spain and Andalusia's first autonomous Chancellor of the Economy, used these arguments to empower the IPIA as the chief development agency of the region. Rodríguez advocated increases in the agency's annual budget and negotiated the provision of commercial credit lines with the powerful Cajas de Ahorros (savings banks). With access to credit, Rodríguez reasoned, the IPIA could directly finance small firms in sectors that its specialists would target. Additionally, the regional government developed its own "regional INI"—a holding company called the Sociedad para la Promoción y Reconversión Económica de Andalucía (Andalusian Economic Promotion and Reconversion Society, SOPREA).

Under Rodríguez's protection, IPIA and SOPREA recruited professional economists, administrators, and engineers and cultivated ties with consulting firms and banks as if it were a private agency. IPIA also created regional offices in Andalusia's seven provinces that acted as contact nodes with the agency's client firms. At first the system worked well, supplying information, inducing multifirm cooperation, and providing modest finance from 1983 through 1985. IPIA's Achilles heel, however, was its arms-length ties with Escudero and the latter's penchant for populism.

Rodríguez and IPIA's first director general, Ricardo Sánchez de la Morena, saw Escudero's support as essential. Yet maintaining it would not be easy. Unlike Asturias, Andalusia was granted access to the "fast track" to regional autonomy. While talk of "economic oppression" could be useful for currying the support of the region's voters, Andalusia faced fewer constraints on its access to national resources, and therefore, PSOE leaders felt less pressure to employ such arguments to *expand* the powers of the statute of autonomy.

Although the reasons to create the IFR and its sister agencies were reinforced *ex ante* by the need to build Asturian autonomy, in Andalusia, "fast track" autonomy minimized similar *ex ante* concerns. IPIA, and not the regional political elite, became most responsible for justifying further expansion of the development agency's resources and agenda (Marquez Guerrero 1997: 113). The IPIA system depended upon the regional president's budget and PSOE support was seen as crucial for extracting resources from Madrid. Neither could be accomplished without Escudero's backing. In order to solicit it, Rodríguez and Morena had IPIA articulate a policy of "endogenous development." The term evoked a distinction with the "exogenous development" historically associated in Andalusia with the export-oriented chemical sector in Huelva, the very symbol of the region's underdevelopment. The new thinking behind the new terminology directed IPIA to develop Andalusia's nascent sectors and raw materials in ways that would create external economies *within* the region. Endogenous development argued that Andalusia would develop if it could only unlock its underutilized resources. The real purpose of the new thinking, however, was to construct a rhetorical defense against the common accusations leveled by the region's politicians that IPIA really worked on behalf of Andalusia's dominant, enclave sectors. In practice, the argument sacrificed the agency's independence by surrendering the principles first conceived by its technocratic leadership to the economic nationalism and populism championed by Escudero and the regional PSOE. This concession would steadily erode IPIA's technocratic capacities and that of its successors.

IPIA's dependency on the PSOE's reluctant political support was exacerbated by the fact that the agency was unable to cultivate horizontal associations with other agencies or organized societal or economic actors in the region. SOPREA remained a dependency of IPIA, just as vulnerable to political intervention as the mother agency itself. The only noteworthy organization that might have supplied an alternative base of support was the Confederación de Empresários de Andalucía (Confederation of Andalusian Business, CEA), Andalusia's chief entrepreneurial association. Although labor organizations in the enclave economies such as the Cádiz shipbuilding industry and the Linares automobile industry were relatively strong, outside of these sectors the region's anemic industrial base limited the capacity of unionism. Basing political support on enclave-sector labor, however, was a limited option as that would undercut the IPIA's claim to be the region's chief articulator of "endogenous development." Garnering CEA's support, however, would generate other difficulties.

The CEA emerged from the ashes of Franquist state corporatism at about the same time that Andalusian autonomy was first created. In its earliest state, CEA was in no position to provide IPIA with significant amounts of political leverage. The association's members were primarily the very same small and medium-sized firms largely ignored by national and regional industrial policy.[35] Moreover, its leadership was suspicious of the development agency. Key to CEA's emerging political power in Andalusia was its capacity to represent and channel regional business interests. CEA sought to be the region's chief articulator of business groups and it saw IPIA as a competitor in this regard. Escudero, for his part, only increased the CEA leadership's sense of encirclement by refusing to negotiate with the business association as the exclusive representative of Andalusian firms. According to its own practices, IPIA *was* a rival to the CEA. The IPIA initiated its sectoral policies by cultivating relations with local authorities and firms and then defending these interests before other public agencies and private sector representatives such as CEA (Marquez Guerrero 1997: 116–17). Antagonistic relations between IPIA

---

35. Among the key representatives of smaller firms inside CEA was the association's president, Manuel Otero Luna, who also acted as the president of the Confederación Española de Pequeños y Medianos Empresarios (Spanish Confederation of Small and Medium-Sized Firms, CEPYME).

and CEA were also reflected in CEA's opposition to PSOE, which the business association campaigned intensively against during the crucial election of 1982.

Through the mid-1980s, Andalusia's industrial policy bureaucracy remained limited in its capacity to cultivate political support. The regional presidency, IPIA and the regional political technocracy, and the CEA maintained arms-length relations that failed to cultivate any broad support for economic policy. Under accusations from his own party that he had engaged in corrupt practices, Escudero soon resigned, opening the door to José Rodríguez de la Borbolla, another Socialist who was hesitant to embrace the rational, bureaucratic model of problem-solving advocated by IPIA and the Chancellery of Economy. Faced with significant levels of conflict with the CEA, nationalists who retained control of the municipal government of Seville, and increasing labor union strife, Rodríguez de la Borbolla became increasingly reliant on the use of ambitious industrialization projects, particularly those involving large investments by foreign firms, to protect his Socialist political base of workers.

Yet the increasing tendency of the Andalusian government to focus its resources on large and multinational firms exacerbated already frayed relations with CEA. Despite the signing of a number of political pacts between the regional government and the CEA during 1984 and 1985, the Andalusian government maintained poor relations with the business association, which repeatedly mounted criticisms and political opposition to Rodríguez de la Borbolla's policies.[36] In 1986, CEA vice president José Bohórquez argued that the Andalusian government was "in a majority of cases a wall of inefficiency and incompetence in public administration."[37] Relations remained poor until early 1990 when the regional government succeeded in establishing a number of accords with CEA. The pacts promised Andalusian business public support during Expo 1992 (the World's Fair in Seville) and resources for research and training. CEA, however, remained suspicious of the Andalusian government's industrial policy, because the large multinational firms the government favored were not connected to the business association. The CEA president, Manuel Otero Luna, argued that the business confederation did not value tripartite agreements and was ready to renounce official subsidies as the exclusive domain of these large firms that CEA did not represent.[38]

---

36. For example, see the criticisms voiced in *El País,* June 12, 1986.
37. See comments in *El País,* April 30, 1986.
38. See the interview with Otero Luna in *El País,* August 24, 1990.

Otero Luna's criticisms extended to Rodríguez de la Borbolla's successor, Manuel Chaves, who the CEA head accused of "ruining Andalusian firms" with his government's "passivity" in the face of financial crisis.[39] In June 1992, Chaves attempted to muster CEA's support by signing an accord that recognized the business association as the "sole representative of the Andalusian business class." Yet CEA remained critical, claiming that it questioned the "public good intentions" of the Chaves government.[40] In May 1993, the CEA and the unions signed a tripartite agreement, but the accords fell apart a few months later under CEA and union opposition to the regional government's industrial plans. In this way, the government's relations with the CEA followed a stop-and-go pattern from the mid-1980s through the 1990s.

The PSOE also faced intense opposition to its economic policies in the regional parliament. Among the most noteworthy critics of Socialist policy was Julio Anguita, the head of the Izquierda Unida Convocatoria (and the future head of the Izquierda Unida, or United Left, national party). The Alianza Popular (AP, the predecessor to the center-right Partido Popular, PP), also did not hesitate to attack the regional PSOE's large industrial policy budgets by citing dozens of cases of wasted public resources in failing firms.[41] Andalusian nationalist parties, and the Seville municipal government under nationalist control, routinely attacked the regional Socialist leadership and its industrial policy. In practice, these criticisms were intended primarily to cut into the PSOE's absolute majority in the regional parliament. Over time, such opposition had an eroding effect on the Socialist's strong grip on power. Opposition parties, particularly the PP and IU, made sizable electoral gains during the late 1980s and early 1990s, eventually breaking the PSOE's absolute majority in 1994.

Yet perhaps the most serious threat to the PSOE's grip on power came from the unions. Key Andalusian unions refused to swing support to the PSOE or the regional government. Comisiones Obreras openly rejected Rodríguez de la Borbolla's pact-making in 1989. The Andalusian PSOE's decision to follow the lead of the national party and back a "moratorium" on direct negotiations with the UGT pushed that confederation closer to CCOO's position in the region during 1989 and afterwards.[42] Yet, unlike the CEA and the PSOE's legislative critics, both UGT and

39. Otero Luna's comments were recorded in *El País*, March 27, 1992.
40. See comments by CEA officials in *El País*, April 1, 1993.
41. See comments by the national president of the AP, Antonio Hernández Mancha, in *El País*, May 2, 1988.
42. See comments by UGT and CCOO leaders in *El País*, February 23, 1989, and March 9, 1989.

CCOO believed the public investments in industry were necessary to begin a "genuine process of industrialization."[43] Such union demands confirmed for the Socialists the political wisdom in expanding the Andalusian public sector.

As the regional government became more reliant on a strong public-sector role in industrial policy, the IPIA's technocracy lost its most inspired leadership. Julio Rodríguez left the Chancellery for the presidency of the Banco Hipotecario, leaving Morena without his chief source of support within the Socialist government. The lack of political support was reflected in the IPIA's budget, which experienced no increases during 1984 and 1985, despite the region's worsening economic conditions. The few ties with firms and provincial and municipal supporters IPIA was able to cultivate in the early 1980s began to decompose. Finally, in a last-ditch attempt to save the agency, Morena proposed that IPIA be merged with SOPREA and made into a singular promoter of industry in Andalusia. Without horizontal associations and with uncertain political support, the outcome of the IPIA-SOPREA fusion—the Instituto de Fomento de Andalucía (Andalusian Institute of Promotion, IFA)—and Socialist interests in manipulating its resources to bolster labor support, would politicize the Andalusian industrial policy system to an unprecedented and costly degree.

Politicizing a Demiurge Industrial Policy in Andalusia

The Rodríguez de la Borbolla government turned to two ultimately ill-fated strategies in reshaping Andalusia's industrial policy. First, the Andalusian government created a strategy of intervention in the market that depended on escalating levels of public ownership and production. Evans (1995: 79) uses the term "demiurge role" to refer to public production, but the term also applies to the *increasing* importance of public sector ownership—a "creeping" demiurge role—in Andalusia. The expansion of the public sector's demiurge role in the region was envisioned by Andalusian leaders, and particularly PSOE politicians, as an essential element in development. Rodríguez de la Borbolla saw it as a mechanism for *creating* a new industrial structure to replace the modest and uneven one in the region.[44] Endogenous growth was replaced with an exogenous strategy that focused on the attraction of high-tech multinationals with few if any suppliers in the region (Marquez Guerrero

43. This was the nature of CCOO and UGT demands in public demonstrations between Andalusia and Madrid in early 1992 (see *El País*, February 9, 1992).

44. See comments by PSOE leaders in *El País*, October 4, 1986.

1997: 128–32).[45] National subsidies, much of which were concentrated in the Cartuja 1993 initiative, a development follow-up to the 1992 World's Fair in Seville, and the Technology Park in Málaga, expanded the IFA's resources. Big and expensive projects became the targets of the IFA's demiurge role. The agency quickly became a de facto holding company for the regional government's expanding list of public firms and joint ventures.[46] More important, in its demiurge capacity the IFA became increasingly valuable to the PSOE's political ambitions in the region.

During the IFA's first years the demiurge role was limited to joint ventures with foreign and some domestic firms. For example, in 1986, IFA, through SOPREA, formed a joint venture with Westinghouse for the production of helicopters. The IFA participated as a 40 percent owner of Aeroversa, the resulting conglomerate.[47] In a similar way, IFA expanded its joint ownership operations in aviation technology, textiles, automobiles, construction, and other sectors. The organizational apparatus of IFA and SOPREA, which fell under the Institute's administration, grew by 30 percent annually.[48] By 1993, IFA owned completely or in part 61 firms and was investing over $100 million per year in its going concerns.[49] These IFA investments, however, represented a concentration of public resources in a small number of large firms. About 99 percent of Andalusian firms, which are small and medium-sized operations, were left out of the IFA's demiurge activities.

Over time the ambitions of the Andalusian government's demiurge interests extended to firms that were politically important but economically unviable. One of the most noteworthy interventions of this type took place in August 1987 when Rodríguez de la Borbolla promised Land Rover Santana, a Japanese-owned automobile manufacturer in Linares, $100 million in subsidies over the next four years. The sizable

45. The Junta made its priorities clear when it commissioned a study from Manuel Castells and Peter Hall in the early 1990s to assess the potential for developing high-tech growth poles in the region. See Castells and Hall (1992).

46. A complete breakdown of the IFA system is not possible in this section. For a more comprehensive analysis of the structure of the IFA and its associated public firms, see Junta de Andalusia (1993) and Marquez Guerrero (1997: 117–27). The latter emphasizes the continuation of the "action plans" that focused on firm clusters in marble, ceramics, cork, olive oil, and furniture. However, most of the IFA's new programs, and its largest projects, took on a demiurge character.

47. Although the joint venture was first done through SOPREA in 1986 (for details, see El País, March 8, 1986; June 10, 1986), IFA took control of the operation when it incorporated SOPREA in 1987.

48. The estimate is based on an author interview with Miguel Rivas, advisor of studies and plans, IFA, April 11, 1996, Seville, Andalusia.

49. For more on the structure and composition of the IFA's firms, see IFA (1994). For figures on IFA's capital spending, see IFA (1994) and El País, May 12, 1992.

commitment was driven by the Socialists' interests in propping up the failing firm, which was the largest employer (with 2,718 workers) in the *comarca* of Linares, a district suffering from 30 percent unemployment.[50] Santana remained through the 1990s the critical hub of auto manufacturing in Andalusia as the only automobile producer in the region. Beyond the firm's economic significance, Santana was of immense symbolic importance to the regional government. The firm became a pillar of Rodríguez de la Borbolla's strategy to bring other Japanese investors to Andalusia. In November 1989, the regional president used the case of Suzuki-owned Santana to motivate Fujitsu to expand its installations in Málaga and to woo Mitsui to the region for the first time.[51] After 1990, Rodríguez de la Borbolla's emphasis on Japanese investment continued under his successor, Manuel Chaves. In order to bolster the region's link to the Japanese, Chaves had the IFA open and expand its office in Tokyo to attract Japanese companies to Andalusia. In 1992 and 1993, Chaves went on junkets to Japan to sell the idea of moving Japanese firms to the region. Despite deep cuts in public spending forced by an economic slowdown in 1993, the IFA began an expansive project to provide industrial infrastructure for Santana's suppliers. It was clear even to the casual observer that the Andalusians entertained the notion of making Andalusia a platform for Japanese investment in the EU.[52] The Socialists did not hesitate to make this one of the most salient aspects of their electoral campaign. The symbol of modern Japanese investors streaming into the poor Andalusian region fed widespread hopes that the PSOE could effectively rewrite the region's history of industrial backwardness.

The extraordinary intervention in the market contemplated by Andalusian leaders underscored the Socialists' model for maintaining control of the regional government. Rodríguez de la Borbolla attempted to institutionalize Escudero's older populist politics into a pact-making process called *vertebración social* (meaning "to provide a social backbone to policy") that was designed to attract the support of the region's major political and economic interests. But the model was hindered by continued conflicts with the CEA, opposition political parties of the right and left, and the region's unions.

For the regional technocracy *vertebración social* meant nothing less than more direct political control over the management of industrial

---

50. *El País*, August 2, 1987, and IEA (1995: 117).

51. *El País*, November 16, 1989.

52. This interest was voiced openly on a number of occasions during 1992 as Andalusian, and particularly Socialist, leaders attempted to use the media focus on Expo 92 to attract the attention of Japanese multinationals.

policy. The IFA's political technocracy had already been substantially weakened by the exit of Julio Rodríguez, but it received a nearly fatal hit when Ricardo Morena abandoned the system for the presidency of one of the INI's public firms, Lactaria Española, in early 1987. Afterwards political leaders consolidated their grip on the economic bureaucracy. The IFA would continue to be operated by political technocrats, but these figures would cease to have the power to shape regional industrial policy as had Rodríguez and Morena. Political interests injected themselves into Andalusian industrial policy to an unprecedented degree, leading to numerous cases of corruption and nepotism in the 1987–95 period.[53]

The weakening of the Andalusian technocracy's control over the IFA, and the super agency's lack of horizontal ties to the CEA or the unions, left the industrial policy system open to political attacks. Increasing political opposition to PSOE management of regional industrial policy created strong incentives for policy-makers to manipulate IFA to fulfill short-term political interests. The politicians on the IFA's administrative council often used agency resources to advance their own political interest, particularly concerning failing firms. As one IFA official confided to the author:

> We have a kind of noose around the necks of the technocrats here and that is the politicians. The IFA is a professional agency but it has not ceased to be an electoral weapon in regional politics. Politics has too much influence over the IFA now. The IFA sometimes supports firms in crisis, not because of technical or economic criteria, but because the politics of the situation demand IFA involvement. Clearly the IFA cannot afford to be autonomous. The IFA is not autonomous. . . . Consider that our Rector's Council is made up of people from the Consejería de Industria, Comercio y Turismo. This creates lots of cross-pressure on what we do here. I would say that four investment decisions per year are clearly shaped by political criteria. Although that seems small, these political investments for firms in crisis consume and waste a tremendous amount of the IFA's resources. (Author interview, April 1996, Seville, Andalusia)

---

53. One prominent case is that of Jaime Montaner, the chancellor of economy under Chaves. Montaner was well connected to a number of regional savings banks (Cajas de Ahorros) and often used these personal associations to extract favorable loans for business associates. The worst charges linked Montaner to a scheme that channeled kickbacks to the PSOE from financial deals involving sales of industrial plots (see *El Mundo,* April 26, 1995).

Another indicator of the politicization of the IFA was the inefficient way its accounts were managed. Already by 1989, three of the IFA's five major public firms were running heavy deficits. These problems were made worse as political interests overrode technical management of industrial policy. Vertical ties between the IFA and client firms were unable to produce sustainable and responsive economic policies because of political manipulation of the system. In this way, IFA's demiurge functions were transformed into costly gambles. This last point is made clear in the case of IFA's intervention in Santana Motors.

During the early 1990s, productivity at Suzuki's Santana plant in Linares (Jaén) lagged behind the company's other global installations. In 1991, Santana reported a loss of $50 million and productivity continued at 75 percent of Suzuki's plants in Japan. Amid rumors that Suzuki was to close the Linares plant, Manuel Chaves and IFA director, Juan Manuel Romero, traveled to Tokyo where the institute maintained an office, and heavily lobbied Suzuki's directors to keep the plant open.[54] Under intense pressure from the Linares unions, the regional government agreed in March 1993 to provide over $100 million in new, subsidized finance to Suzuki in order to avoid a salary freeze and wholesale job cuts. Despite the infusion, the firm lost $59 million in the first nine months of 1993 and nursed a debt that topped $161 million. A year after the March accords, Suzuki abandoned the agreement, claiming that it needed to eliminate 1,400 workers and procure an outside partner to provide over $317 million in capital to save Santana. In response, UGT and CCOO led a demonstration of 70,000 in Linares on February 24, 1994, to protest Suzuki's decision. The protesters soon turned their ire on Chaves, whom they depicted as an *entreguista* (turncoat). Union leaders claimed that the regional government had been duped into providing millions to Suzuki without any mechanism for leveraging the firm to act as it promised.[55] The union-led protests sparked a guarantee by Jaime Montaner, the regional chancellor of economy, that the Chaves government would not close Santana's doors. Montaner's bold statement harkened back to Escudero's populism. The guarantee was itself not backed by either the firm or the national government. Officials of the latter argued that the Andalusian government could not prevent Santana from shutting down. Unlike his chancellor of economy, Chaves remained adamant during the following weeks that the regional government would not intervene directly in Santana. Yet the unions escalated their pressure on the regional

---

54. These events are chronicled in *El País*, February 3, 1993.
55. See comments by Antonio Gutiérrez, CCOO secretary general, in *El País*, February 25, 1994.

president with a general strike in late March. After a much-publicized and emotional march of 250 Santana workers from Linares to Seville, Chaves offered a plan involving paid preretirement of 900 Santana workers and official finance to the firm. The unions, however, rejected the plan as too austere. Facing an expanding base of opposition during a critical election year, the Chaves government had the IFA intervene and purchase controlling shares of Santana. By September 1994, however, IFA representatives claimed that Santana could not continue production due to the fact that the Santana 2000, the four-wheel land rover produced by Suzuki in Linares, was obsolete and no longer met environmental standards.[56] Since IFA was not able to sell off a significant segment of its shares, the Andalusian government was left with a barely functional automobile firm that generated huge losses. In March 1995, Suzuki abandoned Santana and left it in the hands of the IFA.

The IFA's intervention in Santana was indicative of a larger demiurge strategy for saving failing firms. For example, between May 1993 and August 1994, the Andalusian government invested over $269 million of the regional budget to save 13 nonviable firms, including Santana.[57] This amount surpassed the total for all of the IFA's other industrial promotion programs in agriculture, industry, and services in 1993 and represented 83 percent of total industrial investment in Andalusia for the same year.[58] Although this seemed economically inefficient, it was politically profitable for the Socialists. Chaves and the PSOE, after losing their absolute majority in June 1994 and despite sweeping victories by the PP in most of Spain's other regions, including Asturias, survived a challenge from the PP in 1995 and remained in power.

Although certainly not determinate, the IFA's demiurge interventions in Linares and other locations avoided the potentially high political costs of a more passive governmental response. Had the Andalusian industrial policy system not been guided by such populist political interests; had it been more horizontally supported by an array of political and economic actors, especially after the exit of Morena, then the costs of politically manipulating the IFA would not have been so great. Centralized, political control of the IFA created a hierarchical-functional horizontal embeddedness that made the agency more vulnerable. The results were politically useful for the Socialists, but fiscally costly and ultimately unimportant to most of Andalusia's firms.

56. See *El Mundo*, September 10, 1994.
57. See *El País*, August 19, 1994.
58. Calculated from ESECA (1994: 103) and IEA (1995: 81), respectively.

Conclusions:

Shifting States in Comparative Perspective

All four of the subnational governments compared in this book had strong economic incentives to build synergy. Severe economic crises with deep historical legacies dominated the development trajectories of Asturias, Minas Gerais, Rio de Janeiro, and Andalusia. Yet only two of these subnational cases created a sustainable system of public intervention in the market based on synergistic ties between development agencies and firms.

In this chapter I begin with a reevaluation of the evidence presented by these four case studies. I highlight the ways in which changes in national institutions and development patterns affected the capacities of subnational governments to (re)organize industrial policies during the 1980s and 1990s. I test the main argument further by extending the range of empirical observations to include additional cases of success and failure in producing subnational synergy in Brazil, Spain, and other countries. Much of this data is based on emerging fieldwork that makes possible only arms-length comparisons. But these are sufficiently suggestive to provide additional clues to the incidence of synergy and its hypothesized political causes.

In the subsequent section I reconsider the limits of analyses that stop with national institutions. I argue that such approaches have limited application in what Locke (1996) calls "composite economies"—highly differentiated domestic markets where regional variations are marked.

At the same time, the role of national institutions cannot be ignored altogether. I follow Locke in his defense of a "micropolitical approach" but my attempt is to include an understanding of how national institutions mattered in shaping subnational industrial policy in Brazil and Spain.

I then examine the populist-dependent and dependent types to highlight the importance of interregional conflict in determining the incidence of delegative government and horizontal embeddedness. I use a brief longitudinal comparison of the Mexican states to illustrate what happens in the "off cell" cases first introduced in Table 1.1.

In the final section I assess the theoretical significance of my findings for emerging research on the political economy of decentralization. I argue that subnational comparisons offer a means for moving scholars beyond the "first wave" analyses of decentralization. These have focused on national electoral and party systems and their effects on "fiscal federalism." Yet they exclude consideration of how composite forms of subnational political interests and institutions and interregional dynamics affect policy-making.

THE CROSS-SUBNATIONAL COMPARISONS
Minas Gerais and Rio de Janeiro

Minas Gerais's development agencies were created in a political context very different from the one that prevailed in Rio de Janeiro. The *mineiro* elite was a relatively cohesive political class, having survived decades as a traditional oligarchy. It was also a diverse elite, including political technocratic elements as well as more purely "traditional" politicians. As such it faced few threats to its cohesion during the 1960s and 1970s, when Minas Gerais's industrial policy agencies were being constructed. Under these conditions, *mineiro* politicians were willing to delegate significant resources and policy responsibilities to agencies such as the INDI, BDMG, CDI, and CEMIG. In Rio de Janeiro, decades of elite polarization among factions led by the *chefes políticos* operating within and between political parties created the conditions for populist government. Political leaders such as Chagas Freitas, Brizola, and Moreira Franco developed strong incentives to centralize their control over the state government's development agencies, thereby reducing the costs of using industrial policy to cultivate clientelistic constituencies.

The comparison between Minas Gerais and Rio de Janeiro demonstrates that the prevalence of clientelism need not derail the building of synergy. While clientelistic politics pervaded Rio's state politics, Minas

Gerais was no stranger to these kinds of relations. Indeed, clientelism, in the form of personal commitments between state and federal officials during the authoritarian period, was an important resource for building Minas's development agencies.[1] Rather, the key distinctions between Rio de Janeiro and Minas Gerais were the degree to which politicians believed they needed to garner industrial policy resources for political purposes and their capacity for doing so.

Horizontal embeddedness regulated the effects of clientelism in Minas Gerais. Creating a plan-oriented horizontal embeddedness was politically and logistically important. The *mineiro* elite, following the "prophets of doom," believed that Minas was the victim of exploitation by other states. As such the state required an aggressive industrial policy during the developmentalist period. Creating a network of specialized but interlinked development agencies reflected the dimensions of Minas's problems and also provided justification for the decentralization of fiscal resources. Logistically, *mineiro* politicians saw these ties as crucial to providing a lasting solution to Minas Gerais's dependency on the industrial markets of São Paulo.

Although Rio de Janeiro's deindustrialization experience would have justified a similar commitment on the part of state government leadership, these actors were more concerned with their short-term political survival. As a result, horizontal embeddedness never developed as extensively as it did in Minas. Elite polarization created overriding incentives for incumbents to use industrial policy resources as part of the larger effort to cultivate clientelistic support.

The Brazilian cases also highlight the legacy or "path dependency" of horizontal embeddedness. Armed with horizontal ties across the agencies, the industrial policy network in Minas could more easily weather the changes in government that would occur in the transition to democracy. During the Newton Cardoso administration, these horizontal ties allowed the agencies to protect their resources from the governor's clientelistic politics. Later, horizontal ties facilitated the transfer of personnel, resources, and information that became crucial to the restructuring of the industrial policy system.

Without these horizontal linkages, CODIN became an isolated development agency in Rio de Janeiro; constantly vulnerable to the particularistic interests of the *chaguistas* and the *brizolistas*. As the party system continued to fragment during the transition to democracy, the absence of horizontal ties became more onerous for CODIN. In contrast to the INDI-BDMG-

---

1. I thank Judith Tendler for suggesting this particular point.

CDI-CEMIG network, CODIN was far too dependent on the state's political leadership to restructure Rio's decaying development policy.

The advent of delegative government at the time the *mineiro* agencies were created produced opportunities for the agencies to forge horizontal ties. The continuation of these linkages even after the mandates of their creators were exhausted explains why Minas was able to maintain an industrial policy network. The persistence of horizontal embeddedness allowed the system the time and opportunity to develop close affiliations with client firms and the knowledge needed to redirect the state's industrial policy from its previous developmentalist framework. These qualities proved crucial in building synergistic public-private ties in the automotive sector in the state. The state government's relationship with Fiat and its suppliers evolved from a time when the state was a financier of the multinational's startup operations to a time when the state government could facilitate the assembler's just-in-time regime by providing support to its suppliers. Meanwhile, the state government maintained its own interests in diversifying the placement of auto parts firms in other locations in Minas. Without a previous history of implementing a developmentalist policy and without the organizational attributes of horizontal embeddedness to maintain and help restructure the agencies over time, these achievements would have been less likely. CODIN had none of these experiences or attributes. It was not able to produce consistent synergistic relations with private firms given the incentives to do so by a declining industrial market in the 1980s. In the 1990s, it could play almost no role in diversifying or accelerating a positive trend of industrial investment.

The comparison of industrial policy in Minas Gerais and Rio de Janeiro provides a rich foundation for numerous conclusions about Brazilian politics. One of the most important conclusions responds to a commonly held view that Brazilian subnational politics is endemically clientelistic (Samuels and Abrúcio 2001; Hagopian 1996). This observation does not explain numerous exceptions involving effective, programmatic policy-making such as the *mineiro* industrial policies analyzed in this study or Tendler's (1997) cases of public procurement, health, and education policies in Ceará (Montero 2000: 72–75). These studies demonstrate that the organizational attributes of bureaucracies and firm networks matter in determining whether collective efficiencies can emerge in this ocean of clientelistic norms. Moreover, the comparison shows that state governments have the capacity to change their development models and assert their interests, even when they partially challenge those of a powerful multinational such as Fiat (Tendler 2000: 47).

Additional Brazilian Cases

The experience of Minas's industrial policy might be considered an outlier within Brazil, but recent scholarship at the subnational level suggests that the politics of the delegative dilemma and horizontal embeddedness are salient features in determining "success" or "failure" across a range of policy areas. Tendler's (1997) study of "good government" in Ceará during the early to mid-1990s represents the most thorough study to date. While it does not focus on political causes but on the developmental effects of innovative policy-making, the Ceará story suggests that political delegation and horizontal embeddedness played important roles in making this a case of policy success.

Tendler notes how reformist governors, specifically Tasso Jereissati (1987–91 and 1995-present) and Ciro Gomes (1991–94), blocked parochial encroachments by political opponents by strengthening the meritocracy of Ceará's civil service. She is silent on the motivations of these seeming "good governors" and their political capacity, but a closer look reveals that the political class they led faced divided partisan opponents and were broadly supported by the electorate and important segments of business. Both "Tasso" and "Ciro" were among a political class of successful entrepreneurs who had since the 1970s become active in discussing the state's economic development as leaders of the most powerful business association in Ceará, the Cearense Industrial Center (CIC).[2] Their rise to power after the 1986 elections followed the decomposition of the formerly hegemonic PDS and infighting among the three military "coronels" (César Cals, Adauto Bezerra, and Virgílio Távora) who had previously controlled state government through an extensive clientelistic network. The reformist coalition of the PMDB and leftist parties almost gained a majority in the state assembly, but succeeded in unseating mayors loyal to the coronels in both Fortaleza, the capital, and the interior. Faced with remaining political opposition in the state legislature, including growing dissension within the PMDB, Jereissati and the reformers joined the Party of Brazilian Social Democrat (PSDB) in 1989 and retained the governorship in 1990 and 1994 with first-turn wins and with increasing popular majorities during the 1990s. Declining electoral volatility in the state assembly, an increasing incidence of straight-ticket voting for federal and state office, the absence of ideological cleavages in the electorate or the political class, and a growing sense among voters of

---

2. The prominent political position of the CIC business leadership was the result of low levels of business dependence on the national state and weak labor organizations. See Abu-El-Haj (1997).

"pro-government" and "opposition" lines gave Ceará an unusually co-herent party system during the early to mid-1990s (Moraes Filho 1997). These trends empowered Ciro Gomes's reformist administration, which enjoyed a majority in the state legislature beginning in 1992. With clear, supportive electoral signals, the backing of the state's business organiza-tions and public opinion, and the absence of labor opposition or rela-tively severe social conflict, the reformist governors could expect to retain power. These conditions created the political security the reform-ers needed to implement their plans for using the public apparatus as an "inducer of new investments" (Gondim 1997: 369–70).

Tendler's analysis of four policy areas—preventive health, emergency employment, agricultural extension, and public procurement for small firms—emphasizes merit-based recruitment into the civil service, self-motivated public servants, official publicity, and close cross-monitoring by suppliers and recipients of public goods as key independent vari-ables. But her cases are also explicit about the role of horizontal ties link-ing public agencies, private clients, producer associations, and neighborhoods in enhancing the effects of publicity, monitoring, and pro-gram follow-through. Her fourth policy area—procurement policies for small firms—most closely approximates the policies analyzed in my own study. Tendler notes that two agencies—the state Department of Industry and Commerce (SIC) and a national, semipublic technical-assistance agency, the Brazilian Small Enterprise Assistance Service (SEBRAE), spearheaded the creation of an industrial district of small furniture pro-ducers in the remote town of São João do Aruaru (SJA) during the 1990s. The story highlights the close connections linking SIC and SEBRAE, par-ticularly the fact that more than 70 percent of the latter's funding in Ceará came from SIC and that the two agencies worked in tandem to secure public contracts and supply technical assistance to the small producers in SJA. These horizontal ties extended to the agencies' role in fostering the formation of small firm associations in SJA to bid for state contracts. The agency-association networks proved successful in garnering state con-tracts and upgrading production to fulfill them; more than this, these ties also provided political protection from the opposition of displaced com-petitors and politicians "representing" them. As Tendler notes:

> The purchasing agencies first contracted with SIC for the goods or
> services. SIC then made a second contract with SEBRAE to pro-
> vide technical assistance to the small firms, paying SEBRAE a 5
> percent commission to purchase the goods or services from an as-
> sociation of small firms, artisans, or building tradesmen located

near each other. Key to the good results of these arrangements, SEBRAE would not contract individually with small firms. It instead sought out existing small-firm associations or encouraged and helped groups of potential suppliers located in one place to organize an association . . . they [SIC and SEBRAE] also encouraged the associations to become a counter-lobby to the hitherto more powerful displaced firms, as well as to lobby in favor of tax exemptions for small firms. For every round of opposition from the previous suppliers, SIC and SEBRAE mobilized a wave of presidents of local small-firm associations to pressure the governor to preserve the program or to extend it to their towns. (116, 130)

Official publicity enhanced the constituency-building effects of horizontal ties.[3] Horizontal ties also limited the costs of hidden information by promoting cross-monitoring, which included feedback from neighborhood associations and producer groups (126–27). Both the organizational attributes Tendler describes among the agencies in Ceará and the effects of these ties on small-firm productivity and the political maintenance of the policy network highlight the central qualities of horizontal embeddedness and its implications for synergy: information flows were symmetrical and frequent, cross-monitoring prevented bureaucratic dysfunction, and agency interconnections reinforced sources of political support.[4]

In another case I have studied elsewhere (Montero 1997: chap. 8)—São Paulo—the persistence of populist government and the absence of horizontal embeddedness produced the same poor results reflected in the Rio case. Since the greater metropolitan area of São Paulo contained over 50 percent of Brazil's industrial activity, the state's chief problem was not attracting new investment but deconcentrating a highly agglomerated industrial sector (Cano 1977, 1994: 226).[5] By the end of the 1960s São

3. As Tendler notes: "publicity also served the purpose of creating a new constituency that would help the governors and agency managers overcome political opposition" (p. 137).

4. An investigation of Ceará's first experience with industrial policy in the 1963–66 period under the governorship of Virgílio Távora will reveal a similar set of conditions undergirding the state development company (CODEC), the hydroelectric company of the São Francisco (CHESF), the federal Bank of the Northeast Region (BNB), and the federal development agency SUDENE. See Soares and Rocha (1989). While this experience was not maintained it established an important precedent. The CIC leadership later in the 1980s and 1990s saw the "horizontalization of organization" as being politically important in "eliminating the last vestiges of *coronelismo* and particularistic manipulation of public institutions" (Abu-El-Haj, 1997: 336).

5. In 1970 the *city* of São Paulo accounted for 28 percent of Brazil's manufacturing. Greater São Paulo and surrounding municipalities represented over 44 percent and 15 percent, respectively.

Paulo's dominance as Brazil's industrial heart began to generate sizable costs. Urban congestion, pollution, and overpopulation produced serious diseconomies in the metropolitan area. Land, rent, and labor costs increased as did the price of basic services such as infrastructure maintenance and sanitation (Secretaria da Indústria e do Comércio 1987; Schwartzman 1975).[6] The rise of an independent labor movement during the end of the 1970s and throughout the transition to democracy in the 1980s produced a series of strikes in São Paulo's industrial centers—the ABC region and surrounding municipalities.[7] Work stoppages increased production costs, creating additional pressures on firms to move away from the metropolitan area.

As in Rio, the persistence of a polarized political class in state government hindered the formation of industrial policies designed to address these problems. The major political figures in state politics during the 1980s and 1990s remained individuals, such as the ex-governors Paulo Salim Maluf (1979–82) and Orestes Quércia (1987–90), who represented competing clientelistic networks. These politicians routinely sublimated the interests of building political party and electoral institutions and state development institutions to their own political interests.[8] Their persisting ambitions to attain national office and keep their supporters in state office produced the most extensive patronage-dispensing apparatus in Brazilian subnational government.[9]

6. One estimate produced by Sabesp, the São Paulo public firm that manages basic sanitation in the metropolitan area, showed that the average costs of water service are 20 percent higher in the city than in the interior of the state; sanitation costs are 17 percent higher and construction costs are between 28 to 52 percent higher (*Veja*, November 9, 1994).

7. For studies of these shifts in the *paulista* union movement, see Alves (1989) and Keck (1992).

8. For example, Quércia used the threat of leaving the PMDB for the PTB in 1982 in order to elicit support for his first run at the governorship. The tactic helped to boost Quércia to the position of Franco Montoro's lieutenant governor at the time and solidified Quércia's dominion over the *paulista* PMDB in 1986 as governor. However, Quércia's self-interested manipulation of party allegiances only served to reduce respect for political parties at a critical point during the Brazilian transition to democracy. Like Quércia, Maluf focused on his campaign for the presidency several times during the 1980's and 1990's, only to divert political attention away from São Paulo's failing infrastructure projects and the metropolitan area's worsening economic problems. For a discussion of these events, see *Veja*, May 5, 1993.

9. The Orestes Quércia and Luiz Antonio Fleury Filho (1991–94) governorships were emblematic examples of how the *paulista* political system operates in this regard. Both governors were infamous during their mandates for channeling lucrative public contracts to political cronies, particularly contractors that contributed millions to both campaigns. Worse still, these governors routinely prevented judicial institutions from prosecuting cases of fraud. Although investigators in 1993 found that over $430 million of Electropaulo contracts were fraught with cases of kickbacks and other payoffs to public officials during the Quércia administration, they were unable to bring a single complaint to trial. As one ju-

Those political technocrats who did emerge to address the issues requiring an industrial policy were politically isolated both within the government and within the political associations of *paulista* business. Emerson Kapaz is the best example. As president of the Industrial Union of Musical Instrument and Toy Producers of São Paulo, Kapaz emerged in the July 1992 internal elections of the Federação de Indústrias do Estado de São Paulo (Federation of Industries of the State of São Paulo, FIESP), the most powerful business association in Brazil, as a dissident voice against the organization's preferred candidate, Carlos Eduardo Moreira Ferreira. During the early 1990s, Kapaz had been a key business proponent of the innovative tripartite industrial relations experiment in the automotive sector (the *câmaras setoriais*—sectoral chambers) and had played a prominent role in launching the toy manufacturers' sectoral chamber.[10] At the time, Kapaz was vocal about the need to create a national and a *paulista* industrial policy to address failures in infrastructure, research and development, and the problems of industrial restructuring.[11] Kapaz criticized the FIESP's tendency to focus on macroeconomic policy and ignore the possibilities of infrastructural and microeconomic policy. Kapaz's view was part of the emerging criticism among segments of organized business of the neoliberal model of national political economy and the patrimonial nature of state-business associations.[12] Along with some prominent *paulista* political technocrats at the national level

rist, Fábio Kander Comparato, noted: "*Quercismo* is noxious. In São Paulo, he eviscerates the investigative capacity of democratic institutions" (*Veja*, January 20, 1993). Employees of the Fleury administration would not aid investigators in collecting evidence against the governor's predecessor. Both governors prevented investigations from going forward by politically controlling the state's Legislative Assembly. In 1987, Quércia's first year as governor, eight separate commissions of inquiry were called to investigate the new governor's history of scandals. Since sixty-one of the eighty-four deputies in the assembly were avowed *quercistas*, the inquiries stalled. Quércia also appointed four of the seven counselors on the Tribunal de Contas do Estado (Tribunal of State Accounts), the public agency that is supposedly a watchdog over the state government's spending. Not surprisingly, Quércia's political influence on the Tribunal produced unanimous approvals of all public contracts sent to the governor and a number of his associates in state government who would later be accused of receiving kickbacks from contractors.

10. For a review of the sectoral chambers experience, see Martin (1996) and E. Diniz (1994).

11. See a couple of Kapaz's editorials: *Gazeta Mercantil*, April 15, 1992, and *Estado de São Paulo*, May 10, 1992.

12. Kapaz was one of the key leaders of the Pensamento Nacional das Bases Empresariais (National Thinking of the Business Community, PNBE) which acted as an opposition to neoliberal and patrimonial segments of the FIESP. For a complete analysis of the PNBE and other anti-neoliberal business groups in Brazil during this time, see Kingstone (1999) and an interview with Paulo Cunha, president of the Instituto de Estudos para o Desenvolvimento Industrial (Institute for the Study of Industrial Development, IEDI), another FIESP rival, in *Folha de São Paulo*, April 19, 1993.

such as José Serra (São Paulo senator and Fernando Henrique Cardoso's first minister of planning) and Dorothea Werneck (one of the original creators of the sectoral chambers and Cardoso's first minister of industry), Kapaz openly rejected neoliberalism in Brazil (Schwartz 1996: 130).

By 1996, however, none of these actors had been able to change the direction of either national or *paulista* economic policy. Werneck's sectoral chambers were largely defunct and the secretary was deposed from her position at the ministry of industry in 1995. Serra left planning and ran for the municipal government of São Paulo in 1996, only to lose to Maluf's hand-picked successor, Paulo Pitta, who would soon face a corruption scandal. And Kapaz, still a key leader of the opposition business associations, ran the State Secretariat of Science and Technology, but a lack of resources and gubernatorial support produced few tangible results.[13] Other state institutions such as the state bank, BANESPA, and the Secretariats of Industry and Planning were also unable to address the state's economic problems due to severe fiscal constraints.[14] The underfinancing of the Secretariat of Science and Technology was so severe that officials told me that all they could do to keep state government accounts designated for industrial policy *open* was to leave a credit balance of R$1![15]

Beyond state-level comparisons in Brazil, some recent comparative studies of municipal-level policy-making, particularly in the well-studied

13. Illustrative of this point is the case of Fairway, a multinational chemical textile firm successfully wooed away from São Paulo by Minas Gerais's state government in 1995. Kapaz intervened with promises of extensive fiscal and financial concessions to convince Fairway's directors to keep the firm in São Paulo. When the state secretary of science and technology was unable to come through with any of the promised items, the firm left for Minas (author interview with Dirk Blaesing, president and director of Fairway Filamentos (Rhodia and Hoescht joint venture), July 3, 1996, São Paulo). Also see a statement of Kapaz's intentions upon assuming his office in *Gazeta Mercantil,* January 24, 1995.

14. The case of BANESPA was particularly disturbing. As part of the division of spoils that marks much of *paulista* politics, the state bank acted as a personal treasure chest for the governors and their political supporters. Loans were offered without sufficient collateral; at times without any collateral whatsoever. As was the case in most of Brazil's public banks during the 1980's, BANESPA financed public expenditures, particularly during election years. Again, some of the country's largest contractors received the lion's share. Quércia's borrowing alone accounted for $600 million of the $1.4 billion of the bank's debt during his term. And the ex-governor was not reticent about expressing his intentions when he admitted in 1990: "I broke the state, but I elected my successor [Fleury]" (*Veja,* March 22, 1995). By the end of Fleury's term, the state government owed over $10 billion to BANESPA, which was by 1994 almost $21 billion in the red. Central Bank inspectors initiated a probe in 1995 that effectively halted the prospects for any new major expenditures (*Veja,* February 22, 1995). BANESPA was finally privatized in 2000.

15. Author interviews at the Secretariat of Science, Technology, and Economic Development, July 1996, São Paulo.

cases of "participatory budgeting," suggest that the logic of the delegative dilemma and horizontal embeddedness are central determinants of success. Renato Boschi (1999), for example, has provided some insights into the diverse performance of local-level participatory budgeting in Belo Horizonte (Minas Gerais) and Salvador (Bahia). Boschi's study finds that while participatory budgeting was fully implemented in Belo Horizonte, the Bahian experiment broke down when the regional sub-units, the "participatory" working groups that are the lifeblood of the process, were unable to claim administrative or financial autonomy from the municipal administration led by the center-left PSDB. The latter centralized its management of the budgeting process in the face of persistent threats from the rival clientelistic network of Bahian senator Antônio Carlos Magalhães. By contrast, the participatory budgeting process in Belo Horizonte became highly decentralized into horizontally connected "popular councils." This transition was buttressed by the coming to power of Patrus Ananias, a candidate of the leftist PT and leader of a coalition of parties organized into the Frente BH Popular. Boschi notes that the combination of a secure political coalition and a decentralized administrative network allowed the participatory budgeting process in Belo Horizonte to be implemented and maintained throughout the 1990s while the experiment in Salvador stagnated.

Asturias and Andalusia

Following the lessons of the Minas-Rio comparison, the key difference between these two cases was the extent to which political incumbents believed they needed to utilize industrial policy to cultivate clientelistic support and their capacity for doing so over time. The Asturian Socialists created a network of development agencies at a time of low elite polarization, when the regional parties and the powerful Asturian unions were agreed on the necessity of providing a united front for the building of regional autonomy. Having been guaranteed access to "fast-track" autonomy and facing nationalist rivals and significant opposition by the region's chief business association at the beginning of the autonomy process, the Andalusian Socialists had fewer incentives (or possibilities) for constructing a united front at the time the region's development agencies were formed. They employed populist mechanisms to build their constituency. Once in power and armed with an absolute majority, the Andalusian Socialists concentrated on using industrial policy to reinforce their electoral position, a strategy that responded to but also propagated conflicts with the region's business association. These conflicts only reinforced, in a self-fulfilling vicious circle, PSOE fears of opposition and the priority of reinforcing the party's "social partnerships" with unions. In Asturias, the PSOE leadership avoided conflicts with the region's key political force, the labor unions in the steel and mining sectors. More important, it used the influence of these actors in its campaigns to draw greater authority and resources from Madrid. At no point did prominent social or partisan conflicts during the building of the subnational industrial policy bureaucracy create incentives for Socialist managers like Pedro de Silva to buttress themselves politically with misappropriations of policy resources.

The Asturians had the opportunity to reconsider their region's development trajectory in a different political context than the one that prevailed in Andalusia. Policy ideas and perspectives cultivated in SADEI during the late-Franquist period played a bigger role in the strategies of regional industrial policy from the beginning. Specifically, the advocacy of prominent SADEI political technocrats against deepening the region's dependence on public mining and steel helped restrain the PSOE from fully embracing the unions' ill-fated defense of employment in these sectors. By contrast, the dominance of populist politics at the beginning of the autonomy process in Andalusia marginalized alternative perspectives of the region's development trajectory. "Endogenous development" as a frame for industrial policy emerged as much as part of the IPIA/IFA attempt to produce and retain the political support of regional politicians for their policy initiatives, than as an outgrowth of an already politically supported agenda. Despite having a history similar to that of Asturias regarding national industrial policy failures and dependence on the public sector, no autonomous development mission based on a rational economic assessment of these legacies could emerge in the politicized context of Andalusia.

The sources of elite conflict in Andalusia were distinct from those that prevailed in Rio de Janeiro, but they produced, nonetheless, strong incentives to centralize control of industrial policy. While levels of partisan fragmentation and elite conflict were much greater in Rio, Andalusia's Socialists were able to maintain a more coherent political party base. In this case, conflicts with rival parties, business, and labor became the key constraints explaining Socialist interests in manipulating industrial policy. Still, IFA was able to garner more resources and become more active in industrial policy than CODIN. This finding suggests that distinct levels of elite conflict affect the politicization of industrial policy differently *across* cases of populist government.

The continuation of a politicized industrial policy in Andalusia and one based on a political technocratic development mission in Asturias led to two very different structures of industrial policy agency networks. While PSOE politicians concentrated their control over the IFA and used the agency in a demiurge capacity to build and keep the political support of workers in the enclave sectors, the development agencies in Asturias constructed an increasingly collaborative set of horizontal ties with each other and with the region's unions. Lacking cross-cutting monitoring functions to stem the abuse of industrial policy for political aims, the IFA's hierarchical-functional structure promoted unsustainable, unaccountable, and fiscally costly investments that failed to build lasting or flexible synergistic ties with the region's firms. This was particularly true of the IFA's ties with small and medium-sized firms, which remained neglected by the agency's programs and, through the CEA, resentful of its focus on large, multinational firms. In Asturias, by contrast, horizontal ties allowed the development agencies to innovate new responses to the region's economic problems and bootstrap resources, including additional political support among the Asturian unions. Even as regional PSOE presidents became less supportive of the agencies, the policy network improved. It maintained a high level of accountability and it offered a more flexible framework for addressing the problems of small and medium-sized firms.

The comparison of Asturias and Andalusia also controls for other variables—particularly national institutions—that might conceivably explain the rise and maintenance of synergy. As the birthplace of the contemporary PSOE and as one of the largest regions in Spain, Andalusia was a privileged recipient of EU cohesion funding and other resources. In comparison to Asturias between 1986–94, Andalusia was more heavily and consistently subsidized. Funding differences, therefore, cannot explain the outcomes.

The distinct experiences in creating synergy in Asturias and Andalusia, both PSOE-led regions, suggest that the identity of the governing party is not determinate. It is in the unpacking of the party leadership, the examination of their particular experiences, and the placement of these understandings in the larger context of political conflict within the region and between the region and the national government, that we get a better idea of how political parties affect the possibilities for building and maintaining synergy. Pedro de Silva's experiences with the PNI, the ZURs, and during the construction of Asturian regional autonomy directly shaped his leadership's industrial policy strategy and, specifically, the extent to which SADEI's emerging development mission would be the basis for the new policy. While Andalusia's government was also led by a strong PSOE, its leadership's interests were shaped to a far greater extent by persisting social conflicts. The comparison of Asturias and Andalusia contests the notion that the politics of PSOE-led regions were mere extensions of a common "socialist" response to development problems.

The comparison also illustrates that analysis of electoral politics does not supply a complete picture of the conditions necessary to create and maintain synergy. While both the Asturian and Andalusian Socialists enjoyed absolute parliamentary majorities in their regions, and this during a time when their national party maintained a similar position in the national Cortes, the Asturians were more successful than the Andalusians in constructing synergistic ties between development agencies and firms.

Additional Spanish Cases

The contrasting experiences of Asturias and Andalusia are not unique when compared with other regions in Spain. A brief look at the politics behind Valencia's innovative policies to increase the productivity of small-firm industrial districts and Madrid's failure to deal with the problems of similar firms illustrates the importance of political delegation and horizontal embeddedness.

As in Minas, Asturias, and Ceará, a reformist leadership led by Joan Lerma of the Valencian PSOE (PSPV-PSOE) pursued a regional industrial policy during the years they held power from 1983–95. Like Silva and the Asturian PSOE, Lerma and the PSPV-PSOE were motivated by the autonomy process and early experiences with the industrial reconversion before they assumed office. After the public steel works at Sagunto were targeted for a complete phase-out in 1981, the PSPV-PSOE and the Valencian UCD negotiated the broad outlines of a regional economic policy as a way of defending Valencian autonomy. Cross-party support for the creation of a regional development apparatus was institutionalized in the regional statute of autonomy in 1982. The agreements stressed the need to develop new ways of promoting innovation in small and medium-sized firm "clusters" located throughout Valencia.[16] Once in power with an overwhelming majority in 1983, the PSPV-PSOE initiated its plans for the creation of regional technology institutes as part of its larger campaign to take full advantage of the economic development clauses built into the statute of autonomy. Lerma and his chancellor of industry, Segundo Bru, took the lead on these projects as an extension of nationally subsidized efforts to relocate downsized Sagunto

---

16. Small firms make up over 97 percent of Valencia's industrial sector. On the importance of such policies for the political parties, see *El Pais*, August 2, 1981. The technical justification for focusing on small firm clusters is summarized in Gabinete Técnico de la Consellería de Industria, Comercio, y Turismo (1989).

workers. These policies were politically significant, as they would consolidate the first major reconversion reforms in Spain and create a strong justification for decentralizing development policy to the Valencian government. The latter was a key regional consideration as interregional and intergovernmental conflicts over the LOFCA/LOAPA rules punctuated by Vice-President Alfonso Guerra's and Industry Minister Carlos Solchaga's public disapproval of further decentralization underscored the Valencian government's efforts to demonstrate its concern and competence with industrial policy.[17]

The earlier Sagunto experience and prolonged fights with the national PSOE government also fostered close relations between the PSPV-PSOE and the region's business associations and labor unions. The attempt to speak for regional interests, derided by Guerra as the creation of "regional PSOE barons," placed a premium on securing better relations between the governing party and the unions than was possible at the national level. Even when relations between the PSOE and the UGT soured during the 1980s, the PSPV-PSOE and the Valencian UGT and CCOO were able to forge a series of accords on public employment, retraining, and reindustrialization policies. The major business associations participated in the organization of the region's technology institutes, thereby creating a set of ongoing working relationships in diverse sectors with state agencies. As in Asturias, peaceful ties with regional labor unions and business avoided the levels of social conflict that encouraged the politicization of industrial policy in Andalusia. The PSPV-PSOE's stable electoral position also granted Lerma the convenience of mapping out a reindustrialization strategy for the long term.

The Valencian industrial policy network emerged around the activities of IMPIVA (the Institute for Small and Medium-Sized Firms), which was created in 1984.[18] IMPIVA coordinates its actions with regional technology institutes and business and innovation centers located near local clusters. Each cluster is represented by a not-for-profit private business association that works closely with the agencies. Representatives from the regional government (through IMPIVA), the Ministry of Industry, local business associations, and the unions sit on the governing bodies of the technology institutes. The result is a horizontally integrated industrial policy network that works to foster and reinforce cooperation

17. I discuss these conflicts elsewhere (Montero 2001b). Also see Ciclo de Conferencias sobre Política Valenciana (1985), *El País*, September 1, 1985, and September 22, 1985, for the Valencian government's view.

18. Between 1985 and 1994, IMPIVA consumed over 71 percent of all funds for industrial promotion in Valencia. See Más (1995).

among small and medium-size producers in ceramics, footwear, textiles, plastics, and other sectors through the provision of public goods in infrastructure and technical support.

The organization and function of the Valencian technology institutes has been well-studied by Spanish and internationally well-known scholars of business such as Michael Porter (1990). Even without venturing into the details, a review of this scholarship reveals that the salient characteristics associated with the success of IMPIVA and local institutes in promoting the coordination of small-firm clusters are symmetric and frequent transfers of information and finance linking public agencies, universities, the institutes, business associations, and labor unions (Rico 1992). These characteristics have fostered appreciable levels of policy feedback and facilitated policy experimentation (Espina 1994; Más 1995). Horizontal ties have also enhanced accountability in the use of public resources. The result has been high levels of business confidence in the performance of the IMPIVA system, an outcome that has continued beyond the end of the PSPV-PSOE mandate in 1995.

In Valencia, the third most industrialized region in Spain, and one without Asturias's extreme dependency on public steel and mining, it might not be surprising to find a successful development apparatus. Yet similar factors did not favor the articulation of a subnational industrial policy in the Community of Madrid, the industrial and administrative heart of Spain. The region's milieu of administrative capacities, both public and private, paved the way for the emergence of Madrid as the headquarters for half of all foreign investors in Spain and the center of the country's financial markets (Sanchez Ortiz 1990). Despite the region's poor rural surroundings, the lack of raw materials, and the center's great distance from the vital ports of Spanish commerce, Madrid's array of industries and administrative and financial services provided a self-sufficient economic base from which the region could adjust to sweeping macroeconomic change. Unlike Asturias, the Community of Madrid was largely spared the throes of the industrial reconversion during the 1980s, as few of the industrial sectors targeted for restructuring after 1983 were located in Madrid. The region's chief industrial problems were similar to those of São Paulo: diseconomies produced by agglomerated investment patterns. Although the national and regional governments were able to create incentives for the deconcentration of industry,[19] they were less successful with directing industrial deconcentration to fa-

___

19. In 1975, Greater Madrid accounted for 95 percent and the remaining areas represented 5 percent of the Community of Madrid's industrial employment. By 1992, however, Greater Madrid generated 85 percent of the region's industrial employment while the sur-

vor poorer areas of the region, and particularly the south. Industrial downsizing during the economic slowdown of the early 1990s produced acute social problems as 45,000 jobs were phased out between 1988 and 1992 alone. Services, which had come to dominate Madrid's economy, absorbed labor at rates below the national average (Méndez and Razquín 1995).

The PSOE controlled the Madrid regional government as it did most other Spanish regions for much of the 1980s and early 1990s. Yet following the party's experience in Andalusia, the PSOE in Madrid became concerned with eliciting business and labor support to calm social conflicts generated by industrial restructuring. Joaquín Leguina, the regional president from 1983 through 1995, faced escalating pressures by business and labor groups to create industrial employment.[20] Leguina focused on creating "political pacts" with the region's chief business association, the Confederación Empresarial de Madrid (Entrepreneurial Confederation of Madrid, CEIM), and the labor unions, but each attempt collapsed due to business and labor claims that the regional government's economic agencies were insufficiently funded and misdirected. Between 1987 and 1992, the failure of three major attempts to form tripartite pacts added to a growing sense of political vulnerability among the leaders of the regional PSOE. Leguina himself identified the inability to form a lasting agreement with the CEIM, UGT, and CCOO during the economic recession of the early 1990s as the chief factor facilitating the growth of the opposition Partido Popular (PP) in the regional parliament.[21]

The Socialist hierarchy's increasing political vulnerability and the advent of greater levels of strike activity and criticism by CEIM and the unions led to a vicious circle. Incumbents manipulated the main industrial promotion agency, the Instituto Madrileño de Desarrollo (Institute of Development of Madrid, IMADE), to cultivate support, but this only

---

rounding areas fostered 15.4 percent. These general figures reflected the increasing movement of industrial firms from the old centers of Madrid's production base. Between 1987 and 1990 alone, 87 percent of all new investments occurred outside areas traditionally allocated to industry. See Méndez and Razquín (1995: 148).

20. A survey of Madrid firms by the Confederación Empresarial de Madrid (Entrepreneurial Confederation of Madrid, CEIM), the region's chief business association, in 1987 found that only 5 percent of the region's firms believed that the regional government was doing important work and only 1.4 percent of responding firms were aware of the extent of the government's activities. The vast majority agreed that the regional government's efforts in the area of industrial policy were weak. Reports of this poll were published in *El País* on June 24, 1987.

21. Leguina expressed this opinion in a private meeting with the minister of industry, Claudio Aranzadi, and the secretary of state for industry, Álvaro Espina Montero, in May 1992 (author interview with Álvaro Espina Montero, May 30, 1996, Madrid).

isolated IMADE, adding to business and labor claims that the regional government was doing nothing to generate additional employment and growth.

IMADE was created in 1983 soon after Leguina and the PSOE secured control of the regional government. Between its founding and 1987, IMADE generated only modest success in subsidizing the finance of small and medium-sized firms through the regional mutual collateral society, Avalmadrid, the agency most responsible for providing guarantees on private finance to small firms. Yet relations between the two agencies were at arms-length. Avalmadrid tended to be conservative in its lending practices, frustrating IMADE staff who could not consolidate financial support for firm projects. Avalmadrid saw IMADE as an agency pushing risky small and medium-sized firm projects, a view that frustrated IMADE's attempts to secure financial support for firm projects.[22]

Without useful horizontal associations and a growing sense of political vulnerability by the regional PSOE leadership after 1987, IMADE would become a target for centralizing industrial policy resources and distributing political patronage. José Luis Fernández Noriega, Leguina's Chancellor of the Economy, made IMADE's directorate a revolving door of political appointments. The agency experienced three changes of director in 1992 and 1993 alone. In October 1993, Fernández Noriega stripped the agency of most of its affiliated public firms. Nine separate societies were closed in an attempt to "rationalize" IMADE's structure.[23] This process was accompanied by growing public knowledge of the extent of fraud among IMADE's administrators.[24] IMADE's directors bitterly attacked regional politicians for their charges, further weakening the ability of the agency to coordinate resources and support. Private firms continued to view the agency as ineffective.[25] By the mid-1990s, the Community of Madrid could boast of few or no meaningful successes in the area of industrial policy.

22. Author interview with Gloria Ruíz Camacho, economist for Avalmadrid, May 14, 1996, Madrid; and with José Javier Peña Linares, director of information services, IMADE, May 13, 1996, Madrid.

23. For more on this episode, see El País, October 30, 1993.

24. Regional politicians accused high-level administrators of subsidizing firms in which they had a private interest. The accusations developed into a full-blown investigation that uncovered a web of corruption far larger than originally suspected. See El Mundo, October and November, 1994, on the case of "Ibercoop."

25. My own preliminary discussions with businesses in Madrid reflected these opinions. Managers of Espindesa, for example, a chemical firm that had received a small subsidy through IMADE in 1991, told me that IMADE's activities were poorly organized and had no effect on production or employment in their case. Agency officials, I was told, showed little interest with Espindesa's concerns.

Additional Cases from Other Countries

The method of qualitative comparison used in this book has enabled me to "process trace" the diverse ways in which subnational industrial policy can be created and maintained despite the very real threats posed by the delegative dilemma and bureaucratic dysfunction. Yet the analysis is limited on the question of how *global* the conditions undergirding the successful cases are. Given the limitations posed by this kind of research and the fragmentary nature of the research program to date, providing a more seamless survey of the universe of cases is problematic. However, in Chapter 1 I referred to earlier case reports that have motivated this study. During the course of my research and writing I encountered numerous scholars producing work akin to this study on different countries and subnational units. While I cannot summarize all of these case reports here, I will highlight briefly some of their findings. These corroborate the importance of horizontal embeddedness in particular.

The essays gathered by Peter Evans and published in a special issue of *World Development* in 1996[26] and a contemporary set organized by Merilee Grindle and published as a Harvard Institute for International Development study in 1997 (Grindle 1997) represent some of the most important of the case reports to go to press. Although the contributions examine distinct areas of policy and in the main emphasize informal, "close," and cooperative ties between public agencies and clients (vertical embeddedness), the case reports, like Tendler's own study of Ceará, highlight the crucial role of what I call horizontal embeddedness. For example, in Evans (1997a), Wai Fung Lam's study of the management of irrigation systems in Taiwan underscores the importance of horizontal coordination and accountability among public managers and client farmers. Elinor Ostrom offers a similar insight in her analysis of "co-production" in water and sanitation systems in developing countries. In the Harvard study, Hilderbrand and Grindle (1997: 37, 46–47) summarize the insights produced by case studies of development policies in Bolivia, the Central African Republic, Ghana, Morocco, Sri Lanka, and Tanzania, by highlighting the role of "task networks"—"organizations within and outside the public sector" whose coordination is a key factor in the performance of development policies in comparative perspective. As in my analysis of horizontal embeddedness, the contributors find significant evidence that hierarchical relations among agencies tend to produce one-way flows of information while horizontal relations make possible the multidimensional communications that enhance coordination and flexibility.

26. These essays were published as Evans (1997a).

Two earlier and influential works on Italy (Putnam 1993; Locke 1995) have added to the state of the art by providing insight into the developmental utility of horizontal ties. Both describe technologically advanced and highly flexible industrial districts in which local governments play a proactive role. Both analyses favor social factors linking firms, but they also provide glimpses of how the public sector's role is enhanced by being part of horizontal ("polycentric," "reciprocal," and so on) networks involving firms and other public agencies. Like my own study, both of these scholars' works emphasize the *composite* nature of national economies and the *subnational contingency* of developmental outcomes. By building on these and other studies, my comparative work has attempted to specify more precisely the role of the subnational public sector, the contingent political conditions that shape development policy institutions, and the variant outcomes that result from distinct subnational policy regimes.

THE CROSS-NATIONAL COMPARISONS

The comparisons of subnational regions in Spain and Brazil, two countries literally an ocean apart, have demonstrated not only the incidence of causal factors such as political delegation and horizontal embeddedness but their *causal weight*. Specifically, the subnational comparisons reveal aspects of the political economy of industrial policy in these two countries that would not have been uncovered by more aggregate, national surveys. Yet some national attributes do matter while others do not. In the subsections that follow I first highlight those national characteristics that do not explain subnational variation. Then I discuss those cross-national attributes that made a difference in the cases.

Contrasting Alternative Explanations

In this section I return to the list presented in Chapter 1 of the national factors for which this study attempted to control: 1) the "strength" of political parties; 2) fiscal resources and the EU factor; and 3) social capital. I also return to some of the points that were presented in Chapter 2 on "dual transitions" in both countries to illustrate how each country's experience with democratization, decentralization, and the erosion of state-led growth affected the range of opportunities and constraints for subnational industrial policy.

While the comparison of Asturias and Andalusia suggested that significant subnational variations in synergy are possible given the rule of the same party, the broader comparison of party systems between Brazil and Spain highlights the limited role of the "party strength" variable more generally. It would be difficult to find two party systems that are more different than those in Brazil and Spain. Brazil's fragmented and mercurial parties lack the discipline and parliamentary cohesion of parties in Spain. To be sure, other forms of elite cohesion may matter more. For example, in Minas Gerais the lack of elite conflict was due to the long evolution of traditional roles for politicians and development agencies, a history of powerful families in *mineiro* politics, and close relations based on personal ties between the state and national governments. The inability of populist politicians in Rio to institutionalize their support base through the construction of disciplined parties certainly helps to explain the continuation of fragmented elite conflict in that state. But more disciplined parties in Spain did not produce the conditions for synergy in Andalusia. Party organization matters for explaining certain distinctions between the Brazilian and Spanish subnational cases, but synergy emerged in Minas and Asturias despite these differences.

An argument based more exclusively on the analysis of fiscal resources, and more broadly, the history of industrial restructuring, in Brazil and Spain might well have concluded that the Spanish regions would be better placed to generate synergy than the Brazilian states. Yet, as the comparison of Asturias and Andalusia showed, resources alone could not explain the pattern of synergistic ties among the four cases. References to fiscal resources and Spain's inclusion in the EC in 1986 explain some of the differences between the Spanish regions and the Brazilian states. The availability of structural funding, EU cohesion monies, and the industrial reconversion program in Spain provided the regions with a much larger array of fiscal resources than was possible in Brazil. Despite these significant differences, the *mineiro* agencies were able to do more with less by allocating scarce resources and focusing strategically on sectors with large positive externalities. Asturias, unlike Andalusia, for all of its resources in comparison to Minas, did not pursue a resource-intensive industrial policy, but rather focused on the small and medium-sized firms that compose most of the region's employment. The choice and organization of industrial policy strategies were not dependent on fiscal resources and the role of supranational entities such as the EU.[27]

27. The role of the EU and other transnational institutional arrangements such as Mercosul, however, are still relevant for thinking about subnational industrial policy. The fact that neither Mercosul nor the EU specifically include subnational industrial policies in their proscriptions against national industrial policies removes potential legal obstacles to the Brazilian states and the Spanish regions. At the same time, these transnational constraints

The classic social capital argument presents another potential alternative explanation for my findings, but the comparison of the four subnational cases provides only mixed support for it. According to the quantitative indicators for social capital in Knack and Keefer's (1997) study of 29 market economies, Spain retains a significantly greater amount of this resource than Brazil. Yet my evidence suggests that reference to national reservoirs of social capital could not explain variations across the two countries or within them. Moreover, the case of high synergy in Brazil—Minas Gerais—also maintained labor repressive structures and limited associational activity in comparison to Asturias. But even Asturias lacked the diffuse cooperative norms common to regions with high levels of social capital. Asturian labor, for example, was constantly at odds with itself and the national government. If not for the regional government's ability to *engineer* cooperative solutions to some of the region's economic problems, Asturias would have failed to develop any kind of synergy. These comparisons serve to illustrate the highly contingent nature of building synergy. No endowed measure of social capital was responsible for it in Minas or Asturias.

The Constraints and Opportunities Created by "Dual Transitions"

Presented with a composite pattern of synergy in Brazil and Spain, I have argued on behalf of a micropolitical approach and against a strictly national-level perspective. The position I have articulated, however, in no way suggests that national institutions and processes do not matter. Explaining why certain subnational cases could produce synergy while others could not requires a focus on how subnational institutions are created and maintained. In this regard, national institutions and experiences produce opportunities and constraints that make particular patterns of subnational economic policy possible.

Both Spain and Brazil underwent multiple and simultaneous transitions during the 1970s, 1980s, and 1990s. Both countries experienced transitions to democracy at the same time that they faced important economic changes. Yet simultaneity was not the only thing linking these processes in both countries. Decentralization of the state played an important role in democratization and economic reform. The erosion of state-led patterns of development created incentives for subnational

---

create incentives for national development authorities such as the Ministry of Industry in Spain and the National Development Bank in Brazil to "decentralize" industrial policy programs by devolving administration of these policies to subnational governments.

governments to organize their own industrial policies just as it helped to weaken all attempts to centralize control over fiscal policy (albeit to a greater degree in Brazil than in Spain). In this sense, the end of statist models, decentralization, and democratization were linked organically. They set the stage for the patchwork pattern of subnational economic policy regimes that would emerge throughout Spain and Brazil.

In Spain, democratization, decentralization, and the crisis of state-led growth empowered new legal entities (the "autonomies") that served a role not just in defusing the problem of regional identity and nationalism during the transition but in evolving a new federal structure for economic policy-making. The decentralized negotiation of the statutes of autonomy with each region compartmentalized the creation of the federal order, dividing policy authorities among the regions in an unequal manner while still bequeathing open-ended authorities in the area of economic development to all of the regions. In part, this explains the greater array of resources Andalusia enjoyed as a "fast track" region in comparison to Asturias, which was placed on the "slow track." These processes also explain the iterative and bargaining-oriented nature of expanding regional policy authorities and resources in Spain. The prolonged evolution of the "state of the autonomies" played out as a larger game in which the Asturians pursued the creation of an industrial policy. This helps to clarify certain distinctions between Minas Gerais and Asturias that I make below.

In Brazil, decentralization enhanced democratization by attacking the centralization associated with the authoritarian period, but it also destabilized the transition by empowering multiple regional interests, and particularly the governors, with an extensive ability to tax and spend. The resulting macroeconomic contradictions produced by such decentralization at the time national governments pursued stabilization of prices were only partially resolved in the 1990s during the Fernando Henrique Cardoso administration. Despite Cardoso's efforts, however, fiscal crises (most notably the January 1999 crisis of the Real Plan), continued to afflict Brazil, leaving macroeconomic stabilization and fiscal reform as the priority of national economic policy-making.

These factors placed several limits on subnational industrial policy. First, the authority to engage in industrial policy became more openended in the Brazilian states than it was in Spain, but the fiscal constraints on subnational spending were more limiting than they became for the Spanish regions. Second, the erosion of the state-led model and the priority given to macroeconomic stabilization limited the extent to which the central government could complement the evolution of a subnational industrial policy with national programs. In contrast to

Spain, there would be no concerted, multisectoral industrial reconversion in Brazil.

THE IMPORTANCE OF INTERREGIONAL COMPETITION: THE DEPENDENT AND POPULIST-DEPENDENT TYPES

Beyond national patterns of institutional change and industrialization, this book has argued that one other dimension of intergovernmental politics affects the incidence of delegative government and horizontal embeddedness. Interregional competition, which is ignored as often as individual subnational experiences are by the national bias in political economy, plays an integral role in determining the correspondence of delegative government and horizontal embeddedness. In Spain and Brazil, interregional competition produced incentives for subnational politicians to create differentiated economic bureaucracies, but only where intraregional elite competition allowed for delegation. Yet, conceivably, even under conditions in which intraregional elite competition is low, the incentives for delegation and the creation of horizontal embeddedness may remain low. This, I argue, is due to the weakness of interregional competition.

Such experiences are typical of unitary or centralized federal states in which the central government effectively constrains the subnational units from competing for fiscal resources and policy authorities. In this context, subnational governments are more likely to be dependent on central government. Intraregional elite competition and subnational policy autonomy may increase over time in such cases, creating political pressures on incumbents to use whatever central or subnational resources and authorities they have at their disposal to cultivate support. This creates a second type: a populist-dependent case. In this section I employ a longitudinal comparison of the Mexican states to demonstrate how both types emerge. The empirical analysis shows that neither case can produce or maintain synergy due to the weakness of political delegation and/or horizontal embeddedness.

Despite its constitutional federalism, Mexico maintains highly centralized policy authorities and fiscal management systems, especially in the arena of economic policy-making. The persistence of an extraordinarily strong presidency, a national legislature oriented to national and not subnational interests, and a high degree of national party discipline, primarily within the Partido Revolucionário Institucional (PRI), have reinforced these centralizing tendencies. The result has been largely closed-ended federal constraints on subnational policy authority and spending and revenue-raising capacities. While the opposition parties were able to assume control of the Chamber of Deputies in 1997, the presidency in 2000, a handful of state governments, and control almost 20 percent of all municipalities, these changes did not substantially shift bargaining leverage to subnational governments. As a result, decentralization has evolved gradually and it has been based on the transfer of expenditures and grants with high levels of federal discretion but little transfer of own-source revenue-raising powers to Mexico's thirty-one states.

Beginning with the José López Portillo *sexenio* (six-year term, 1976–82) and extending into the terms of his successors, Miguel de la Madrid (1982–88) and Carlos Salinas de Gortari (1988–94), Mexican governments embraced decentralization as a mechanism of promoting efficiency and "democratization" (Rodríguez 1993: 134). These reforms, however, maintained, and in some cases extended, federal discretion over subnational taxation and spending. In 1980, President López Portillo expanded the powers of state and municipal governments. Under a new Ley de Coordinación Fiscal, the federal government allocated more of its revenue to the states.[28] In return, the states surrendered their more than one-third share of the federal sales tax and their excise taxes on consumption and production. This continued a historical trend in which, by 1991, state tax revenues were just over a third less than what they had been before 1940 and municipal revenues were a quarter of what they had been prior to the revolution (Díaz Cayeros 1995: 81–82). Under the new Sistema Nacional de Coordinación Fiscal (National System of Fiscal Coordination), intergovernmental contracts coordinated by the federal Secretaría de Hacienda y Crédito Público (SHCP) required states to trade constitutionally protected tax authorities for increases in federal transfers. These nominally voluntary provisions known as *convenios de adhesión* were accompanied by strict federal guidelines that required the states to pursue tax evaders (*convenio de colaboración administrativa*).[29] Under the new

28. The 1980 reform changed the tax system, granting the states the task of collecting the federal value-added tax (*impuesto al valor agregado*, IVA), which substituted the federal sales tax (*impuesto sobre ingresos mercantiles*, ISIM). The states would then forward IVA revenues to the federal treasury, which would then transfer a portion of these resources to the states and municipalities according to a national formula. The states were also required to transfer 20 percent of the federal revenues they collected to the municipalities. Under the new Ley de Coordinación Fiscal, federal transfers were organized into three funds—the Fondo General de Participaciones (FGP), the Fondo Financiero Complementário (FFC), and the Fondo de Fomento Municipal (FFM). A reform in 1990 grouped the FGP and the FFC into a single fund that retained the name FGP. The 1990 reform also centralized collection of the IVA.

29. Although these contracts were "voluntary," the states' failure to adhere to them would require the surrender of all claims to federal funding. See Elías (1997).

formulaic revenue-sharing system, the federal government maintained control over the tax system, including collection of the country's chief tax, the Value-Added Tax. Constitutional constraints on foreign borrowing and substantial discretion by the Ministry of Finance and the national development bank (Banobras) over the contracting of subnational debt created hard budget constraints that kept the states' debt to only 2 percent of GDP during the 1990s (Dillinger, Perry, and Webb 2000: 20–21). These practices added to existing constitutional prohibitions on state duties on internal and external trade such as sales taxes, and taxes on natural resources. They also upheld exclusive federal authorities to regulate financial institutions, impose taxes on foreign trade, and natural resources (Díaz Cayeros 1999).

Federal discretion over the new revenue-sharing system made the states "dependent sovereignties," as it kept the power of the purse firmly in the hands of the president and his chief economic ministries (Rodríguez 1997). Federal discretion also favored PRI-affiliated states and severely constrained the activities of state governments under the command of the opposition Partido Acción Nacional (PAN) and the Partido de la Revolución Democrática (PRD). National ministries in health and education set standards that limited state authority over the spending of monies in these areas.

While social spending became increasingly decentralized, control over the earmarking of these funds continued to be strongly centralized. De la Madrid, while still secretary of programming and the budget (SPP) for López Portillo, organized joint federal-state financing of public works through a series of agreements known as *convenios*.[30] These were later consolidated into a singular "regional development" budget (*ramo* 26) that was directly managed by federal officials. Through joint private-public "planning cells" and local offices of the Secretariat of Programming and the Budget, the *convenios* financed projects first defined by SPP officials in the National Development Plan and later allocated after bargaining between federal and state authorities. This system produced patterns of social spending that have upheld federal priorities, whether these are based on objective criteria or particular political interests (Elías 1997: 18–19; Díaz Cayeros 1999).

Numerous studies of the Salinas *sexenio*'s best-known contribution to this decentralized system of social spending—the Program of National Solidarity (PRONASOL)—have shown that discretion over the funding

---

30. These were initially organized as Convenios Unicos de Desarrollo (CUDs) but were later renamed Convenios de Desarrollo Social (CDSs) during the Salinas *sexenio*.

and management of this program was centralized and closed-ended. The program was directly administered by the SPP, and later by its successor, the Ministry of Social Development (SEDESOL).[31] Once funded by the Treasury with federal transfers, SEDESOL, along with governors and federal agency officials involved with the local "planning cells," selected candidate municipalities for PRONASOL funding. By requiring "grass-roots participation" at the local level of decision-making and by centralizing budgeting decisions, the bureaucratic structure of PRONASOL undercut the authority of state legislatures and municipal governments. This reduced the costs of allocating PRONASOL funding, particularly for the most expensive projects, according to federal priorities and the interests of national PRI politicians (Rodríguez 1997: 104; Bailey 1994; Molinar and Weldon 1994; Bruhn 1996).[32]

Although transfers to municipalities increased during the 1990s and the 1983 reform of article 115 of the constitution granted municipalities exclusive authority over property taxes, the federal government retained some indirect control over the management of these funds. Municipal governments remained dependent upon state legislatures and the governors who retained veto power over changes in property tax rates and, in practice, assessed taxes as few municipalities maintained up-to-date property cadastres. The state governments also maintained control over the allocation of discretionary grants to municipalities (Elías 1997: 5–6). While the formulas for distributing these funds are based on objective criteria of population size and tax receipts, incentives exist for the use of more political criteria (Rodríguez 1997: 107–10). This constraint encourages municipal politicians to remain loyal to their governors, but they also are limited by three-year terms and no reelection, which creates a counter-tendency not to cooperate with state politicians when they seek municipal support for long-term projects (Elías 1998: 8; Ward 1995). When disputes arise, local governments have little recourse through the courts, as no municipality has ever made a claim successfully against a higher level of government (Rowland 1998: 13). Given these constraints and extant federal leverage over the states, the center maintains much indirect control over municipalities.

Federal control over revenue-sharing and collection have limited the extent of interregional competition in Mexican federalism. Even attempts by the states to levy "temporary" taxes (for example, the proposal in Chihuahua to impose a tax on the *maquiladoras*) have been stymied by

31. SEDESOL was created to replace SPP in 1992. During the Salinas *sexenio* both PRONASOL and the CDSs and their "planning cells" functioned simultaneously.

32. The Zedillo administration has slashed SEDESOL funding and redirected funds to municipal governments through targeted federal grants (*ramo* 33).

federal fiscal discretion (Ward and Rodríguez 1999b: 97–124). This has helped Mexican federalism avoid cross-state rivalries that have fueled sometimes destructive "devil take the hindmost" scenarios elsewhere. But it has also created few incentives for subnational politicians to delegate authority to horizontally embedded industrial policy-making networks. In the rare cases that subnational industrial policy is designed, fiscal dependency on federal programs has limited funding and creates countervailing incentives to shape these policies in ways that please federal authorities. Perhaps the most studied case is that of the Jorge Treviño (PRI) governorship (1985–91) in the state of Nuevo Leon, the second most important industrial economy in Mexico. Treviño's administration attempted to create "business-friendly" policies through financial and technical aid agencies run out of the Secretariats of Industrial and Commercial Promotion and Labor Services and Productivity. The "two-tiered system" was hierarchical, underdeveloped, and depended upon the distribution of rewards to the governor's allies. This political *raison d'etre*, and not the pressures of interregional competition, has more often been at the center of such experiences. In the Nuevo Leon case, fiscal constraints and political loyalties to the national PRI hierarchy severely limited funding and innovation in industrial policy (Méndez 1997). This experience is indicative of other Mexican states, since the most prominent cases of subnational industrial policy in Mexico emerge in core economies such as Nuevo Leon. In the most dynamic manufacturing sector in Mexico—the *maquiladora* sector in the northern states—subnational governments (both state and municipal) have played little role in promoting the diversification and growth of industrial activity (Carrillo and Micker 1997).[33] Federal industrial policy mechanisms have been far more important in these cases, but many of these have either bypassed subnational governments or made them mere implementers of national policy (Ward and Rodríguez 1999b).

During the 1990s, an additional dimension was added to the limits on subnational industrial policy created by dependent government. The gradual liberalization of the political system, escalating conflicts between PRI presidents and governors, and increasing electoral competition from the opposition PAN and PRD in both national and subnational elections created incentives for the governors to pursue populist campaigns. In 1989 the first opposition party assumed control of the first state governorship (the PAN in Baja California Norte). By early 1999, the

33. Author interview with Luis D. Nava, director of the Asociación de Maquiladoras (AMAC), Ciudad Juárez, December 4, 2000. I thank the ten Carleton students who traveled with me to Mexico in December 2000 for their inspired questions and insights.

Intraregional Competition

High   Low

Populist Government	Delegative Government + Horizontal Embeddedness
Cases: Rio de Janeiro, Andalusia, São Paulo, Community of Madrid	Cases: Minas Gerais, Asturias, Ceará, Valencia
Populist-Dependent Government	Dependent Government
Cases: Mexican states during the 1990s	Cases: Mexican states before t he 1990s

Low

FIG 6.1   Distribution of Cases

opposition had won seven more state governorships. In June 1997 the PRI lost control over the Chamber of Deputies. These changes in intergovernmental relations altered the structure of political careers by elevating the authority of the governors (Ward and Rodríguez 1999a).[34] In the current period of increasing partisan fragmentation, governors more often than not face state legislatures under the command of rival parties, weak support even from their own state congressional parties, and a federal presidency that, until Vicente Fox's victory in 2000, remained in the hands of the PRI. For all three major parties, democratization increased the competitiveness of the subnational political game and made gaining and retaining governorships a necessity for garnering national power.

A more competitive subnational political arena coupled with the continuation of central constraints on state spending have created stronger incentives for the governors, even those from the opposition PAN and PRD, to employ economic policy for political purposes. The populist tenor of several subnational campaigns, including those of PRI candidates who have even taken on their party's national hierarchy in states

34. Evidence of this is the fact that the major contenders for the presidency, including the two primary candidates of the PRI in 1999, have held gubernatorial office. Díaz Cayeros (1999) has shown that Mexican politicians tend to run for governor after finishing their terms in the Senate. Given the increased contestability and importance of gubernatorial seats, senators now have more incentives to satisfy subnational interests and particularly those of incumbent governors, even if such actions clash with presidential preferences.

such as Tabasco, is indicative that the politics of the Mexican states are moving into a populist-dependent framework. Richard Snyder (1999a, 1999b) has found that in order to manage the new imperatives of incumbency, subnational executives may unintentionally create opportunities for social actors (as in his case of Oaxaca, small coffee producers) to transform neocorporatist institutions into participatory regimes. Yet neither neocorporatist retrenchment nor the advent of participatory regimes has created the kind of subnational agency networks seen elsewhere. The new incentives facing incumbents have only encouraged the politicization of economic policies in a range of policy areas. Nevertheless, new research on the decentralization of fiscal resources and policy authorities in the future might indicate that in an era of increasing interregional competition, some incumbents might become better placed than others to embrace industrial policies with long time horizons.

In comparative perspective, the changing role of the Mexican states in economic policy-making fills out the "off cells" of Table 1.1. Table 6.1 updates the distribution of cases, including some of the cases of populist and delegative government covered in this chapter.

RESEARCH IMPLICATIONS FOR THE POLITICAL ECONOMY OF DECENTRALIZATION

The study of "decentralization" in developing countries is quickly becoming a focus of much work in political economy (for instance, Willis, Garman, and Haggard 1999; Garman, Haggard, and Willis 2001; IDB 1994; Montero and Samuels, forthcoming). What might be called the "first wave" of this literature has concentrated on the political determinants of decentralization; how distinct national institutions (for instance, political party systems, patterns of malapportionment, and electoral rules) shape the devolution of fiscal resources and policy responsibilities. The study in this book, while more focused on subnational capacity for taking advantage of decentralization, offers some research implications for the emerging comparative literature on decentralization.

First, this study provides further support for a corrective to analyses that focus exclusively on national electoral and partisan institutions. It is evident here that such analyses lose much of the richness of the politics of decentralization. The comparisons of regions within Spain and Brazil suggest that similar national institutions can produce composite patterns of subnational policy-making. By focusing on a top-down approach (that is, national institutions shape subnational capacities), many recent studies of decentralization fail to account for the variables that are endogenous to subnational politics: the role of political interests, organizational attributes, and ideas. These are the factors that will tell us more about the *implications* of decentralization for developing countries. They will also demonstrate that overly simplifying arguments about the efficiency gains from decentralization based either on "competitive" or "fiscal federalist" models must be qualified. Similar caveats must also be reserved for observations based on the assumption that subnational politics are endemically clientelistic. Under the conditions of delegative government and horizontal embeddedness, some subnational governments can develop the efficiencies that competitive and fiscal federalism scholars hold forth as outcomes of decentralization. Where these conditions are absent, populist government will make decentralization look like a mechanism for reinforcing subnational clientelism.

As the decentralization literature moves from the "first wave" studies of political determinants to the "second wave" assessments of policy implications, scholars will need to ask how subnational political economies should be studied. In Chapter 1 I contrasted the approach taken in this study with several articulated by authors such as Putnam, Tendler, Locke, and Evans. Each of these authors (and others not mentioned here) have contributed vastly to our understanding of how subnational politics and institutional arrangements affect patterns of economic change. The approaches they have pursued, however, are still too tethered to one of two frameworks, which Granovetter (1985) calls the "oversocialization" or "undersocialization" of politics. Associational approaches that favor the analysis of social organizations and their attributes support our observations about the importance of the form of ties (horizontal embeddedness). But these approaches have neglected the role of subnational states, even as Evans (1997b) has asserted that the ability of public agencies to scale up social action may be more important than the organization of interfirm collective action and social organizations (for example, soccer clubs and bowling leagues) in developing countries. Associational approaches also envision patterns of social interaction that might be trust-building when observed in their societal context but these same networks can also become Olsonite distributional coalitions when they assert their interests in the economic bureaucracy. Hence, these perspectives tend to oversocialize political economy.

The countertendency, to "undersocialize" political economy, emerges from efforts to give analytical pride of place to the technical adeptness of "professionals" and their relative autonomy from undue sources of societal influence. While corporately coherent Weberian states are important to policy formulation and implementation, "technopols" and their agencies do not operate ensconced from politics. Rather, their authorities and resources come from political support, which relies as much upon individual politicians and their strategic ability to beat out their rivals as it does on the capacity of these leaders to keep their core constituency satisfied (Bates and Krueger 1993b). "Autonomy" of state agencies is unworkable in this context. Not only would it deny these agencies access to the information and contact with the real economy they require to compose and implement policy, but it would undermine their political survival.

Based on these observations, our understanding of subnational political economy can only be enhanced by taking certain attributes from each of these approaches without slipping into the tendency to "oversocialize" or "undersocialize." Associational approaches are correct about the role of horizontal ties, but state organizations are also potential players in such networks, and not just as *primus inter pares*. The state continues to have a unique role in development. Meanwhile, Weberian models are correct to identify distributive struggles over policy as a threat to the consolidation of development missions. Yet the corporate coherence that is a *sine qua non* of Weberian states is a function of the interests of politicians and the political context in which they function. In the face of escalating levels of elite conflict, these structures can be undermined in the interests of cultivating societal support for the incumbent.

The current study has attempted to provide a generalizable approach to explain patterns of subnational political economy. By emphasizing the role of state agencies, the interests of politicians, the role of contending social actors such as business and labor, and the effects of national and subnational institutional change, the theory explains the dynamics of political conflict and cooperation that produce synergy. As the research program into subnational political economy and decentralization in developing countries continues, it will become more important to understand these dynamics.

Aguirre Prado, Carlos, economist for SODECO, June 28, 1995, Langreo, Asturias.

Bañuelos, Belén Menéndez, chief of statistics and documentation, Regional Directorate of Economy and Planning, Chancellery of the Economy and Planning, July 26, 1994, Oviedo, Asturias.

Bayón Mariné, Ignacio, former minister of industry under second UCD government, July 7, 1994, Madrid.

Cañes, Encarna Rodriguez, Regional Directorate of Economy and Planning, Chancellery of the Economy and Planning, July 26, 1994, Oviedo, Asturias.

Carasco, Nieves, former director of industry, Asturias 1988–91; director of Instituto Tecnológico de Materiales (ITMA), June 28, 1995, Llanera, Asturias.

Casado, Miguel Rivas, advisor of studies and plans, IFA, April 11, 1996, Seville, Andalucía.

Cienfuegos-Jovellanos, Pedro de Silva, former president of the Principado de Asturias (1982–90), June 26, 1995, Gijón, Asturias.

Dario Díaz, CCOO organizer, June 27, 1995, Oviedo, Asturias.

Espina Montero, Álvaro, secretary of state for industry, MINER, June 29, 1994, May 30, 1996, Madrid.

Fanjul, Óscar, president of REPSOL, economist and advisor to minister of industry, Carlos Solchaga, July 18, 1994, Madrid.

Feliz, José, Socialist deputy for Asturias, June 15, 1995, Madrid.

Fernández, Javier, CREP director, May 31, 1995, Oviedo, Asturias.

Fernández, Purificación, UGT representative on CES, Secretariat of Organization, UGT, May 9, 1996, Madrid.

García Fernández, Severino, administrative director of the SRP, June 26, 1995, Llanera, Asturias.

Gómez González, Consuelo "Cielo", engineer for SODECO, June 28, 1995, Langreo, Asturias.

Corujedo, María Rosa, economic advisor, Presidency of the Principado de Asturias, May 31, 1995, Oviedo, Asturias.

González-Rico Herrero, Javier, assistant director, SAYPE, June 26, 1995, Llanera, Asturias.

Gutiérrez Palacios, Rodolfo, sociologist, Universidad de Oviedo, July 26, 1994, May 29, 1995, Oviedo, Asturias.

Maravall, Fernando, Former economist for MINER and special advisor to Carlos Solchaga, June 27, 1994, Madrid.

Martín Pascual, Gonzalo, coordinator of the Secretariat of Organization, UGT, May 9, 1996, Madrid.

Martín, Paloma, UGT economist, June 7, 1994, Madrid.

Martins, Carlos Alberto, adjunct director of the Office of Cinematic and Audiovisual Promotion, Chancellery of Culture (Community of Madrid), May 20, 1996, Madrid.

Mendoza, Javier Larraya, director of economics, IKEI (Basque Country), July 21, 1994, San Sebastian, Basque.

Mestanza, Gervásio Cordero, subdirector general of regional planning, Ministry of Economy, July 11, 1994, Madrid.

Miguel, Sonia Cano, technical assistant, CESGAR, March 27, 1996, Madrid.

Molinas Sans, César, director general of planning, Ministry of Economy, July 11, 1994, Madrid.

Moys, Ronald, director of Directorate General 16, Regional Policy, European Union, June 23, 1995, Oviedo, Asturias.

Pedreira, Manuel Sesto, economist, UNED, March 27, 1996, Madrid.

Peña Linares, José Javier, geographer and director of information services, IMADE, May 13, 1996, Madrid.

Pérez, Juan, technical assistant, General Directorate of Industry, Energy and Mines, Chancellery of Economy (Community of Madrid), April 25, 1996, Madrid.

Pérez, Manuel Alfredo, economist and Socialist deputy in the Asturian Junta, May 30, 1995, Oviedo, Asturias.

Rincón, Donald Alfred, technical counselor, Ministry of Industry, June 30, 1994, Madrid.

Rojas Sánchez, Rosendo, director of the Area of Business Information and Research, December 11, 1998, Madrid.

Ruíz Camacho, Glória, economist, Avalmadrid, May 14, 1996, Madrid.

Suárez González, José Manuel, Metallurgical Federation, UGT, June 7, 1994, March 26, 1996, Madrid.

Suárez Puente, María José, director of technical services, IFR, July 26, 1994, May 17, 1995, Llanera, Asturias.

Firm interviews

Arbesú, Pelayo Roces, Juan Roces, S.A., March–April, 1996, Asturias.

Arcillas Refractarias, S.A. (Arciresa), March–April, 1996, Asturias.

Astur Calco, S.A., March–April, 1996, Asturias.

Asturpharma, S.A., March–April, 1996, Asturias and Madrid.

Auxquimía, S.A., March–April, 1996, Asturias.

Compania Electrometálica Asturiana, S.A.L., March–April, 1996, Asturias.

De la Lama, Alejandra, Department of Public Relations, Kodak, May 16, 1996, Madrid.

Espindesa, March–April, 1996, Madrid.

Muebles Campa, S.A., March–April, 1996, Asturias.

Ortega González, Juan Antonio, Construcciones Metalicas Joama, S.L., March–April, 1996, Asturias.

Pérez Díaz, Jesús Serafín, manager, Aguas de Fuensanta, S.A., March–April, 1996, Asturias.

Rodríguez Obejero, Juan Carlos, executive, Du Pont, Ibérica, May 31, 1995, Asturias.

Seresco Asturiana, S.A., March–April, 1996, Asturias.

Tamargo, Sérgio, Electro Materiales KLK, S.A., March–April, 1996, Asturias.

Affonso, Rui de Britto Alvares, director, Fundação do Desenvolvimento Administrativo-Instituto de Economia do Setor Publico (FUNDAP-IESP), July 4, 1996, São Paulo, SP.

Alves Castanheira, José Afonso, former CDI head and BNDES executive, March 6, 1995, São Paulo, SP.

Barbosa, Kenneth Albernaz, manager of external relations, INDI, January 31, 1995, June 13, 1996, Belo Horizonte, Minas Gerais.

Barros de Castro, Antônio, economist and former president of the BNDES under the Itamar Franco government, March 27, 1995, Rio de Janeiro, RJ.

Brant, Paulo Eduardo Rocha, director of credit, BDMG, June 21, 1996, Belo Horizonte, Minas Gerais.

Bresciani, Luiz Paulo, Metallurgy Union of São Bernardo, CUT, July 27, 1993, São Bernardo do Campo, São Paulo.

Brunelli, Audenir Antonio, executive secretary of the National Forum of State Secretaries of Science and Technology and director general of the Secretariat of Science and Technology of the State of São Paulo, July 3, 1996, São Paulo, SP.

Carneiro, Maria Christina, advisor for the Planning Directorate, BNDES, June 7, 1996, Rio de Janeiro, RJ.

Castro, Levy Pinto de, ex-finance director of Rio de Janeiro's Metro and retired BNDES economist; currently works for the Rio state government task force on privatization, June 4, 1995, Rio de Janeiro, RJ.

Castro, Vanessa R.S., marketing advisor, CODIN, May 30, 1996, Rio de Janeiro, RJ.

Chaves, Benjamin Collares, director of special projects, INDI, February 22, 1995, Belo Horizonte, Minas Gerais.

Chaves, Marilena, chief advisor, Secretariat of Planning, SEPLAN, June 14, 1996, Belo Horizonte, Minas Gerais.

Cooperman, Hélio, director of the Economics Department of the FIESP, November 29, 1994, São Paulo, SP.

Costa Avila, Jorge de Paula, director of economic studies and business promotion, CODIN, May 30, 1996, Rio de Janeiro, RJ.

Costa, Ricardo de Castro, operational superintendent, AD-Rio, May 31, 1996, Rio de Janeiro, RJ.

Costa, Rodrigo Fiuza, chemical engineer, INDI, June 18, 1996, Belo Horizonte, Minas Gerais.

Cruz, Eduardo Mello da Costa, director, INDI, June 18, 1996, Belo Horizonte, Minas Gerais.

Cunha, Patricia, economist at FUNDAP-IESP, February 7, 1995, São Paulo, SP.

Cunha Filho, Jorge Fernandes da, chief of staff, Secretariat of State for Economic Development and Tourism, Government of the State of Rio de Janeiro; ex-President of CODIN (Moreira Franco and second Brizola governments), August 2, 1999, Rio de Janeiro, RJ.

Diniz, Clélio Campolina, professor of economics, CEDEPLAR, February 22, 1995, June 20, 1996, Belo Horizonte, Minas Gerais.

Diniz, Eli Roque, professor of sociology and political science, IUPERJ, July 10, 1996, Rio de Janeiro, RJ.

Dulci, Otávio, professor of sociology and political science, UFMG, June 24, 1996, Belo Horizonte, Minas Gerais.

Ferreira, Carlos Mauricio C., special advisor to the Secretariat of State for Industry and Commerce; ex-president of the Fundação João Pinheiro, June13, 1996, Belo Horizonte, Minas Gerais.

Fonseca, Juarez Boaventura, economist and assistant to the Executive Board, INDI, June 14, 1996, Belo Horizonte, Minas Gerais.

Gomes de Figueiredo, Paulo Henrique, director of the Development Agency of Itabira, March 2, 1995, April 6, 1995, Itabira, Minas Gerais.

Holanda, Felipe de, economist at the FUNDAP-IESP, February 7, 1995, São Paulo, SP.

Kux, Dieter, mechanical engineer, INDI, February 22, 1995, June 18, 1996, Belo Horizonte, Minas Gerais.

Lima, Marco Antonio de Araujo, president of CODIN and ex-BNDES executive director, June 5, 1996, Rio de Janeiro, RJ.

Longobucco Teixeira, Iolanda, economist in the division of industrial technology, BNDES, May 28, 1996, Rio de Janeiro, RJ.

Lopes, Edmar Vidigal, engineer and director of the Development Agency of Timóteo, April 7, 1995, Timóteo, Minas Gerais.

Meilman, Doris Lustman, director of planning, BNDES, June 5, 1996, Rio de Janeiro, RJ.

Monteiro Rego, Carlos Alberto, director of economic development, Institute of Planning of Rio de Janeiro, former chemical engineer in the Institute of Planning and Applied Economics (IPEA), June 5, 1996, Rio de Janeiro, RJ.

Montenegro Filho, José, researcher, National Confederation of Industries (CNI), May 28, 1996, Rio de Janeiro, RJ.

Moreira, Márcio, metallurgy engineer, INDI, February 22, 1995, Belo Horizonte, Minas Gerais.

Nardim, Marcelo, chief of the planning area, BNDES, July 14, 1999, Rio de Janeiro, RJ.

Oliveira Filho, Gesner José, adjunct secretary, Secretariat of Economic Policy, Ministry of Economy (Itamar Franco administration), December 7, 1994, Brasília, Federal District.

Oliveira, Maria de Fatima, Division of Industrial Technology, CNI, May 28, 1996, Rio de Janeiro, RJ.

Paiva Ferreira, Claudio de, superintendent of industrialization, Secretariat of State for Industry and Commerce, June 26, 1996, Belo Horizonte, Minas Gerais.

Peregrino, Paulo, marketing chief, CODIN, July 20, 1999, Rio de Janeiro, RJ.

Pordeus, Iran Almeida, chief executive, BDMG, June 13, 1996, Belo Horizonte, Minas Gerais.

Ramalho, Yolanda Maria Melo, chief of the Department of Entrepreneurial Research, BNDES, June 5, 1996, Rio de Janeiro, RJ.

Ramos de Oliveira, Carlyle, general coordinator of agroindustry, Ministry of Industry (Itamar Franco administration), December 9, 1994, Brasília, Federal District.

Ribeiro, José Carlos Gomes, agroindustrial engineer, INDI, February 22, 1995, Belo Horizonte, Minas Gerais.

Rodrigues da Cunha, Francisco, mayor of Mateus Leme, June 19, 1996, Mateus Leme, Minas Gerais.

Rodriguez, Vicente, sociologist, FUNDAP-IESP, February 17, 1995, São Paulo, SP.

Rossi, Charles, chief of the Department of Industrial Promotion and New Investments, FIRJAN, May 29, 1996, Rio de Janeiro, RJ.

Sacenco Kornijezuk, Nilton, adjunct secretary, Secretariat of Industrial Policy, Ministry of Industry (Itamar Franco administration), December 9, 1994, Brasília, Federal District.

Salej, Stefan Bogdan, President of FIEMG, April 6, 1995, Belo Horizonte, Minas Gerais.

Sato, Heroyuge, director of the Subsection on the Textile Industry, ABIMAQ-SINDIMAQ, January 11, 1995, São Paulo, SP.

Suzigan, Wilson, economist, University of Campinas (UNICAMP); former economist at IPEA, December 12, 1994, Campinas, São Paulo.

Teixeira, Carlos Alberto, ex-president of BDMG (1988–90); ex-secretary of the Secretariat of State for Industry and Commerce, June 25, 1996, Belo Horizonte, Minas Gerais.

Tomas Salles, Ana Beatriz, advisor of entrepreneurial planning, CODIN, May 30, 1996, Rio de Janeiro, RJ.

Valladares, Paulo, advisor to the executive board, INDI; former president of BDMG and INDI, June 18, 1996, Belo Horizonte, Minas Gerais.

Vieira, Cláudio Felix, researcher at Price Waterhouse do Brasil, July 31, 1993, July 3, 1996, São Paulo, SP.

Firm Interviews

Araújo, Murilo, manager, Nansen (electric parts), June 17, 1996, Belo Horizonte, Minas Gerais.

Blaesing, Dirk, president, Fairway Filamentos (Rhodia and Hoescht joint venture) (industrial textiles/chemicals), July 3, 1996, São Paulo, SP.

Marcucci, Paulo, manager, Kadron (auto parts), June 17, 1996, Belo Horizonte, Minas Gerais.

Pereira, José Eduardo de Lima, director of external relations, FIAT (automobiles), April 4, 1995, Betim, Minas Gerais.

Rossi, Nelson, Jr., director, American National Cans (aluminum containers), July 1, 1996, São Paulo, SP.

Salej, Stefan Bogdan, CEO of Technowatt (illumination), April 6, 1995, Belo Horizonte, Minas Gerais.

Santos, Alzimir Mello, Brasif (construction equipment), June 20, 1996, Belo Horizonte, Minas Gerais.

Sumiden Tokai do Brasil Indústrias Elécticas (electronic components), June 25, 1996, Mateus Leme, Minas Gerais.

Torres, Marco Antônio, director, Aymoré (food processing), June 17, 1996, Belo Horizonte, Minas Gerais.

Zica, Petrônico, director, Delp Engenharia (mechanical parts), June 20, 1996, Belo Horizonte, Minas Gerais.

BIBLIOGRAPHY

Abrúcio, Fernando Luiz. 1998. *Os Barões da Federação: O Poder dos Governadores no Brasil Pós-Autoritário*. São Paulo: Editora Hucitec.
Abu-El-Haj, Jawdat. 1997. "Neodesenvolvimentismo no Ceará: Autonomia Empresarial e Política Industrial." *Revista Econômica do Nordeste* 28, no. 3 (July–September): 327–45.
Aceña, Pablo Martín, and Francisco Comín. 1990. "La acción regional del Instituto Nacional de Industria, 1941–1976." In *Pautas regionales de la industrialización española (Siglos XIX y XX)*. Barcelona: Editorial Ariel.
———. 1991. *INI: 50 años de industrialización en España*. Madrid: Espasa Calpe.
Addis, Caren. 1999. *Taking the Wheel: Auto Parts Firms and the Political Economy of Industrialization in Brazil*. University Park: Pennsylvania State University Press.
Affonso, Rui de Britto Álvares. 1995. "A Federação no Brasil: Impasses e Perspectivas." In Rui de Britto Álvares Affonso and Pedro Luiz Barros Silva, eds., *A Federação em Perspectiva: Ensaios Selecionados*. São Paulo, SP: FUNDAP.
———. 1988. "Federalismo Tributário e Crise Econômica: Brasil 1975–1985." Masters' thesis. Campinas, S.P.: Instituto de Economia, UNICAMP (Universidade Estadual de Campinas).
Afonso, José Roberto Rodrigues. 1995. "A Questão Tributária e o Financiamento dos Diferentes Níveis de Governo." In Rui de Britto Álvares Affonso and Pedro Luiz Barros Silva, eds., *A Federação em Perspectiva: Ensaios Selecionados*. São Paulo, S.P.: FUNDAP.
———. 1994. "Descentralização Fiscal: Revendo Idéias." *Ensaios FEE* 15, no. 2: 353–89.
Afonso, José Roberto Rodrigues, Júlio César Maciel Ramundo, and Erika Amorim Araujo. 1998. "Breves Notas Sobre o Federalismo Fiscal no Brasil." Mimeo.

Aghion, Philippe, and Jean Tirole. 1997. "Formal and Real Authority in Organizations." *Journal of Political Economy* 105, no. 1: 1–29.

Agranoff, Robert. 1996. "Federal Evolution in Spain." *International Political Science Review* 17, no. 4: 385–401.

Alesina, Alberto and Alex Cukierman. 1990. "The Politics of Ambiguity." *The Quarterly Journal of Economics* 105, no. 4 (November): 829–50.

Allen, David. 2000. "Cohesion and the Structural Funds." In Helen Wallace and William Wallace, eds., *Policy-Making in the European Union.* Fourth ed. New York: Oxford University Press.

Alves, Maria Helena Moreira. 1989. "Trade Unions in Brazil: A Search for Autonomy and Organization." In Edward C. Epstein, ed., *Labor Autonomy and the State in Latin America.* Boston: Unwin Hyman.

Ames, Barry. 2001. *The Deadlock of Democracy in Brazil: Interests, Identities, and Institutions in Comparative Politics.* Ann Arbor: University of Michigan Press.

———. 1995. "Electoral Strategy Under Open-List Proportional Representation." *American Journal of Political Science* 39, no. 2 (May): 406–33.

———. 1987. *Political Survival: Politicians and Public Policy in Latin America.* Berkeley: University of California Press.

Amsden, Alice. 1989. *Asia's Next Giant: South Korea and Late Industrialization.* New York: Oxford University Press.

Anes Alvarez, Rafael. 1987. "Límites de la primera industrialización en Asturias." In Nicolás Sánchez-Albornoz, ed., *La modernización económica de España, 1830–1930.* Madrid: Alianza.

Angel Rojo, Luis. 1987. "La crisis de la economía española, 1973–1984." In Jordi Nadal and Jaume Torras, eds., *La economía española en el siglo 20: una perspectiva histórica.* Barcelona: Editorial Ariel.

Arias Fernández, Angel M. 1989. "El desarrollo tecnológico de Asturias ante Europa (pretexto para una evaluación empírica)." *Economía y Sociedad* 2 (June): 119–32.

Arias Fernández, Angel M., and Juan A. Vázquez García. 1988. "Asturias: crisis y declive industrial." *Economía Industrial* 263–64 (September–December): 110–25.

———. 1986. "Situación y perspectivas del sector industrial en Asturias." *Información Comercial Española* 635 (July): 127–43.

Aríztegui, Javier. 1988. "La política monetaria." In José Luis García Delgado, ed., *España: economía.* Madrid: Espasa-Calpe.

Arretche, Marta T. S. 1996. "Mitos da Descentralização: Mais Democracia e Eficiência nas Políticas Públicas?" *Revista Brasileira de Ciências Sociais* 11, no. 31 (June): 44–66.

Asturgar, S. G. R. 1995. *Informe anual—1994.* Oviedo: Asturgar, S. G. R.

Baer, Werner. 1965. *Industrialization and Economic Development in Brazil.* Homewood, Ill.: Richard D. Irwin.

————. 1969. *The Development of the Brazilian Steel Industry.* Nashville, Tenn.: Vanderbilt University Press.

————. 1989. *The Brazilian Economy: Growth and Development.* Third ed. New York: Praeger.

————. 1990. "A Industrialização Brasileira e a Nova Política Industrial." *Ensaios FEE* (August): 83–96.

————. 1995. *The Brazilian Economy: Growth and Development.* Fourth ed. New York: Praeger.

Bailey, John. 1994. "Centralism and Political Change in Mexico: The Case of National Solidarity." In Wayne Cornelius, Ann L. Craig, and Jonathan Fox, eds., *Transforming State-Society Relations in Mexico: The National Solidarity Strategy.* La Jolla: Center for U.S.-Mexican Studies, University of California, San Diego.

Ballesteros, A. 1989. "La función pública de las comunidades autónomas." In S. Martin-Retorrillo, ed., *Pasado, presente y futuro de las comunidades autónomas.* Madrid: Instituto de Estudios Económicos.

Barrio Alonso, María de los ángeles, and Manuel Suárez Cortina. 1989. "Asturias." In Juan Pablo Fusi, ed., *España: Autonomías.* Madrid: Espasa-Calpe.

Barzelay, Michael, and José María O'Kean. 1989. *Gestión pública estratégica: Conceptos, análisis y experiencias: El Caso IPIA (Strategic Public Management in Andalusia: Concepts, Experience and Analysis,* English version). Madrid: Instituto de Estudios Fiscales.

Bates, Robert H. 1989. *Beyond the Miracle of the Market: The Political Economy of Agrarian Development in Kenya.* New York: Cambridge University Press.

Bates, Robert H., and Anne O. Krueger. 1993. "Generalizations Arising from the Country Studies." In Robert H. Bates and Anne O. Krueger, eds., *Political and Economic Interactions in Economic Policy Reform: Evidence from Eight Countries.* Oxford: Basil Blackwell.

BDMG (Banco de Desenvolvimento de Minas Gerais). 1964. *Relatório de Suas Atividades.* Document prepared for the First Latin American Meeting of the Financial Institutions of Development. Belo Horizonte: Governo Magalhães Pinto.

————. 1989a. *Economia Mineira 1989: Diagnóstico e Perspectivas. Vol. I: Síntese e Propostas.* Belo Horizonte: Governo de Minas Gerais.

————. 1989b. *Economia Mineira 1989: Diagnóstico e Perspectivas. Vol. II: Indústria. Tomo I—Novos Desafios.* Belo Horizonte: Governo de Minas Gerais.

———. 1989c. *Economia Mineira 1989: Diagnóstico e Perspectivas. Vol. II: Indústria. Tomo II—Estudos Setoriais*. Belo Horizonte: Governo de Minas Gerais.

———. 1995. *Banco de Desenvolvimento de Minas Gerais, S.A.* Belo Horizonte: Governo de Minas Gerais.

Benito del Pozo, Paz. 1995. "La industria en Asturias: Un declive prolongado." In Joaquín Bosque and Ricardo Méndez, eds., *Cambio industrial y desarrollo regional en España*. Barcelona: Oikos-Tau.

Bermeo, Nancy. 1994. "Sacrifice, Sequence, and Strength in Successful Dual Transitions: Lessons from Spain." *The Journal of Politics* 56, no. 3 (August): 601–27.

Bermeo, Nancy, and José García-Durán. 1994. "Spain: Dual Transition Implemented by Two Parties." In Stephan Haggard and Steven B. Webb, eds., *Voting for Reform: Democracy, Political Liberalization, and Economic Adjustment*. New York: World Bank/Oxford University Press.

Boix, Carles. 1999. "Setting the Rules of the Game: The Choice of Electoral Systems in Advanced Democracies." *American Political Science Review* 93, no. 3: 609–24.

Boschi, Renato Raul. 1999. "Modelos Participativos de Políticas Públicas: Sociedade Civil, Conselhos e Descentralização." Paper presented at the Brazil in the Twenty-first Century Meeting at the CPDOC/Fundação Getúlio Vargas in Rio de Janeiro, Brazil, September 2–3.

Boyer, Miguel. 1975. "La empresa pública en la estrategia industrial española: el INI." *Información Comercial Española* (April): 94–123.

Boylan, Delia. 1998. "Preemptive Strike: Central Bank Reform in Chile's Transition from Authoritarian Rule." *Comparative Politics* 30, no. 4 (July): 443–62.

Brandão, Carlos Antônio, Eduardo Nunes Guimarães, Heládio José de Campos Leme, and Vitorino Alves da Silva. 1998. "Os Eixos Nacionais de Integração e Desenvolvimento do Programa `Brasil em Ação': Possíveis Impactos sobre Minas Gerais." In *VIII Seminário Sobre a Economia Mineira*. Vol. 2. Belo Horizonte: UFMG/CEDEPLAR.

Brant, Paulo. 1983. "O Setor Industrial em Minas Gerais: Características, Desempenho Recente e Perspectivas." In *II Seminário sobre a Economia Mineira: Historia Econômica de Minas Gerais; A Economia Mineira dos Anos 80*. Belo Horizonte: Diamatina/CEDEPLAR.

Brennan, Geoffrey, and James Buchanan. 1980. *The Power to Tax: Analytical Foundations of a Fiscal Constitution*. New York: Cambridge University Press.

Bresser Pereira, Luiz Carlos. 1993. "Economic Reforms and Economic

Growth: Efficiency and Politics in Latin America." In Luiz Carlos Bresser Pereira, José María Maravall, and Adam Przeworski, eds., *Economic Reforms in New Democracies: A Social-Democratic Approach.* Cambridge: Cambridge University Press.

Brito, Fausto. 1984. "O Estado Tutelar: o INDI na Experiência Mineira de Industrialização na Década de 70." *Revista Brasileira de Estudos Políticos* 58 (January): 241–57.

———. 1988. "Minas Gerais: O Retrocesso Político Recente." In *IV Seminário sobre a Economia Mineira.* Belo Horizonte: CEDEPLAR/ FACE/UFMG.

Brú Parra, Segundo. 1988. "La dimensión espacial de la política industrial." *Economía Industrial* (March-April): 33–43.

Bruhn, Kathleen. 1996. "Social Spending and Political Support: The `Lessons' of the National Solidarity Program in Mexico." *Comparative Politics* 28, no. 2 (January): 151–77.

Brusco, Sebastiano. 1982. "The Emilian Model: Productive Decentralisation and Social Integration." *Cambridge Journal of Economics* 6, no. 2 (June): 167–84.

Brusco, Sebastiano, and Ezio Righi. 1989. "Local Government, Industrial Policy, and Social Consensus: The Case of Modena (Italy)." *Economy and Society* 18, no. 4 (November): 405–24.

Buchanan, James M., Robert D. Tollison, and Gordon Tullock, eds. 1980. *Toward a Theory of the Rent-Seeking Society.* College Station: Texas A&M University Press.

Burgess, Katrina. 1999. "Loyalty Dilemmas and Market Reform: Party-Union Alliances Under Stress in Mexico, Spain, and Venezuela." *World Politics* 52, no. 1 (October): 105–34.

Callaghy, Thomas M. 1988. "The State and the Development of Capitalism in Africa." In Donald Rothchild and Naomi Chazan, eds., *The Precarious Balance: State and Society in Africa.* Boulder, Colo.: Westview Press.

Cano, Wilson. 1994. "Concentración, desconcentración y descentralización en Brasil." In José Luis Curbelo, Francisco Alburquerque, Carlos A. de Mattos, and Juan Ramón Cuadrado, eds., *Territorios en Transformación: Análisis y Propuestas.* Madrid: Fondo Europeo de Desarrollo Regional (FEDER).

———. 1977. *Raízes da Concentração Industrial em São Paulo.* Rio de Janeiro: Difel.

Caravaca Barroso, Inmaculada. 1995. "Industrialización y desarrollo en Andalucía." In Joaquín Bosque and Ricardo Méndez, eds., *Cambio industrial y desarrollo regional en España.* Barcelona: Oikos-Tau.

Carey, John. 2000. "Parchment, Equilibria, and Institutions." *Comparative Political Studies* 33, no. 6–7 (August–September): 735–61.

Carrillo, Jorge, and Marta Micker. 1997. "Exportaciones automotrices y formación de *clusters* en el norte de México: El caso de Ciudad Juárez." Paper presented at the conference, "Produção Flexível e Novas Institucionalidades na América Latina." Rio de Janeiro, September 18–20.

Castells, Antoni. 1990. "Transición democrática y descentralización del sector público." In José Luis García Delgado, ed., *Economía española de la transición y la democracia 1973–1986*. Madrid: Centro de Investigaciones Sociologicas.

Castells, Antoni, and Ferran Bel. 1991. "El proceso de descentralización ante el mercado único europeo." *Papeles de Economía Española* 48: 220–36.

Castells, Manuel. 1989. *The Informational City: Information Technology, Economic Restructuring, and the Urban-Regional Process*. Cambridge: Blackwell.

Castells, Manuel, and Juan Antonio Vázquez. 1994. *Estrategias para la Reindustrialización de Asturias*. Madrid: Editorial Civitas.

Castells, Manuel, and Peter Hall, eds. 1992. *Andalucía: innovación tecnológica y desarrollo económico*. Vols. 1 and 2. Madrid: Espasa Calpe.

Castillo, Jaime del. 1987. "Regiones industrializadas en declive: el caso del Norte de España." *Información Comercial Española* 645 (May): 9–18.

Castillo, Jaime del and Juan A. Rivas. 1988. "La Cornisa Cantábrica: Una macro-región industrial en declive." *Papeles de Economía Española* 34: 115–40.

Castro, Antônio Barros de. 1999. "O Lado Real do Real: O Debate e Algumas Surpresas." In João Paulo de Almeida Magalhães, Adhemar dos Santos Mineiro, and Luiz Antônio Elias, eds., *Vinte Anos de Política Econômica*. Rio de Janeiro: Contraponto.

———. 1994. "Renegade Development: Rise and Demise of State-Led Development in Brazil." In William C. Smith, Carlos H. Acuña, and Eduardo A. Gamarra, eds., *Democracy, Markets, and Structural Reform in Latin America*. New Brunswick: Transaction Publishers.

CEOE. 1992. "Financiación y gasto de las Comunidades Autonomas." *Informes y estudios de CEOE* 2, no. 65: 7–100.

Chhibber, Pradeep, and Samuel Eldersveld. 2000. "Local Elites and Popular Support for Economic Reform in China and India." *Comparative Political Studies* 33, no. 3 (April): 350–73.

Chubb, John E. 1991. "How Relevant Is Competition to Government Policymaking?" In Daphne A. Kenyon and John Kincaid, eds., *Competi-*

tion Among States and Local Governments: Efficiency and Equity in American Federalism. Washington, D.C.: The Urban Institute Press.

Ciclo de Conferencias sobre Política valenciana. 1985. *¿Es posible una convergencia social y política valenciana?* Valencia: Asociación Cultural Valencia 2000.

Cienfuegos-Jovellanos, Pedro de Silva. 1977. *El regionalismo asturiano.* Salinas: Ayalga.

———. 1994. "La economía asturiana durante la construcción autonómica (década de los 80)." In La Nueva España, eds., *Historia de la economía asturiana. Tomo III.* Oviedo: La Nueva España.

CNI (Confederação Nacional da Indústria). 1998. *Políticas Estaduais de Apoio à Indústria.* Rio de Janeiro: CNI.

———. 1995. *Políticas Estaduais de Apoio à Indústria.* Rio de Janeiro: CNI.

CODIN (Companhia de Desenvolvimento Industrial). 1987. *Histórico.* Rio de Janeiro: CODIN.

Conniff, Michael L. 1981. *Urban Politics in Brazil: The Rise of Populism, 1925–1945.* Pittsburgh: University of Pittsburgh Press.

Consejería de Hacienda y Economía, Principado de Asturias. 1994. *Plan de Desarrollo Regional de Asturias 1994–1999.* Vols. 1, 2. Oviedo: Principado de Asturias.

———. 1993. *Presupuestos Generales del Principado de Asturias: 1993.* Vol. 3. Oviedo: Principado de Asturias.

———. 1989. *Programa de Desarrollo Regional del Principado de Asturias 1989–1993.* Vol. 1. Oviedo: Principado de Asturias.

———. 1986. *Programa de Desarrollo Regional 1985–88.* Oviedo: Principado de Asturias.

Corona, Juan F., Luis M. Alonso, and Pedro Puy. 1998. *Hacia un federalismo competitivo: Propuesta para reformar el sistema de financiación autonómica.* Madrid: Círculo de Empresarios.

Cox, Gary W. 1997. *Making Votes Count: Strategic Coordination in the World Electoral Systems.* New York: Cambridge University Press.

CREP (Comisión de Coordinación de los Representantes del Principado en la Empresa Pública). 1992. *Informe sobre la empresa pública industrial del INI en el Principado de Asturias: antecedentes y perspectivas de futuro.* Unpublished document. (December). Oviedo: CREP.

———. 1987. *Dictamen de la CREP sobre el documento "Para un planteamiento global de la empresa pública industrial del INI en Asturias."* Unpublished document. Oviedo: CREP.

Coutinho, Luciano, and João Carlos Ferraz. 1994. *Estudo da Competitividade da Indústria Brasileira.* São Paulo: Papirus.

Curbelo, José Luis. 1994. "Las regiones en la transición española." *Revista*

Latinoamericana de Estudios Urbano Regionales (EURE) 20, no. 61 (December): 5–26.

Delgado Cabeza, Manuel. 1993. "Las tres últimas decadas de la economía andaluza." In Manuel Martín Rodríguez, ed., *Estructura Económica de Andalucía.* Madrid: Espasa Calpe.

Deyo, Frederic C., ed. 1996. *Social Reconstructions of the World Automobile Industry: Competition, Power, and Industrial Flexibility.* New York: St. Martin's Press.

————. 1987. *The Political Economy of the New Asian Industrialism.* Ithaca: Cornell University Press.

Díaz Cayeros, Alberto. 1999. "Do Federal Institutions Matter? Rules and Political Practices in Mexico." Paper presented for the workshop "Federalismo, Democracia, y Políticas Públicas: Perspectivas Comparadas," CIDE, Mexico City, June 14–15.

————. 1995. *Desarrollo económico e inequidad regional: Hacia un nuevo pacto federal en México.* Mexico City: Miguel ángel Porrúa.

Diaz-López, César Enrique. 1981. "The State of the Autonomic Process in Spain." *Publius: The Journal of Federalism* 11 (Summer): 193–217.

Dillinger, William, and Steven B. Webb. 1998. "Fiscal Management in Federal Democracies: Argentina and Brazil." Mimeo.

Dillinger, William, Guillermo Perry, and Steven B. Webb. 2000. "Macroeconomic Management in Decentralized Democracies: The Quest for Hard Budget Constraints in Latin America." Paper presented at the 2000 meeting of the Latin American Studies Association, Hyatt Regency Miami, March 16–18.

Diniz, Clélio Campolina. 1981. *Estado e Capital Estrangeiro na Industrialização Mineira.* Belo Horizonte: Universidade Federal de Minas Gerais (PROED).

————. 1984. "Economia e Planejamento em Minas Gerais." *Revista de Estudos Políticos* 58 (January): 259–89.

————. 1986. "O Paradoxo Mineiro: Fortalecimento Econômico e Enfraquecimento Político." In *III Seminário sobre a Economia Mineira.* Belo Horizonte: CEDEPLAR/FACE/UFMG.

————. 1994. "Reversión de la polarización y reconcentración regional en Brasil." In José Luis Curbelo, Francisco Alburquerque, Carlos A. de Mattos, and Juan Ramón Cuadrado, eds., *Territorios en Transformación: Análisis y Propuestas.* Madrid: Fondo Europeo de Desarrollo Regional (FEDER).

Diniz, Clélio Campolina, and Fabiana Borges Teixeira dos Santos. 1994. "Região Sudeste: Desempenho Econômico, Heterogeneidade Estrutural e Perspectivas." In *Evolução e Perspectivas das Desigualidades Regionas no Desenvolvimento Brasileiro*. São Paulo: FUNDAP.

Diniz, Eli. 1994. "Reformas Econômicas e Democracia no Brasil dos Anos 90: As Câmaras Setoriais como Fórum de Negociação." *Dados* 37, no. 2: 277–315.

———. 1982. *Voto e Máquina Política: Patronagem e Clientelismo no Rio de Janeiro*. Rio de Janeiro: Paz e Terra.

Domínguez, Jorge I. 1997. "Technopols: Ideas and Leaders in Freeing Politics and Markets in Latin America in the 1990s." In Jorge Domínguez, ed., *Technopols: Freeing Politics and Markets in Latin America in the 1990s*. University Park: Pennsylvania State University Press.

Duarte Filho, Francisco Carvalho. 1986. "Desempenho e Fontes de Crescimento da Indústria Mineira no Período Pós-75." *Analise e Conjuntura* 1, no. 2 (May–August): 31–52.

Duarte Filho, Francisco Carvalho, Marilena Chaves, and Rosamaria Roedel Silva. 1979. "A Industrialização Mineira e os Incentivos Fiscais: Avaliação da Lei 5.261/69." *Fundação João Pinheiro* 9, no. 12 (December): 925–51.

Dulci, Otávio Soares. 1988. "Identidade Regional e Ideologia: O Caso de Minas Gerais." *Textos Sociologia e Antropologia* 27, Universidade Federal de Minas Gerais (UFMG), Faculdade de Filosofia e Ciências Humanas.

———. 1992. "Elites e Políticas de Desenvolvimento em Minas Gerais." *Ciências Sociais Hoje, 1992*. São Paulo: ANPOCS.

Dye, Thomas R. 1990. *American Federalism: Competition Among Governments*. Lexington: Lexington Books.

Elías, Emily Edmonds. 1998. "The Implications of Electoral Competition for Fiscal Decentralization and Subnational Autonomy in Mexico." Paper presented at the 1998 meeting of the Latin American Studies Association, The Palmer House Hilton Hotel, Chicago, September 24–26.

———. 1997. "Fiscal Decentralization and Municipal Governance in Mexico: The Case of Chihuahua." Paper presented at the 1997 meeting of the Latin American Studies Association, Continental Plaza Hotel, Guadalajara, Mexico, April 17–19.

Encarnación, Omar G. 1996. "The Politics of Dual Transitions." *Comparative Politics* 28, no. 4 (July): 477–92.

ESECA (Sociedad de Estudios Económicos de Andalucía, S.A.). 1994. *Informe económico financiero de Andalucía 1993*. Granada: Caja General de Ahorros de Granada.

Espina Montero, Álvaro. 1994. "Una política de cooperación para los sistemas productivos locales." *Economía y Sociedad* 11 (December): 149–72.

Estado de Minas Gerais. 1995. *Plano Mineiro de Desenvolvimento Integrado—PMDI.* Belo Horizonte: Government of Minas Gerais.

———. 1993. *Diretrizes para a Política Industrial do Estado de Minas Gerais.* Belo Horizonte: Government of Minas Gerais.

———. 1982. *Diretrizes para um Plano de Governo em Minas.* Belo Horizonte: Government of Minas Gerais.

Estado do Rio de Janeiro, Governo Chagas Freitas. 1979. *Diretrizes Gerais de Governo: Bases para o Plano de Desenvolvimento Econômico e Social, 1980–1983.* Rio de Janeiro: Government of Rio de Janeiro.

Estado do Rio de Janeiro, Governo Brizola (1983–87). 1983. *Plano de Desenvolvimento Econômico e Social.* Rio: Government of Rio de Janeiro.

Estado do Rio de Janeiro, Governo Moreira Franco (1987–91). 1987. *Plano de Desenvolvimento Econômico e Social, 1988–1991.* Rio: Government of Rio de Janeiro.

Esteban, Marisol, and Roberto Velasco. 1996. "La política industrial en la España de las autonomías." *Papeles de Economía Española* 67: 288–301.

Evans, Peter B., ed. 1997a. *State-Society Synergy: Government and Social Capital in Development.* Berkeley: IAS/University of California at Berkeley.

———. 1997b. "Introduction: Development Strategies Across the Public-Private Divide." In Peter B. Evans, ed., *State-Society Synergy: Government and Social Capital in Development.* Berkeley: IAS/University of California at Berkeley.

———. 1996. "Government Action, Social Capital and Development: Reviewing the Evidence on Synergy." *World Development* 24, no. 6 (June): 1119–32.

———. 1995. *Embedded Autonomy: States and Industrial Transformation.* Princeton: Princeton University Press.

———. 1992. "The State as Problem and Solution: Predation, Embedded Autonomy and Structural Change." In Stephan Haggard and Robert R. Kaufman, eds., *The Politics of Economic Adjustment: International Constraints, Distributive Conflicts, and the State.* Princeton: Princeton University Press.

———. 1979. *Dependent Development: The Alliance of Multinational, State, and Local Capital in Brazil.* Princeton: Princeton University Press.

Fernández, Zulima. 1994. "La empresa pública en Asturias." In La Nueva España, eds., *Historia de la economía asturiana. Tomo IV.* Oviedo: La Nueva España.

Fernández, Zulima and Juan A. Vázquez. 1990. "La empresa pública en Asturias." *Economistas* 45–46 (August–November): 152–57.

Fernández Fernández, Felipe, and Francisco Macías Mateo. 1986. "Situación actual de la economía asturiana." *Información Comercial Española* 635 (July): 101–9.

Fernández de Pinedo, Emiliano, and José Luis Hernández Marco, eds. 1988. *La industrialización del norte de España*. Barcelona: Editorial Crítica.

Ferreira, Marieta de Morães, ed. 1999. *Conversando sobre Política: Hamilton Xavier e Saramago Pinheiro*. Rio de Janeiro: Fundação Getúlio Vargas.

Fiat. 1995. *Mineirização: Fiat*. February (internal document).

Figueiredo, Argelina Cheibub, and Fernando Limongi. 1997. "O Congresso e as Medidas Provisórias: Abdicação ou Delegação." *Novos Estudos CEBRAP* 47 (March): 127–54.

Fishman, Robert M. 1990. *Working-Class Organization and the Return to Democracy in Spain*. Ithaca: Cornell University Press.

Fosler, R. Scott. 1988. *The New Economic Role of the American States*. New York: Oxford University Press.

Fox, Jonathan. 1996. "How Does Civil Society Thicken? The Political Construction of Social Capital in Rural Mexico." *World Development* 24, no. 6 (June): 1089–103.

Freire, Américo, ed. 1998. *Conversando sobre Política: José Talarico*. Rio de Janeiro: Fundação Getúlio Vargas.

Frieden, Jeffry A. 1991. *Debt, Development, and Democracy: Modern Political Economy and Latin America, 1965–1985*. Princeton: Princeton University Press.

Fuentes Quintana, Enrique. 1990. "De los pactos de la Moncloa a la Constitución (julio 1977–diciembre 1978)." In José Luis García Delgado, ed., *Economía española de la transición y la democracia*. Madrid: Centro de Investigaciones Sociológicas.

Fuentes Quintana, Enrique, and Jaime Requeijo. 1984. "La larga marcha hacia una política económica inevitable." *Papeles de Economía Española* 21: 2–39.

Fuhr, Harald. 1993. "Mobilizing Local Resources in Latin America: Decentralization, Institutional Reforms and Small-Scale Enterprises." In Brigitte Spath, ed., *Small Firms and Development in Latin America: The Role of the Institutional Environment, Human Resources and Industrial Relations*. Geneva: International Institute for Labour Studies.

Gabinete Técnico de la Consellería de Industria, Comercio, y Turismo. 1989. *La industria valenciana 1980–85: sectores de demanda fuerte, media, y débil*. Valencia: Consellería de Industria, Comercio, y Turismo.

Gama de Andrade, Luis Aureliano. 1980. "Technocracy and Development: The Case of Minas Gerais." Ph.D. diss., University of Michigan.

García Blanco, José María, and Rodolfo Gutiérrez. 1990. "El declive de las áreas de antigua industrialización." *Sociología del Trabajo* 8 (Winter): 3–29.

Garman, Christopher, Stephan Haggard, and Eliza Willis. 2001. "Fiscal Decentralization: A Political Theory with Latin American Cases." *World Politics* 53 (January): 205–36.

Garrett, Geoffrey. 1998. *Partisan Politics in the Global Economy.* New York: Cambridge University Press.

———. 1995. "Capital Mobility, Trade and the Domestic Politics of Economic Policy." *International Organization* 49, no. 4 (Autumn): 657–87.

Garrett, Geoffrey, and Peter Lange. 1996. "Internationalization, Institutions, and Political Change." In Robert O. Keohane and Helen V. Milner, eds., *Internationalization and Domestic Politics.* Cambridge: Cambridge University Press.

Gay, Robert. 1988. "Political Clientelism and Urban Social Movements in Rio de Janeiro." Ph. D. diss., Brown University.

Geddes, Barbara. 1994. *Politician's Dilemma: Building State Capacity in Latin America.* Berkeley: University of California Press.

Gerschenkron, Alexander. 1963. *Economic Backwardness in Historical Perspective.* Cambridge: Harvard University Press.

Gondim, Linda Maria de Pontes.1986. *Planners in the Face of Power: The Case of the Metropolitan Region of Rio de Janeiro, Brazil.* Ph. D. diss., Cornell University.

———. 1997. "Os `Governos das Mudanças' no Ceará: Socialdemocracia ou populismo?" In Eli Diniz and Sérgio de Azevedo, eds., *Reforma do Estado e Democracia no Brasil.* Brasília: UnB/ENAP.

Gourevitch, Peter. 1986. *Politics in Hard Times: Comparative Responses to International Economic Crises.* Ithaca: Cornell University Press.

Graham, Lawrence S. 1990. *The State and Policy Outcomes in Latin America.* New York, N.Y.: Praeger.

Granovetter, Mark. 1973. "The Strength of Weak Ties." *American Journal of Sociology* 78, no. 6 (May): 1360–80.

———. 1985. "Economic Action and Social Structure: The Problem of Embeddedness." *American Journal of Sociology* 91, no. 3 (November): 481–510.

Grindle, Merilee, ed. 1997. *Getting Good Government: Capacity Building in the Public Sectors of Developing Countries.* Cambridge: Harvard University Press.

Gutiérrez, Rodolfo. 1994. "Mercado de trabajo y relaciones laborales." *Historia de la Economía Asturiana. Tomo IV.* Oviedo: La Nueva España.

———. 1993. "Mercado de trabajo y relaciones laborales." In SADEI, ed., *Datos y cifras de la economía asturiana—1993.* Oviedo: Principado de Asturias.

Gutiérrez, Rodolfo, and Juan A. Vázquez. 1991. "La gestión del declive minero." *Revista de Economía* 11: 89–93.

Haddad, Paulo. 1985. *Dimensões do Planejamento Estadual no Brasil: Analise de Experiencias.* Rio de Janeiro: IPEA/INPES.

Haggard, Stephan, and Robert R. Kaufman. 1995. *The Political Economy of Democratic Transitions.* Princeton: Princeton University Press.

———. 1992. "Institutions and Economic Adjustment." In Stephan Haggard and Robert R. Kaufman, eds., *The Politics of Economic Adjustment: International Constraints, Distributive Conflicts, and the State.* Princeton: Princeton University Press.

Haggard, Stephan, and Steven B. Webb, eds. 1994. *Voting For Reform: Democracy, Political Liberalization, and Economic Adjustment.* New York: World Bank / Oxford University Press.

Hagopian, Frances. 1996. *Traditional Politics and Regime Change in Brazil.* Cambridge: Cambridge University Press.

———. 1992. "The Compromised Consolidation: The Political Class in the Brazilian Transition." In Scott Mainwaring, Guillermo O'Donnell, and J. Samuel Valenzuela, eds., *Issues in Democratic Consolidation: The New South American Democracies in Comparative Perspective.* Notre Dame: University of Notre Dame.

Heller, Patrick. 1996. "Social Capital as a Product of Class Mobilization and State Intervention: Industrial Workers in Kerala, India." *World Development* 24, no. 6 (June): 1055–71.

Herrigel, Gary. 1995. *Reconceptualizing the Sources of German Industrial Power.* New York: Cambridge University Press.

Hilderbrand, Mary E., and Merilee S. Grindle. 1997. "Building Sustainable Capacity in the Public Sector: What Can Be Done?" In Merilee Grindle, ed., *Getting Good Government: Capacity Building in the Public Sectors of Developing Countries.* Cambridge: Harvard University Press.

Holman, Otto. 1989. "In Search of Hegemony: Socialist Government and the Internationalization of Domestic Politics in Spain." *International Journal of Political Economy* 19, no. 3 (Fall): 76–101.

Horta, Cid Rebelo. 1986. "Familias Governamentais de Minas Gerais." *Analise & Conjuntura* 1, no. 2 (May–August): 111–45.

IDB (Inter-American Development Bank). 1994. *Economic and Social*

Progress in Latin America, 1994 Report. Special Report: Fiscal Decentralization. October. Washington, D.C.: IDB/Johns Hopkins University Press.

———. 1997. *Economic and Social Progress in Latin America, 1997 Report. Latin America After a Decade of Reforms.* September. Washington, D.C.: IDB/Johns Hopkins University Press.

IEA (Instituto de Estadística de Andalucía). 1995. *Indicadores económicos de Andalucía.* Fourth trimester 17.

IFA (Instituto de Fomento de Andalucía). 1994. *Memoria 1993.* Seville: IFA.

———. 1993. *Agencias regionales de desarrollo en España.* October. Seville: IFA.

IFR (Instituto de Fomento Regional). 1998. *Memoria de actividades—1997.* Llanera: IFR.

———. 1997. *Memoria de actividades—1996.* Llanera: IFR.

———. 1994. *Boletín de información* 9 (June).

———. 1995. *Memoria de actividades—1994.* Llanera: IFR.

———. 1994. *Memoria de actividades—1993.* Llanera: IFR.

———. 1993. *Memoria de actividades—1992.* Llanera: IFR.

INDI (Instituto de Desenvolvimento Industrial). 1998. *Perfil da Indústria de Autopeças em Minas Gerais 1996.* Belo Horizonte: INDI.

———. 1995. *Relatório Anual 94.* Belo Horizonte: INDI.

———. 1994. *Os Setores de Material de Transporte e Mecânico em Minas Gerais.* Belo Horizonte: INDI.

INDI Informa. 1993. "Kadron Implanta Segunda Fase do Projeto" 15, no. 74 (September–October): 3.

Jayme Junior, Frederico Gonzaga, and Hugo Eduardo A. Gama Cerqueira. 1995. "Bancos Estaduais e Federalismo: Um Estudo dos Bancos Mineiros." In *VII Seminário sobre a Economia Mineira.* Vol. 2. Belo Horizonte: UFMG/CEDEPLAR.

Jiménez-Blanco, A. 1989. "La distribución de competencias económicas entre el estado y las Comunidades Autónomas." In S. Martin-Retorrillo, ed., *Pasado, presente y futuro de las Comunidades Autónomas.* Madrid: Instituto de Estudios Económicos.

Johnson, Chalmers. 1982. *MITI and the Japanese Miracle: The Growth of Industrial Policy, 1925–1975.* Stanford: Stanford University Press.

Junta de Andalucía. 1993. *Sector público empresarial de la Junta de Andalucía.* Seville: Junta de Andalucía.

Katzenstein, Peter J., ed. 1978. *Between Power and Plenty: Foreign Economic Policies of Advanced Industrial States.* Madison: University of Wisconsin Press.

————. 1985. *Small States in World Markets: Industrial Policy in Europe.* Ithaca: Cornell University Press.

Keck, Margaret E. 1992. *The Workers' Party and Democratization in Brazil.* New Haven: Yale University Press.

King, Gary, Robert O. Keohane, and Sidney Verba. 1994. *Designing Social Inquiry: Scientific Inference in Qualitative Research.* Princeton: Princeton University Press.

Kingstone, Peter R. 1999. *Crafting Coalitions for Reform: Business Preferences, Political Institutions, and Neoliberal Reform in Brazil.* University Park: Pennsylvania State University Press.

Kitschelt, Herbert, Peter Lange, Gary Marks, and John D. Stephens, eds. 1999. *Continuity and Change in Contemporary Capitalism.* New York: Cambridge University Press.

Knack, Stephen, and Philip Keefer. 1997. "Does Social Capital Have An Economic Payoff? A Cross-Country Investigation." *Quarterly Journal of Economics* (November): 1251–88.

Knight, Jack. 1992. *Institutions and Social Conflict.* New York: Cambridge University Press.

Krueger, Anne O. 1974. "The Political Economy of the Rent-Seeking Society." *American Economic Review* 64 (June): 291–303.

Krugman, Paul. 1991. *Geography and Trade.* Cambridge: MIT Press.

Lafuente Félez, Alberto, and Ramón Pérez Simarro. 1988. "Balance y perspectivas de las ZUR." *Papeles de Economía Española* 35: 219–34.

Lagemann, Eugênio. 1995. "O Federalismo Fiscal Brasileiro em Questão." In Rui de Britto álvares Affonso and Pedro Luiz Barros Silva, eds., *A Federação em Perspectiva: Ensaios Selecionados.* São Paulo, S.P.: FUNDAP.

Lam, Wai Fun. 1996. "Institutional Design of Public Agencies and Co-production: A Study of Irrigation Associations in Taiwan." *World Development* 24, no. 6 (June): 1039–54.

Lamounier, Leonardo Alves. 1997. "Minas Gerais: O Sistema Partidário nas Duas últimas Décadas." In Olavo Brasil de Lima Júnior, ed., *O Sistema Partidário Brasileiro: Diversidade e Tendências—1982–94.* Rio de Janeiro: Fundação Getúlio Vargas.

Lee, Naeyoung, and Jeffrey Cason. 1994. "Automobile Commodity Chains in the NICs: A Comparison of South Korea, Mexico, and Brazil." In Gary Gereffi and Miguel Korzeniewicz, eds., *Commodity Chains and Global Capitalism.* Westport: Praeger.

Lerena, Luis A. 1988. "Ideas matrices de la nueva política industrial regional." *Economía Industrial* (March-April): 45–54.

Libânio, Gilberto de Assis. 1998. "Evolução Recente das Contas Externas do Brasil e de Minas Gerais." In *VIII Seminário Sobre a Economia Mineira.* Vol. 2. Belo Horizonte: UFMG/CEDEPLAR.

Light. 1985. *Perfil Sócio-Econômico do Estado do Rio de Janeiro.* Rio: Light.

Locke, Richard M. 1995. *Remaking the Italian Economy.* Ithaca: Cornell University Press.

———. 1996. "The Composite Economy: Local Politics and Industrial Change in Contemporary Italy." *Economy and Society* 25, no. 4 (November): 483–510.

Longo, Carlos Alberto. 1994. "Federal Problems with VAT in Brazil." *Revista Brasileira de Economia* 48, no. 1 (January–March): 85–105.

López Murphy, Ricardo ed. 1995. *Fiscal Decentralization in Latin America.* Washington, D.C.: Inter-American Development Bank.

Lukauskas, Arvid J. 1997. *Regulating Finance: The Political Economy of Spanish Financial Policy from Franco to Democracy.* Ann Arbor: University of Michigan Press.

Magalhães, João Paulo de Almeida. 1983. *Projeto Pro-RIO: Problemas e Potencialidades do Estado do Rio de Janeiro.* Rio: Instituto de Estudos Políticos e Sociais.

Mainwaring, Scott. 1999. *Rethinking Party Systems in the Third Wave of Democratization: The Case of Brazil.* Stanford: Stanford University Press.

———. 1997. "Multipartism, Robust Federalism, and Presidentialism in Brazil." In Scott Mainwaring and Matthew Soberg Shugart, eds., *Presidentialism and Democracy in Latin America.* New York: Cambridge University Press.

———. 1993. "Brazilian Party Underdevelopment in Comparative Perspective." *Political Science Quarterly* 107: 677–707.

Maravall, José María. 1993. "Politics and Policy: Economic Reforms in Southern Europe." In Luiz Carlos Bresser Pereira, José María Maravall, and Adam Przeworski, eds., *Economic Reforms in New Democracies: A Social Democratic Approach.* Cambridge: Cambridge University Press.

Maravall, José María, and Julián Santamaría. 1986. "Political Change in Spain and the Prospects for Democracy." In Guillermo O'Donnell, Phillippe Schmitter, and Laurence Whitehead, eds., *Transitions from Authoritarian Rule: Southern Europe.* Baltimore: Johns Hopkins University.

Marquez Guerrero, Carolina. 1997. "Regional Development Strategies of a New Regional Government: The Junta de Andalucía, 1984–1992." *Progress in Planning* 48, no. 2: 69–159.

Martín Rodríguez, Manuel, and Antonio Martín Mesa. 1993. "Sistema financiero." In Manuel Martín Rodríguez, ed., *Estructura Económica de Andalucía.* Madrid: Espasa Calpe.

Martin, Scott. 1996. "As Câmaras Setoriais e o Meso-Corporativismo." *Lua Nova: Revista de Cultura e Política* 38: 139–70.

Martins, Luciano. 1985. *Estado Capitalista e Burocracia no Brasil pós 64.* Rio de Janeiro: Paz e Terra.

Más, Francisco. 1995. "Enterprise Support Structures in Spain: The Case of Valencia." Mimeo, September.

Mata-Machado, Bernardo. 1987. "O Poder Político em Minas Gerais: Estrutura e Formação." *Análise e Conjuntura* 2, no. 1 (January–April): 91–124.

Maxfield, Sylvia. 1997. *Gatekeepers of Growth: The International Political Economy of Central Banking in Developing Countries.* Princeton: Princeton University Press.

McCubbins, Matthew D., Roger G. Noll, and Barry R. Weingast. 1987. "Administrative Procedures as Instruments of Political Control." *Journal of Law, Economics, and Organization* 3, no. 2 (Fall): 243–77.

McCubbins, Matthew D., and Thomas Schwartz. 1984. "Congressional Oversight Overlooked: Police Patrols versus Fire Alarms." *American Journal of Political Science* 28 (February): 165–79.

Medeiros, Antonio Carlos. 1983. "Politics and Intergovernmental Relations in Brazil, 1964–1982." Ph.D. diss., London School of Economics and Political Science.

Méndez, Ricardo, and Jaime Razquín. 1995. "Crisis y renovación industrial en Madrid: Balance y perspectivas." *Economía y Sociedad* 12 (June): 133–57.

Méndez, José Luis. 1997. "Subnational and International Industrial Policy by the State of Nuevo Leon, Mexico." Paper presented at the conference, "Rights versus Efficiency in a Globalized Era," Columbia University, New York City, September 11.

Migdal, Joel S. 1988. *Strong Societies and Weak States: State-Society Relations and State Capabilities in the Third World.* Princeton: Princeton University Press.

Miller, Gary J. 1992. *Managerial Dilemmas: The Political Economy of Hierarchy.* New York: Cambridge University Press.

MINER (Ministerio de Industria). 1995. *Programa de Reindustrialización y Dinamización Económica de Asturias. Balance 1994 y previsiones 1995.* Comisión Mixta de Seguimiento. May. Madrid: MINER.

Ministerio de Economía y Hacienda. 1995. *La descentralización del gasto público en España: período 1984–1994.* Madrid: Ministerio de Economía y Hacienda, Dirección General de Coordinación con las Haciendas Territoriales.

Moe, Terry M. 1984. "The New Economics of Organization." *American Journal of Political Science* 28 (November): 739–77.

Molinar Horcasitas, Juan, and Jeffrey A. Weldon. 1994. "Electoral Determinants and Consequences of National Solidarity." In Wayne Cornelius, Ann L. Craig, and Jonathan Fox, eds., *Transforming State-Society Relations in Mexico: The National Solidarity Strategy.* La Jolla: Center for U.S.-Mexican Studies, University of California, San Diego.

Monasterio Escudero, Carlos. 1994. "La hacienda del Principado de Asturias." *Papeles de Economía Española* 59: 267–76.

———. 1996. "Los límites al endeudamiento de los gobiernos subcentrales: teoría y evidencia para el caso Español." *Papeles de Economía Española* 67: 275–85.

Montero, Alfred P. 2001a. "Making and Remaking `Good Government' in Brazil: Subnational Industrial Policy in Minas Gerais." *Latin American Politics and Society* 43, no. 2 (Summer): 49–80.

———. 2001b. "Decentralizing Democracy: Spain and Brazil in Comparative Perspective." *Comparative Politics* 33, no. 2 (January): 149–69.

———. 2000. "Devolving Democracy? Political Decentralization and the New Brazilian Federalism." In Peter R. Kingstone and Timothy J. Power, eds., *Democratic Brazil: Actors, Institutions, and Processes.* Pittsburgh: University of Pittsburgh Press.

———. 1998. "State Interests and the New Industrial Policy in Brazil: The Privatization of Steel, 1990–1994." *Journal of Interamerican Studies and World Affairs* 40, no. 3 (Fall): 27–62.

———. 1997. "Shifting States in Uneven Markets: Political Decentralization and Subnational Industrial Policy in Contemporary Brazil and Spain." Ph.D. diss., Columbia University.

Montero, Alfred P., and David Samuels, eds. Forthcoming. *Decentralization and Democracy in Latin America.* Notre Dame: University of Notre Dame Press.

Moraes Filho, José Filomeno de. 1997. "O Subsistema Partidário e o Retorno ao Multipartidarismo." In Olavo Brasil de Lima Júnior, ed., *O Sistema Partidário Brasileiro: Diversidade e Tendências—1982–94.* Rio de Janeiro: Fundação Getúlio Vargas.

Motta, Marly Silva da, ed. 1998. *Conversando sobre Política: Erasmo Martins Pedro.* Rio de Janeiro: Fundação Getúlio Vargas.

Musgrave, Richard A., and Peggy B. Musgrave. 1989. *Public Finance in Theory and Practice.* Fifth ed. New York: McGraw-Hill.

Navarro Arancegui, Miquel. 1990. *Política de reconversión: balance crítico.* Madrid: EUDEMA.

———. 1988. "La política de reconversión en España: El caso de la siderurgia." Ph.D. diss., Universidad de Deusto, Bilbao.

Nelson, Joan M., ed. 1990. *Economic Crisis and Policy Choice: The Politics of Adjustment in the Third World*. Princeton: Princeton University Press.

Niskanen, William A. 1971. *Bureaucracy and Representative Government*. Chicago, Ill.: Adine.

Oates, Wallace E. 1972. *Fiscal Federalism*. New York: Harcourt Brace Jovanovich.

Ojeda, Germán, and Juan A. Vázquez. 1990. "Asturias: Una industrialización intervenida." In *Pautas regionales de la industrialización española (Siglos 19 y 20)*. Barcelona: Editorial Ariel.

————. 1988. "La economía." In *Historia de Asturias: Edad contemporánea II*. Vol. 9. Salinas, Asturias: Ayalga Ediciones.

Oliveira Junior, Márcio de, and Marcelo Petersen Cypriano. 1995. "Finanças Públicas do Estado de Minas Gerais: Um Estudo da Evolução da Receita, Despesa e Endividamento—1987–1994." In *VII Seminário sobre a Economia Mineira*. Vol. 2. Belo Horizonte: UFMG/CEDEPLAR.

Olson, Mancur. 1982. *The Rise and Decline of Nations*. New Haven: Yale University Press.

Ostrom, Elinor. 1997. "Crossing the Great Divide: Coproduction, Synergy, and Development." In Peter B. Evans, ed., *State-Society Synergy: Government and Social Capital in Development*. Berkeley: IAS / University California at Berkeley.

Pajuelo Gallego, Alfonso, and José Villena Peña. "La industria." In Manuel Martín Rodríguez, ed., *Estructura Económica de Andalucía*. Madrid: Espasa Calpe.

Pereira de Melo, Hildete, and Cláudio Monteiro Considera. 1986. "Industrialização Fluminense 1930–1980." *Revista do Rio de Janeiro* 1, no. 3 (May–August): 111–21.

Pérez, Sofia A. 1997. "From Cheap Credit to the EC: The Politics of Financial Reform in Spain." In Michael Loriaux, Meredith Woo-Cumings, Kent E. Calder, Sylvia Maxfield, and Sofía Pérez, eds., *Capital Ungoverned: Liberalizing Finance in Interventionist States*. Ithaca: Cornell University Press.

Pérez-Díaz, Victor. 1984. "Gobernabilidad y mesogobiernos: autonomías regionales y neocorporatismo en España." *Papeles de Economía Española* 21: 40–76.

Piore, Michael J., and Charles F. Sabel. 1984. *The Second Industrial Divide: Possibilities for Prosperity*. New York: Basic Books.

Porter, Michael. 1990. *The Competitive Advantage of Nations*. New York: Free Press.

Prates, Fernando Martins, and Maria Luiza de Aguiar Marques. 1995. "A Indústria Mineira no Contexto de um Novo Ciclo de Crescimento no País: Estudo de Caso da Indústria de Autopeças." In *VII Seminário sobre a Economia Mineira*. Vol. 2. Belo Horizonte: UFMG/CEDEPLAR.

Principado de Asturias. 1995. *Información: Programa de Reindustrialización y Dinamización Económica de Asturias*. Oviedo: Principado de Asturias.

———. 1994. *Plan de Apoyo a las PYMES: 1994–1996*. Oviedo: Principado de Asturias.

Prud'homme, Rémy. 1995. "The Dangers of Decentralization." *The World Bank Research Observer* 10, no. 2 (August): 201–20.

Pyke, Frank, Giacomo Becattini, and Werner Sengenberger. 1990. *Industrial Districts and Inter-Firm Cooperation in Italy*. Geneva: International Institute for Labour Studies.

Putnam, Robert D. 1993. *Making Democracy Work: Civic Traditions in Modern Italy*. Princeton: Princeton University Press.

Remmer, Karen L., and Erik Wibbels. 2000. "The Subnational Politics of Economic Adjustment: Provincial Politics and Fiscal Performance in Argentina." *Comparative Political Studies* 33, no. 4 (May): 419–51.

Rico, Antonio. 1992. "Política industrial, servicios y regiones." *Economía Industrial* (July–August): 123–35.

Rodden, John. 2000. "The Dilemma of Fiscal Federalism: Hard and Soft Budget Constraints Around the World." Paper prepared for the conference "Decentralization and Democracy in Latin America," University of Minnesota, February 6–8.

Rodriguez, Vicente. 1995. "Federalismo e Interesses Regionais." In Rui de Britto Álvares Affonso and Pedro Luiz Barros Silva, eds., *A Federação em Perspectiva: Ensaios Selecionados*. São Paulo, S.P.: FUNDAP.

Rodríguez, Victoria E. 1997. *Decentralization in Mexico: From Reforma Municipal to Solidaridad to Nuevo Federalismo*. Boulder, Colo.: Westview Press.

———. 1993. "The Politics of Decentralization in Mexico: From Municipio Libre to Solidaridad." *Bulletin of Latin American Research* 12, no. 2: 133–45.

Rosell, Jordi and Lourdes Viladomiu. 1991. "La política regional en los ochenta: continuidad o ruptura?" In M. Etxezarreta, ed., *La reestructuración del capitalismo en España, 1970–1990*. Barcelona: Economía Crítica.

Rowland, Allison M. 1998. "Decentralized Urban Service Provision: What Can We Learn from Mexico?" Paper presented at the 1998 Latin American Studies Association, The Palmer House Hilton Hotel, Chicago, September 24–26.

Rueschemeyer, Dietrich, and Peter B. Evans. 1985. "The State and Economic Transformation: Toward an Analysis of the Conditions Underlying Effective Intervention." In Peter B. Evans, Dietrich Rueschemeyer, and Theda Skocpol, eds., *Bringing the State Back In.* New York: Cambridge University Press.

Ryff, Tito. 1995. "O Estado, A Fusão e a Região Metropolitana." In *O Estado do Rio de Janeiro: Primeiro Debate Fundação Getúlio Vargas.* Rio de Janeiro: Fundação Getúlio Vargas.

Sabel, Charles F. 1989. "Flexible Specialisation and the Re-emergence of Regional Economies." In Paul Hirst and Jonathan Zeitlin, eds., *Reversing Industrial Decline? Industrial Structure and Policy in Britain and Her Competitors.* New York: St. Martin's Press.

———. 1995. "Bootstrapping Reform: Rebuilding Firms, the Welfare State, and Unions." *Politics and Society* 23, no. 1 (March): 5–48.

SADEI (Servicio de Publicaciones del Principado de Asturias). 1993. *Estadísticas laborales: 1993; Evolución del empleo en Asturias (1985–1993).* Oviedo: Principado de Asturias.

———. 1990a. *HUNOSA y ENSIDESA: La incidencia de dos empresas públicas en Asturias.* Oviedo: Principado de Asturias.

———. 1990b. *Cuentas regionales de Asturias—1990. Metodología y fuentes estadísticas. Análisis de resultados.* Oviedo: Principado de Asturias.

———. 1983. *Estudio económico sobre la actividad industrial asturiana.* Oviedo: Principado de Asturias.

———. 1974. *La incidencia del sector público en la economía asturiana.* Oviedo: Caja de Ahorros de Asturias.

———. 1972. *La economía asturiana en el II y III Plan de Desarrollo.* Oviedo: Caja de Ahorros de Asturias.

———. 1970. *Estudio sobre la situación y perspectivas de la economía asturiana ante el Polo de Desarrollo de Asturias.* Oviedo: Caja de Ahorros de Asturias.

Samuels, David J. 2000. "The Gubernatorial Coattails Effect: Federalism and Congressional Elections in Brazil." *The Journal of Politics* 62, no. 1 (February): 240–53.

———. 1998. "Careerism and Its Consequences: Federalism, Elections, and Policy-Making in Brazil." Ph.D. diss., University of California, San Diego.

Samuels, David J., and Fernando Luiz Abrúcio. 2001. "The `New' Politics of the Governor: Federalism and the Brazilian Transition to Democracy." *Publius: The Journal of Federalism* 30, no. 2 (Spring): 46–61.

Samuels, Warren J., and Nicholas Mercuro. 1984. "A Critique of Rent-Seeking Theory." In *Neoclassical Political Economy: The Analysis of Rent-*

Seeking and DUP Activities, ed. David C. Collander. Cambridge: Ballinger.

San Miguel Cela, José Luis. 1994. "La política de promoción económica en Asturias." In José Luis García Delgado and Luis Fernández de la Buelga, eds., *Economía y empresa en Asturias: Homenaje a Ignacio Herrero Garralda, Marqués de Aledo.* Madrid: Editorial Civitas.

Sanchez Ortiz, Luis J. 1990. "Madrid, capital del capital." *Economía y Sociedad* 4 (December): 25–36.

Saxenian, AnnaLee. 1994. *Regional Advantage: Culture and Competition in Silicon Valley and Route 128.* Cambridge: Harvard University Press.

SAYPE (Servicio de Asesoramiento y Promoción Empresarial). 1998. *SAYPE 1997.* Oviedo: Consejería de Economía.

———. 1997. *SAYPE 1997.* Oviedo: Consejería de Economía.

———. 1994. *Memoría de Actividades—1993.* Oviedo: SAYPE.

———. 1993. *Memoria de Actividades—1992.* Salinas: SAYPE.

———. 1992. *Memoria de Actividades—1991.* Gijón: SAYPE.

Schmitt, Rogério Augusto. 1997. "Rio de Janeiro: Multipartidarismo, Competitividade, e Realinhamento Eleitoral." In Olavo Brasil de Lima Júnior, ed., *O Sistema Partidário Brasileiro: Diversidade e Tendências—1982–94.* Rio de Janeiro: Fundação Getúlio Vargas.

Schmitter, Philippe C. 1997. "Civil Society East and West." In Larry Diamond, Marc F. Plattner, Yun-han Chu, and Hung-mao Tien, eds., *Consolidating the Third Wave Democracies: Themes and Perspectives.* Baltimore: Johns Hopkins University Press.

Schneider, Ben Ross. 1999. "The *Desarrollista* State in Brazil and Mexico." In Meredith Woo-Cumings, ed., *The Developmental State.* Ithaca: Cornell University Press.

———. 1998. "Elusive Synergy: Business-Government Relations and Development." *Comparative Politics* (October): 101–22.

———. 1993. "The Career Connection: A Comparative Analysis of Bureaucratic Preferences and Insulation." *Comparative Politics* (April): 331–50.

———. 1991. *Politics Within the State: Elite Bureaucrats and Industrial Policy in Authoritarian Brazil.* Pittsburgh: University of Pittsburgh Press.

Schwartz, Gilson. 1996. "Brazil, MERCOSUR, and SAFTA: Destructive Restructuring or Pan-American Integration?" In Shoji Nishijima and Peter H. Smith, eds., *Cooperation or Rivalry? Regional Integration in the Americas and the Pacific Rim.* Boulder, Colo.: Westview Press.

Schwartzman, Simon. 1975. *São Paulo e o Estado Nacional.* São Paulo: Difel.

———. 1973. "Regional Cleavages and Political Patrimonialism in Brazil." Ph. D. diss., University of California, Berkeley.

Secretaria da Indústria e do Comércio. 1987. *A Interiorização da Indústria no Estado de São Paulo*. São Paulo: Government of São Paulo State.

Secretaria de Estado de Indústria, Comércio, Ciência e Tecnologia. 1991. *Política Industrial para o Estado do Rio de Janeiro*. Unpublished internal document.

Segura, Julio. 1989. *La industria española en la crisis 1978–1984*. Madrid: Alianza Editorial.

Serra, José and José Roberto R. Afonso. 1991. "Trajetória e Mitos." *Conjuntura Econômica* (October): 44–50.

Serrano Sanz, José María. 1988. "La intervención económica en el Estado de las Autonomías." In José Luis García Delgado, ed., *España: Economía*. Madrid: Espasa-Calpe.

Servén, Luis. 1989. "La empresa pública en un sector estratégico: HUNOSA." *Papeles de Economía Española* 38: 383–88.

Shah, Anwar. 1991. *The New Fiscal Federalism in Brazil*. World Bank Discussion Papers, no. 124.

Silva de Mattos, Rogério, Lourival Batista de O. Júnior, and Suzana Quinet de A. Bastos. 1995. "Tentativas de Reindustrialização em Juiz de Fora: As Experiências da Siderúrgica Mendes Júnior e da Cia. Paraibuna de Metais." In *VII Seminário sobre a Economia Mineira*. Vol. 2. Belo Horizonte: UFMG/CEDEPLAR.

Silva, Pedro Luiz Barros, and Vera Lúcia Cabral Costa. 1995. "Decentralização e Crise da Federação." In Rui de Britto Álvares Affonso and Pedro Luiz Barros Silva, eds., *A Federação em Perspectiva: Ensaios Selecionados*. São Paulo: FUNDAP.

Skidmore, Thomas E. 1988. *The Politics of Military Rule in Brazil, 1964–85*. New York: Oxford University Press.

———. 1967. *Politics in Brazil, 1930–1964: An Experiment in Democracy*. New York: Oxford University Press.

Smith, W. Rand. 1998. *The Left's Dirty Job: The Politics of Industrial Restructuring in France and Spain*. Pittsburgh: University of Pittsburgh Press.

———. 1995. "Industrial Crisis and the Left: Adjustment Strategies in Socialist France and Spain." *Comparative Politics* 28, no. 1 (October): 1–24.

Smith, William C., and Nizar Messari. 1998. "Democracy and Reform in Cardoso's Brazil: Caught Between Clientelism and Global Markets?" *The North-South Agenda Papers* 33 (September).

Snyder, Richard. 2001. "Scaling Down: The Subnational Comparative Method." *Studies in Comparative International Development* 36, no. 1 (Spring): 93–110.

———. 1999a. "After Neoliberalism: The Politics of Reregulation in Mexico." *World Politics* 51, no. 2 (January): 173–204.

———. 1999b. "Reconstructing Institutions for Market Governance: Participatory Policy Regimes in Mexico's Coffee Sector." In Richard Snyder, ed., *Institutional Adaptation and Innovation in Rural Mexico.* La Jolla: Center of U.S.-Mexican Studies, University of California, San Diego.

Soares, Francisco de Assis, and Euripedys Ewbank Rocha. 1989. "O pioneirismo do Ceará em programas de industrialização." *Revista Econômica do Nordeste* 20, no. 3 (July–September): 247–65.

Soares, Gláucio Ary Dillon. 1984. *Colégio Eleitoral, Convenções Partidárias e Eleições Diretas.* Petrópolis: Vozes.

Soares, Gláucio Ary Dillon, and Nelson do Valle e Silva. 1985. "O Charme Discreto do Socialismo Moreno." *Revista de Ciências Sociais* 28, no. 2: 253–73.

Sola, Lourdes. 1995. "Estado, Regime Fiscal e Ordem Monetária: Qual Estado?" *Revista Brasileira de Ciências Sociais* 10, no. 27 (February): 29–60.

Solchaga, Carlos. 1997. *El final de la edad dorada.* Madrid: Taurus.

Solnick, Steven L. 1996. "The Breakdown of Hierarchies in the Soviet Union and China: A Neoinstitutional Perspective." *World Politics* 48 (January): 209–38.

Souza, Celina. 1997. *Constitutional Engineering in Brazil: The Politics of Federalism and Decentralization.* New York: St. Martin's Press.

Souza, Amaury de, Olavo Brasil de Lima Júnior, and Marcus Figueiredo. 1985. "Brizola e as Eleições de 1982 no Rio de Janeiro." Instituto Universitário de Pesquisas do Rio de Janeiro (IUPERJ) *Série Estudos* 40 (August).

Souza, Amaury de. 1972. "Determinismo Social e o Voto Flutuante em 1960." *Dados* 9: 61–75.

Stallings, Barbara, and Robert Kaufman, eds. 1989. *Debt and Democracy in Latin America.* Boulder, Colo.: Westview Press.

Starling, Heloisa Maria Murgel. 1986. *Os Senhores das Gerais: Os Novos Inconfidentes e o Golpe de 1964.* Belo Horizonte: Vozes.

Subirats Humet, Joan. 1992. *Un problema de estilo: la formación de políticas públicas en España.* Madrid: Centro de Estudios Constitucionales.

———. 1991. "Evaluación del proceso autonómico: algunos indicadores." In A. F. Laraudogoitia and E. M. Artaraz, eds., *Poder Político y Comunidades Autónomas.* Vitoria-Gasteiz: Eusko Legebiltzarra Parlamento Vasco.

Suzigan, Wilson. 1992. "Política Comercial e Perspectivas da Indústria Brasileira." UNICAMP *Textos para Discussão* 13 (December):1–20.

Swyngedouw, Erik A. 1992. "The Mammon Quest. `Glocalisation,' Interspatial Competition and the Monetary Order: The Construction of

New Scales." In Mick Dunford and Grigoris Kafkalas, eds., *Cities and Regions in the New Europe: The Global-Local Interplay and Spatial Development Strategies*. New York: John Wiley.

Tamames, Ramón. 1986. *Estructura Económica de España*. Madrid: Alianza Universidad Textos.

Tendler, Judith. 2000. "The Economic Wars Between the States." Paper prepared for the MIT/Bank of the Northeast Project, Massachusetts Institute of Technology, September 3.

———. 1997. *Good Government in the Tropics*. Baltimore: Johns Hopkins University Press.

———. 1968. *Electric Power in Brazil: Entrepreneurship in the Public Sector*. Cambridge: Harvard University Press.

Thomas, Kenneth P. 1997. *Capital Beyond Borders: States and Firms in the Auto Industry, 1960–94*. New York: St. Martin's Press.

Tiebout, Charles. 1956. "A Pure Theory of Local Government Expenditures." *Journal of Political Economy* (October).

Treisman, Daniel. 1999. "Political Decentralization and Economic Reform: A Game-Theoretic Analysis." *American Journal of Political Science* 43, no. 4: 488–517.

Trullen i Thomas, Joan. 1994. *Fundamentos económicos de la transición política española: la política económica de los acuerdos de la Moncloa*. Madrid: Ministerio de Trabajo y Seguridad Social.

Tsoukalis, Loukas. 1993. *The New European Economy: The Politics and Economics of Integration*. Second ed. New York: Oxford University Press.

Tuman, John P., and John T. Morris, eds. 1998. *Transforming the Latin American Automobile Industry: Unions, Workers, and the Politics of Restructuring*. Armonk: M. E. Sharpe.

Vázquez, Juan A. 1993. "Asturias: La reindustrialización como objetivo." *Papeles de Economía Española* 55.

———. 1992. "La economía asturiana: En la encrucijada de los nuevos ajustes." *Papeles de Economía Española* 51.

———. 1988. "Regiones de tradición industrial en declive: la Cornisa Cantábrica." In José Luis García Delgado, ed., *España: Economía*. Madrid: Espasa Calpe.

von Mettenheim, Kurt. 1995. *The Brazilian Voter: Mass Politics in Democratic Transition, 1974–1986*. Pittsburgh: University of Pittsburgh Press.

Wade, Robert. 1990. *Governing the Market: Economic Theory and the Role of Government in East Asian Industrialization*. Princeton: Princeton University Press.

Ward, Peter. 1995. "Policy Making and Policy Implementation Among Non-PRI Governments: The PAN in Ciudad Juarez and in Chihuahua." In Victoria Rodríguez and Peter Ward, eds., *Opposition Government in Mexico*. Albuquerque: University of New Mexico Press.

Ward, Peter M., and Victoria E. Rodríguez. 1999a. "New Federalism, Intra-governmental Relations and Co-governance in Mexico." *Journal of Latin American Studies* 31: 673–710.

———. 1999b. *New Federalism and State Government in Mexico: Bringing the States Back In*. Austin: University of Texas Press.

Werlang, Sergio R., and Armínio Fraga Neto. 1995. "Os Bancos Estaduais e o Descontrole Fiscal: Alguns Aspectos." *Revista Brasileira de Economia* 49, no. 2 (April–June): 265–75.

Werneck, Rogério. 1991. *Empresas Estatais e Política Macroeconômica*. Rio de Janeiro: Editora Campus.

Weyland, Kurt. 1996. *Democracy Without Equity: Failures of Reform in Brazil*. Pittsburgh: University of Pittsburgh Press.

Willis, Eliza, Christopher da C. B. Garman, and Stephan Haggard. 1999. "The Politics of Decentralization in Latin America." *Latin American Research Review* 34, no. 1: 7–56.

Willis, Eliza J. 1996. "Influencing Industrial Location Through Regional and Local Development in Federal States: Some Lessons." *International Review of Administrative Science* 62: 401–11.

Wirth, John D. 1977. *Minas Gerais in the Brazilian Federation 1889–1937*. Stanford: Stanford University Press.

Wise, Carol. 1998. "NAFTA, Mexico, and the Western Hemisphere." In Carol Wise, ed., *The Post-NAFTA Political Economy: Mexico and the Western Hemisphere*. University Park: Pennsylvania State University Press.

World Bank. 1997. *Decentralization in Latin America: Learning through Experience*. Washington, D.C.: The World Bank.

Wozniak, Lynne. 1993. "The Dissolution of Party-Union Relations in Spain." *International Journal of Political Economy* (Winter): 73–91.

INDEX

accountability. *See* horizontal embeddedness

Acesita steel, 41

Açominas steel, 65, 72

Addis, Caren, 90

Afonso Bicalho da Silva, José, 82, 84

Agência de Desenvolvimento do Rio. *See* Development Agency of Rio (AD-Rio)

Alencar, Marcello, 159–60

Aliança Nacional Renovadora. *See* National Renovation Alliance (ARENA)

Alianza Popular (Spain). *See* Popular Party (PP, Spain)

Almeida Pordeus, Iran, 80

Ananias, Patrus, 187

Anastasia, Antônio Agusto, 82

Andalusia, 3–5, 23–25, 26, 29–30, 52 n. 25, 54, 57, 59, 129, 143, 177, 187–90

automotive industry, 163, 167, 171–72, 174. *See also* Land Rover Santana

business associations, 30, 161, 167, 187. *See also* Confederation of Andalusian Business (CEA)

Cádiz, 163, 167

chemical industry, 163, 166

corruption, 173, 173 n. 53

European Union funds in, 163–64, 189, 197

foreign investment, 168, 170–72

Huelva, 163, 166

industrial development, 160–63, 166–67

industrial policy-making in, 30, 161, 163–64, 167–75, 197

infrastructure, 164

labor unions, 30, 161, 167–70, 172–75, 187

Linares, 163, 167, 171–72, 173–75

Málaga, 171–72

nationalism, 30, 164–65, 167–69, 187

political class of, 164

populist government, 4, 30, 143, 161, 165–67, 172, 174–75, 187–88

public sector spending, 170–71, 174–75

regional autonomy, 164–67, 187–88, 199

regional parliament, 169

savings banks, 165

Seville, 168–69, 171, 175

ship-building industry, 163, 167

small and medium-sized firms, 166–67, 189

Socialist Party (PSOE) in, 30, 161, 164–73, 175, 187–90

technocracy, 164–68, 170, 172–74, 189. *See also* horizontal embeddedness, Andalusia and

technology park. *See* Andalusia, Málaga

unemployment, 161–62, 172

Andalusian Economic Promotion and Reconversion Society (SOPREA), 166–67, 170–71

Andalusian Institute of Industrial Promotion (IPIA). *See* Andalusian Institute of Promotion (IFA)

Andalusian Institute of Promotion (IFA), 30, 164–68, 170–71, 173–75, 188–89

Andalusian Socialist Party (PSA), 164–65

Anguita, Julio, 169

Aranzadi, Claudio, 108, 126 n. 46

Araújo Jorge, J. G. de, 150

Araújo Lima, Marcos Antonio de, 159

Arthur D. Little Co. (ADL), 70, 73

Asia, East, 20 n. 25

Asturgar, S. G. R., 134–36

Asturian Socialist Federation (FSE-PSOE). *See* Asturias, Principado of, Socialist Party (PSOE) in